John Henry Parker

The Architectural History of the City of Rome

John Henry Parker

The Architectural History of the City of Rome

ISBN/EAN: 9783744784863

Printed in Europe, USA, Canada, Australia, Japan

Cover: Foto ©ninafisch / pixelio.de

More available books at **www.hansebooks.com**

THE ARCHITECTURAL HISTORY

OF THE

CITY OF ROME.

ABRIDGED FROM

J. H. PARKER'S "ARCHÆOLOGY OF ROME."

FOR THE USE OF STUDENTS.

PARKER AND CO.
OXFORD, AND 6 SOUTHAMPTON-STREET,
STRAND, LONDON.
1881.

PREFACE.

THE object of this little Handbook is to put before Students an account of the growth of the City of Rome, as it can be gathered from the combined record of writings and stones. Hitherto it has been scarcely possible to do this, for it is mainly in recent times that the early remains of the City's construction have been sought out and found. The excavations which have of late years been pursued around the most ancient portions of the site of Rome, enable us now for the first time to see how the traditions of its people, as they are fragmentarily preserved by historians, agree with those remains. There are acknowledged principles of Archæology, such as that a certain style of building is assignable to a certain age; varying degrees of rudeness in construction indicate successive changes in the art of masonry. These principles have been applied to Rome, and lead to definite results. And again, when the sites on which the early remains are found are compared with the notices given by historians of the successive enlargements of the City, we are then entitled to draw conclusions whether the buildings fit in with the traditions.

Old Rome has been buried, but comes partly to sight again in our own day; and wherever this investigation has been pursued, it has been rewarded, for the most part, by the testimony that the stones maintain the stories. And on the whole, it does not seem presumption or credulity to maintain, that the main facts delivered by Roman writers as to the formation and growth of their capital City are borne out by the walls, banks, fosses, and gates still traceable within it.

The contents of these pages are little else than a condensation of the large works on Roman Archæology by Mr. J. H. Parker of Oxford, who has lately received from the Italian authorities a high recognition of his services in restoring the "true history of the City of Rome." And this abridgment of his book is undertaken at his desire, simply to put before readers, in small compass, the elementary information necessary for understanding the history of the rise and progress of the great City on the Seven Hills. At the same time, it is well to state that the compiler has passed some seasons in Rome, and is satisfied from personal knowledge of the truth of the principles here applied to the very early history of the material growth of the place.

PREFACE.

The Plates were necessarily prepared under my direction. They are chiefly taken from photographs, but photographs alone can only shew the *exterior* of any object, whereas plans and sections are quite necessary to explain many of them. They are to be considered as *diagrams* only, to explain the text to students who have not been in Rome, and are not to be judged as pictures. The attempt has been to explain everything as completely as possible; the only chapter that is not explained by these diagrams is that on the Mamertine Prison, the remains of which, though extensive, are entirely subterranean (now for the most part cellars under houses), and it did not seem practicable to explain these by one or two small plates. My account of this ancient prison has been published separately, with the Plates of it, so that any one interested in the subject can easily obtain the information.

The excavations made for me in 1868, in search of the remains of the PORTA CAPENA, and which I succeeded in finding, led to enormous results. These were the first excavations that had been made in Rome for *historical objects only*, and not in search of statues or other works of ancient art for museums, &c. The PORTA CAPENA is in the *inner* wall of Rome, just a mile within the PORTA APPIA in the *outer* wall; this name was also given to the whole of that district, which formed the first Regio of Augustus.

It is hoped that this Abridgment will open the eyes of many English students to the delusion by which they have been blinded, and will convince them that the early history of Rome, which for the last half-century has been considered as fabulous only, is *the true history*. There is no other manner of explaining the remains now brought to light by the excavations; even the *measurements* of important objects were found to agree exactly with the legendary history preserved by Dionysius and Livy.

JOHN HENRY PARKER, C.B.

ASHMOLEAN MUSEUM, OXFORD.
October, 1881.

CONTENTS.

CHAPTER I.
	PAGE
OF THE MATERIALS USED IN BUILDING AT ROME, AND OF THE VARIOUS STYLES OF CONSTRUCTION	1
MODES OF CONSTRUCTION	4

CHAPTER II.
ROMA QUADRATA	11

CHAPTER III.
THE CITY ON THE TWO HILLS	23

CHAPTER IV.
THE FORTIFICATIONS ON THE OTHER FIVE HILLS, AND ON THE HEIGHTS ADJACENT	32

CHAPTER V.
THE CITY ON THE SEVEN HILLS WITHIN ONE ENCLOSURE	46

CHAPTER VI.
THE AGGER OF TARQUINIUS THE SECOND	55
LATER FORTIFICATIONS	59

CHAPTER VII.
THE WALLS OF AURELIAN AND HONORIUS	67

CHAPTER VIII.
                                                              PAGE
THE STREETS AND ROADS 79

CHAPTER IX.
THE AQUEDUCTS 93

CHAPTER X.
THE THERMÆ 115

CHAPTER XI.
FORUM ROMANUM 122

CHAPTER XII.
THE MAMERTINE PRISON 137

CHAPTER XIII.
THE MAUSOLEA AND TOMBS OF ROME . . 140

CHAPTER XIV.
THE COLOSSEUM, OR FLAVIAN AMPHITHEATRE . 151

CHAPTER XV.
PALACES OF THE CÆSARS 162

ALPHABETICAL INDEX 177

PLATES, WITH DESCRIPTIONS . . . 193

LIST OF PLATES

TO ILLUSTRATE

CHAPTER I.—OF THE MATERIALS USED IN BUILDING AT ROME, AND OF THE VARIOUS STYLES OF CONSTRUCTION.

		Referred to in the text at p.
PLATE		
I.	I. Opus Quadratum.—Squared Work, A.U.C. 3, B.C. 750	4
	II. Opus Incertum.—Irregular Work, A.U.C. 558, B.C. 750	5
II.	III. Opus Reticulatum.—Reticulated, or Net-work, A.U.C. 725, B.C. 28 to A.D. 118	6
	IV. Opus Lateritium.—Brickwork, A.U.C. 810, B.C. 57	7

CHAPTER II.—ROMA QUADRATA.

III.	I. Roma Quadrata.—Plan of the Surface and the Sides	12
	II. ——— Details of the Sides of the Primitive City	*ib.*
IV.	——— Details of the Great Foss	*ib.*
	III. ——— Bath-chambers of Livia, made in that Foss	*ib.*
	IV. ——— Section of it, at the West End	*ib.*

CHAPTER III.—THE CITY ON THE TWO HILLS.

V.	Plan of the City on the Two Hills	24—31
VI.	I. Tower of the same in the Forum of Augustus	26
	II. Part of the Second Wall of Rome, with remains of a Gateway (afterwards in the Forum of Nerva, with the figure of Pallas over it)	*ib.*
VII.	III. Cloaca Maxima, the part visible in the Forum Romanum	27
	IV. Pulchrum Littus, and exit of the River Almo into the Tiber (near the Forum Boarium)	*ib.*

CHAPTERS IV. AND V.—THE FORTIFICATIONS ON THE OTHER FIVE HILLS AND ON THE HEIGHTS ADJACENT. THE CITY ON THE SEVEN HILLS WITHIN ONE ENCLOSURE.

VIII.	I. Wall of the Latins on the Aventine	33
	II. Muro-Torto, at the N. E. corner of the Wall of Rome	61

PLATE		Referred to in the text at p.
IX.	I. Porta Capena, in the Wall of Servius Tullius, Exterior of the lower part of the Western Tower of the Gate, with the Excavations of 1868	53
	II. ———— Interior of the same Tower, with the Aqueduct passing through it	54
X.	III. Porta Capena—A. Part of the Aqueduct, near the Gate	52
	———— B. Section of the Eastern Tower of that Gate	ib.
	———— C. Part of the Arcade of the Aqueduct, and of the *crepido*, or footpath of the Via Appia	53
	IV. Rampart of Servius Tullius, on the Viminal (near the Railway Station)	50
XI.	V. Part of the Agger or Rampart, and Wall of Servius Tullius (in the Exquiliæ), near the Porta Tiburtina	51
	VI. Plan and Section of the Horn-work at the north end of the Rampart—the north-east corner of Rome (on which the House of Sallust was built)	47

CHAPTER VI.—THE AGGER OF TARQUINIUS THE SECOND. LATER FORTIFICATIONS.

XII.	I. Part of the Wall of Tarquinius II., between the Prætorian Camp and the Porta Tiburtina. General View in 1880	56
	II. Section of the same part of the Wall and Rampart	57

CHAPTER VII.—THE WALLS OF AURELIAN AND HONORIUS.

XIII.	I. PORTA MAGGIORE (Prænestina, Labicana, Esquilina, Sessoriana)	78
	II. Porta Asinaria (of the Asinii)	68
XIV.	III. Porta Appia (or di S. Sebastiano)	71
	IV. Wall of Aurelian, part of Exterior	67
XV.	V. ————Corridor (for the Sentinel's path)	68
	VI. Another part of the Corridor of Aurelian	ib.

Chapter VIII.—The Streets and Roads.

PLATE		Referred to in the text at p.
XVI.	I. Part of the Via Appia, near Ariccia—work of Appius Claudius, on an embankment, passing across a swamp	88
	II. Ponte Nono, on the Via Gabina, or Praenestina; a Bridge of very early character, crossing the river Anio near Gabii, at nine miles from the original Gate in the Inner Wall of Rome	86

Chapter IX.—The Aqueducts.

XVII.	I. Arcade of the Aqueducts Claudia and Anio Novus, near Roma Vecchia	99
	II. Arches of Nero, near the Porta Maggiore, crossing the Great Foss of the Sessorium	109
XVIII.	III. Septizonium, or Sette Basse, on the Esquiline Hill	117
	IV. Interior of a Castellum Aquae, or Reservoir	ib.

Chapter X.—The Thermae.

XIX.	I. The Pantheum, Front, with Portico	116
	II. Back of the Pantheum, time of Agrippa, shewing the original construction and fine cornice	ib.
XX.	III. Thermae of Caracalla, part of the Porticus added by Alexander Severus	118
	IV. ——— Part of the Hot-air Chamber on the western side of the Thermae	ib.

Chapter XI.—Forum Romanum.

XXI.	I. Forum Romanum, General View from the Palatine, looking north, in 1878	122
XXII.	II. ——— View of a Rostrum (from Sculpture on the Arch of Constantine)	125
	III. The Emperor Marcus Aurelius addressing the Citizens (from Sculpture on one of the Marble Walls, excavated in 1872)	126
XXIII.	Forum of Trajan, the three Tiers of Shops at the east end. Plan and Section	133

		Referred to
PLATE		in the text at p.

CHAPTER XIII.—THE MAUSOLEA AND TOMBS OF ROME.

XXIV. I. Columbaria in a public Burial-vault on the Via Appia, just within the Porta Appia . . 144
II. Tomb of the Lateran Family, on the edge of the Great Foss that separated the Lateran Palace and garden from the Celian Hill . . . *ib.*

XXV. Tomb of the Baker Eurysaces and his wife Aristia, at the Porta Maggiore 147

CHAPTER XIV.—THE COLOSSEUM, OR FLAVIAN AMPHITHEATRE.

XXVI. I. The Colosseum, General View of the north-east side, the most perfect part of the Exterior in 1870 151
II. ——— Part of the Interior, shewing the early walls to support the floor, and the dens for Lions under the lower gallery, as excavated in 1878 . 152

XXVII. ——— Probable restoration of part of the Sub-structure, with wild animals carried up in cages, and then leaping on to the stage . . . 156

CHAPTER XV.—PALACES OF THE CÆSARS.

XXVIII. I. Chambers in the House of Hortensius, afterwards of Augustus. The walls are faced with *opus reticulatum* of the time of Augustus . . 163
II. Part of the Palace of Tiberius on the Palatine Hill. The palace nearly joins to that of Augustus; the Substructure corresponds with that of the Guard-chambers in the Prætorian Camp, on the north side, built by Tiberius 164

CHAPTER II.—ROMA QUADRATA.

IV*. I. Roma Quadrata.—A Cave-reservoir of rain-water, with a well descending into it from the surface of the hill, and a peculiar hollow cone at the foot of the well 16
II. A similar Cave-reservoir at Alba Longa—with a similar well and hollow cone, on the bank of the Lake of Albano 17
III. Remains of the Primitive Fortifications on the east end of the Capitoline Hill, long concealed in the cellars of Ara Cœli 23

CHAPTER I.

OF THE MATERIALS USED IN BUILDING AT ROME, AND OF THE VARIOUS STYLES OF CONSTRUCTION.

THE principal sorts of stone occurring in Roman edifices are six in number, namely,—

I. *Tophus*. A sandstone of volcanic origin, abounding on the hills of Rome, and over the neighbouring district, sometimes of a deep red, and sometimes of a lighter and yellowish colour. It is called by Vitruvius, the Roman writer on architecture, **Lapis ruber.** It is sometimes hard, but usually very soft, and easy to excavate. The primitive walls around the Palatine, which are now partly visible, were entirely of this material, and were probably built from quarries in the hill itself. There were also ancient quarries of it in the Capitoline, Cœlian, and Aventine Hills; the modern ones are in the Ager Romanus, or Campagna of Rome. On the bank of the Anio, about the sources of the earliest aqueduct, Aqua Appia, are many ancient caves made out of this rock; and it is observable, that the stones in the earliest of these caves have not been cut, but split off the solid mass by wedges. For it is the property of this stone to cleave readily into blocks of four regular sides, so as to require no farther squaring for rude building. This quality made it available for the first settlers of Rome, in an age when iron tools were not yet in use. The modern name is Tufa.

II. *Lapis Albanus*, another kind of volcanic stone, being a conglomerate of ashes and small stones, very hard and rough; the colour is grey, with a tinge of green. The old quarries of it are close to Alba Longa, on the Mons

Albanus; it is still worked at Marino, on the northern slope of that range. The modern name, Peperino, signifies the occurrence on the surface of it of flinty nodules, like peppercorns. The wall backing the agger of Servius Tullius, part of the Mamertine Prison, and the Temple of Jupiter Victor, on the top of the Palatine, are of this material.

III. *Lapis Gabinus*, resembling the last, but with nodules of larger size, and somewhat blacker in colour. As its name shews, it was quarried at Gabii. The triple arch of the Cloaca Maxima, and the substructure of the massive Tabularium on the Capitoline, are built of this stone. Both this and the last-mentioned stone are fireproof, and consequently, after the great conflagration at Rome, A.D. 64, Nero ordered them to be employed in certain portions of the buildings reconstructed. The modern name is Sperone. This is also believed to have been used originally, even before the Peperino.

IV. *Lapis Tiburtinus*, a species of limestone, when freshly hewn, of white colour; which, after exposure, deepens into a yellow tinge. The Romans quarried it very largely from the beds near Tibur, or Tivoli, in the valley of the Anio. It is the best stone obtainable in this part of Italy, being of the highest durability, and admitting the use of very large blocks. Fine examples of it occur in the well-known tomb of Cæcilia Metella, on the Via Appia, and in the Colosseum, the external wall of which is wholly built of it. So are the finest palaces of modern Rome, and many of the best specimens of churches. The modern name is Travertino.

V. *Silex*, flint, but also a basaltic lava, black, and almost as hard as iron. The crater, now the lake of Albano, poured forth several streams of this lava across the Campagna, and nearly as far as Rome. One such current is traceable to the tomb of Cæcilia Metella, two miles from the city on the Via Appia, where quarries of this stone are still in use. This material was used for concrete and for pavements. The modern name is Selce.

VI. *Pumex*, or pumice-stone, was used for internal vaulting, for which its great lightness made it suitable. It is thrown out of the crater of Mount Vesuvius during its eruptions, in the form of white ashes, and, being deposited in thick layers, forms into beds, out of which it is quarried. The vaults of the Colosseum and Pantheon are made of this material.

For more than five hundred years cut stone was used, after which it gradually gave way to other substances: first, concrete; and later on, brick, both of which will be spoken of under the head of Modes of Construction.

The Roman mortar, Materia, was made of lime, mixed with sand, which was either Fossicia, river-sand, or Pulvis Puteolanus, rock-sand, Pozzolana. The latter is found in deposits of great depth over the Campagna, and its quarries on the eastern and southern sides of Rome extend in galleries sometimes miles long. These, when disused, were afterwards in some instances converted into Catacumbæ, catacombs, or places of burial. The best pozzolana sand is rough, crackles in the hand when rubbed, and, as Vitruvius mentions, leaves no stain on a white dress. This sand is of a deep red-and-brown colour, and used properly in the proportion of three to one of lime, and while the lime is quite fresh, becomes a mortar as hard and durable as the stone it cements. Large stones were often held together with clamps of metal, or with bolts of wood let in between two stones, as in the Claudian aqueduct. In the wall of Servius Tullius—where the stones were very large, eleven or twelve feet long—iron clamps were used, also in the Colosseum. In the Pantheon they were of bronze.

Modes of Construction.

The methods of using the fore-mentioned materials are sufficiently distinct to allow of classification. *Opus quadratum* is the name given to the earliest kind of construction, in which the stones are rectangular blocks of Tufa, put together without any cementing substance, and maintained in their places by their own weight only. The earliest and best example is the wall known as that of Romulus, on the Palatine hill, found at intervals at the foot of the cliffs. Such rude masonry lasted, it is believed, for about a hundred years after the foundation of the colony. It is usually called the Etruscan style, being represented in the walls of Fiesole, Perugia, Cortona, Volterra, and other Etrurian towns. The next division of this style differs from the first in the smaller size of the stones, and these are not exclusively of Tufa: the Peperino, from Albano, comes into use. Examples of this second stage occur in the wall of the kingly times on the Aventine, sometimes called the Wall of the Latins, after the first settlers on that hill; this seems next in age to the Palatine walls. Also the Pulchrum Littus, on the bank of the Tiber, built as a protection against inundations; and a wall, with a tower deep in the earth below the church of St. Anastasia, at the foot of the Palatine, are specimens of the second style of the Kings; and again, the wall of Servius Tullius, built against his agger. Here the masonry shews great advance in style. Portions of the old walls of the Kings against the cliffs of the hills in various parts of Rome, and notably on the Viminal, belong to this second style, the stones being gradually smaller as the buildings were later, and being cut with a tool, not split off the parent rock.

Besides the use of rectangular split or hewn blocks,

there occurs another style of early construction, in the form of small stones in irregular polygons. In some districts this is made of the hard mountain limestone, in Rome it is of the Silex or Lava; and where found, it is proof that the material was not cleavable or readily shaped, and was therefore walled-in as the blocks came to hand. These are not cemented, but fitted together with small splinters of stones, wedged into the joints when necessary. But it is very rare in Rome, a small portion existing only on the Viminal; and there is something resembling it in the Emporium, near the port of Rome on the eastern bank of the Tiber, below the Aventine.

The next mode of construction is that called by Vitruvius *Opus Incertum* and *Opus Antiquum*, in which the stones are set in lime-mortar. That material was not brought into general use until between two and three centuries before the Christian era; and when the process of making *concrete* was understood, the advantages of it were seen at once. Walls could be built of rough stone without the trouble of cutting it, and could be as strong and durable as the best wall of cut stone. The earliest example remaining of this mode of construction in concrete is believed to be the lofty wall on the Palatine Hill, by the side of the wall of Romulus. It is extremely rude, and there is no attempt at ornamenting its surface. The earliest use of lime-mortar that can be fixed with a date is in the Emporium, B.C. 175; and here the surface of the wall is faced with the *Opus Incertum*, which preceded reticulated or network. The mass of the wall is concrete, of rough stone and mortar, but the rough surface is not allowed to appear. The same construction is admirably illustrated in the lofty wall called the Muro Torto, of the time of Sylla, against the face of the Pincian Hill, close to the Porta Flaminia, or northernmost gate of Rome. From that time forward the mass of a Roman wall is almost always of concrete, though generally faced with reticulated-work or brick.

The reason that the Roman walls are so durable is, that they were made of concrete, the lime for which was burnt on the spot, and used quite fresh. Every hour that lime is kept, it loses some of its strength: it absorbs moisture from the atmosphere, which causes it to expand, and form crystals rapidly; and after it is once crystallised its binding power is gone: the more rough the material that it has to combine with, the stronger is the concrete. The *Opus reticulatum* is often supposed by casual observers to be of brick, as the small diamond-shaped blocks or wedges of Tufa look very like brick at first sight; there are also at the angles blocks of larger size, closely resembling modern English bricks, but rather larger; they are, however, of stone, with a flat surface, and wedged or pointed off at the back, and being driven into the concrete while wet, before the lime had set, the whole wall, including the surface, is bound together in the firmest manner.

Opus lateritium succeeded to stonework about the time of Augustus, and from that time was most generally used. The Romans excelled in brick-making and in brick-walling, as conspicuously as in stone. The earliest bricks, *lateres*, are said to have been made of the mud in the Tiber's bed, a natural compound of clay and sand. While the bricks used in the walls of Babylon and Persepolis were sun-dried only, the Roman bricks were well burnt in kilns. The earliest examples are in the form of thin flat tiles, mixed with Pozzolana sand, very well made and very hard. In the first century, the Imperial brickwork attained its greatest excellence. No better specimen of it can be seen than in the magnificent arcade of Nero's aqueduct—his continuation of the Aqua Claudia, within the walls, near the Porta Præ-nestina, now Porta Maggiore, and along the Cœlian Hill.

After the early part of the second century the **workmanship** declines, and the very fine brickwork of the time of **Hadrian** is not maintained in **the** Colosseum, **towards the end of** the second century.

It may be here mentioned that the Colosseum, **faced on** the exterior with cut Travertine stone, while the main structure is concrete, has its inner walls faced with bricks, some of which are of the time of Nero. In the third and fourth centuries, although most important buildings were still erected, the brick walls in them were of very inferior quality to what had gone before. The Thermæ of Caracalla and of Diocletian, still standing in enormous masses, the later palaces of the Cæsars on the south-eastern part **of the Palatine, and** the grand villa of the Imperial Gordian family, splendid as they must have been, **were not equal in** construction to the Neronian aqueduct, **or the Thermæ of** Titus, or the Castra Prætoria of **Tiberius's time, or the** Porta Ardeatina, all in the circuit **of the walls of Rome,** and all shewing the same fine character of **the early brickwork.** One test of the age to which bricks belong, adopted upon the careful observation of Roman antiquaries, is to count the number of bricks occurring in a foot or yard of wall-work as it stands: the more bricks, the earlier and better the **style.** Those of Nero usually number nine or ten to the English foot; **in** later work the bricks become thicker, and more mortar is used between them; until **in** the time of Constantine, **and** in the fourth century generally, there are frequently only four **bricks** to the foot, as in modern building; and while the brick itself **is** coarser and more spongy in appearance, the mortar is an inch thick between the courses, or **more,** whereas **in** the early work it **is scarcely shewn.**

Another method of obtaining the dates of brick buildings **is derived from the** usage that prevailed of stamping the bricks in the centre with the names of the maker, usually a slave, and of the owner of the property where the brick-kiln stood; to these, in the time of Hadrian and onwards, it became customary to add the names of the Consuls. A sufficient number of stamped bricks were used in each edifice to record its date with certainty. But, after the transference of the seat of government to Constantinople, the decay of Rome set in, and this care was no longer exhibited. While the custom lasted, the greatest persons in the empire, even members of the reigning family, were not ashamed to have their names thus stamped on their manufactures. The kilns were valuable property, and the word Prædium, often met with in the history of that period, frequently includes the brick-kiln.

Opus mixtum was another method of construction, in which bricks and rough stones were set in alternate layers at regular intervals. It occurs in many parts of the walls of Rome, and in the Circus of Maxentius, A.D. 310. This style is usually attributed to the fourth century, because of this dated example in the first quarter of it; but it occurs also at Pompeii, which was destroyed A.D. 79, and in many parts of the substructure of the wall of Aurelian, which in various places is evidently built upon an earlier wall. It may be seen also in some of the foundation-walls of Hadrian's villa at Tivoli, and at Ostiá in tombs of the second century. It is known in Rome as the style of the Decadence, because it was much used in late Imperial times; but it may be properly regarded as a natural development of the mere concrete wall, which forms the core, or central mass of nearly all Roman walls; and, like other cheap natural modes of building, it affords in itself no evidence of date. It may be added, that it is the style of construction most commonly adopted by the Romans in Gaul and in Britain.

Opus signinum was the name given to the peculiar cement used in lining the channels of aqueducts, so as to make them impermeable by water. It was composed of pounded fragments of brick tiles reduced to powder, and mixed with fresh lime. It is still known in Rome by the name of Cocciopesto.

Something must be said on the use of marble at Rome. It is a mistake to suppose that it ever was used commonly as a building material; but it was used as an ornamental facing to temples, palaces, and thermæ, and also in sumptuous private houses; the core of the wall being stone, and laid over with slabs of marble, and sometimes with square or oblong blocks of it. The cornices and columns are of marble, and all that was visible was so, while the main body of the cella, or shrine, was solid stonework, and this sometimes remains when the ornamental portions have been rebuilt. This is the case with some of the churches which are temples converted to Christian use. The earliest mention of marble is about B.C. 150. Up to that time not only the finest buildings, but sculpture also, had been confined to stone. The great lions' heads in the bank of the port of Rome in the Tiber, B.C. 175, are of stone: so are the tombs of the Scipios, and the temples built up to the date A.U.C. 573 had no marble. Monumental arches, such as that of Drusus, were of stone; that of Dolabella on the Cœlian, the earliest dated building of the Christian era, A.D. 10, is of massive Travertine stone. The theatre of Marcellus is of stone. The Colosseum is externally of stone, internally of brick. The round temple, usually called of Vesta, but more properly that of Hercules in the Forum Boarium, and the Mausoleum of Hadrian were overlaid with marble. The magnificent Thermæ of Antoninus Caracalla were cased with marble to a great extent; the brick walls and plaster, with the marks of the marble slabs, shew what they once were. In the later palaces of the Cæsars on the Palatine some of the columns still standing are of solid marble, and some shew a marble coating over a stone centre. The ruins of the temples supplied many Christian churches with the grandest marble columns for supporting the clerestory walls and for ornament.

The Romans, after the taste for marbles had once set in, ransacked the distant parts of their empire for every variety of them: the names of distinct sorts compose a long list, the most beautiful and costly coming from Africa. There was a wharf on the Tiber devoted entirely to the landing of such sea-borne stones. This wharf, called the Marmorata, was found and excavated in the time of Pius IX., and on being cleared from the sands of the Tiber, exhibited a vast store of marble blocks in different degrees of rudeness and finish, with some specimens of the very finest kinds known, now wholly unobtainable. It is believed also that the Romans imported by sea granite stone from the same quarries as are still wrought near the Lacus Verbanus, or L. Maggiore. The Devonshire marble, called on the spot *Pudding-stone*, was highly esteemed in ancient Rome, and was very scarce *there*.

CHAPTER II.

ROMA QUADRATA.

IT was the constant tradition of Rome's inhabitants that their original city was planted on the Palatine Hill, and the presence of the rudest kind of masonry, still visible round portions of an oblong space at the north end of that hill, confirms the tradition. The position of that eminence is clearly defined upon Mr. Parker's map of Rome; it is the most central of the seven hills composing the complete City; the others, as the Italians say, stand round and pay court to her as queen; and when the whole area was filled up, this, the most ancient of all its divisions, still retained something of a sacred character as the original home of the nation. The form of the Palatine is that of a diamond or lozenge-shaped parallelogram, with its upper apex pointing nearly due north; its height above the sea is 170 feet, and its surface contains about sixty-five acres. But the primitive fortifications occupied only a portion of that extent, namely, the north-western, and this did not contain more than one-third of the whole. What was formerly supposed to be a natural depression is found to have been a very wide and deep foss across the centre of the hill at least 100 feet wide and 30 feet deep, separating the northern portion from the remainder of the hill. This trench is discernible as a deep cutting across the middle of the hill. The space so defined constituted the Arx, or citadel of the colony, into which the settlers, living in their huts on the slopes around, could drive their cattle and conduct their families in time of war. The same principles of fortification as those adopted by the first Romans were universally applied by settlers in the Italian peninsula. First of all, a hilly site was chosen, and if its sides were not sufficiently steep by nature, they were dug away, or scarped into perpendicular cliffs, and against these a wall was built up, where necessary, to prevent landslips. The earth thrown down formed a terrace at the foot, and beyond the terrace a trench was excavated with a road usually in the bottom, and the soil thrown up out of it formed an agger, or bank. Not the Palatine alone, but each of the other hills of Rome, was, as there is reason to believe, originally a separate fortress of this character; and the strong places of Etruria, of which Veii, so long the powerful rival of Rome, is the chief example, were similarly defended. Usually, each hill-town consisted of three parts: 1. The Arx, or citadel, on the highest ground, and most strongly fortified; 2. The dwelling portion, or town around the first, and lower down, also with its strong lines of defence; 3. The pasture-ground, naturally of larger area than the other two, with a single line of protection. And if there was other prominently rising ground near at hand, it was usually occupied as a detached fort for additional security.

The Arx, or citadel of the colony on the Palatine, is called by Roman writers, Roma Quadrata. A fragment of Ennius, quoted by Festus, runs, "Qui se sperat Romæ regnare quadratæ." One interpretation of this phrase is that the wall of circumvallation is of the kind of masonry called *Opus quadratum*, i.e. formed of rectangular blocks of stone. But Dionysius of Halicarnassus, with more probability, refers the name to the shape of the first enclosure on the hill,—" Roma quadrata, which means quadrangular," a four-sided city. It is, however, this wall-work, now made visible by excavations, that is so highly interesting from its great antiquity, as testified by its rude nature. The work consists of oblong blocks of Tufa stone, which, as was said, when split by wedges, cleaves readily into rectangular blocks. Such material would be used by a primitive people, not possessed of iron tools, for the fortification of their newly-founded city. Accordingly, we find round three sides of their fortress remains of walls, built of stones four feet long by two feet wide, or more exactly, as a competent authority states, twenty-three inches wide, being the regular Etruscan measure; each stone is about a ton weight, or, as Dionysius says, a load for a one-horse cart. On the fourth side, looking south-east, any possible remains are concealed by the Palaces of the Cæsars. These stones are laid together against the cliff alternately lengthwise and crosswise, for greater strength. For such interlacing work the name *Emplecton* has been proposed. No mortar is used between the courses, and the blocks are placed so artlessly that the vertical joints between them frequently occur immediately over each other, so that there is a continuous open fissure through the wall, running down past two courses of stones. Moreover, not having been sawn out, or dressed with a chisel, their surfaces are not smooth and close-fitting, so that a cane can be passed through the openings between the blocks. This, the earliest type of *Opus quadratum*, is best seen on the north-west face of the hill; and these peculiarities of ancient rudeness are easily recognised upon the photograph supplied to illustrate them. Such simple remains are of the utmost importance in estimating the antiquity of the city's foundation. The legends preserved by historians attribute to the founder a continuous wall round the settlement on the Palatine. There must of necessity be a wall of considerable strength from the commencement of the colony, for its existence depended on its defences, and the Palatine was neither high enough nor steep enough by nature to dispense with earthworks and walls. The people believed the walls to have been built, and before the concrete work of the Republic had re-faced a great part of the hill-side looking towards the Capitol, they must have seen the continuous line of wall. Indeed, it is probable that the primitive line of defence was always partly visible: for it is indicated by Theodoric the Ostrogoth, in a letter preserved by Cassiodorus, his minister, that a portion of the founder's wall was still in existence. That prince had a jealous veneration for the monuments of the city's fame; but the seat of government had been already transferred elsewhere, and Rome being wholly deserted and neglected by its masters, the process of decay set in, the cliffs of the Palatine in many places slipped, and covered the masonry round the foot of the hill. Fragments of this ancient work are now again exposed to view; and to understand and estimate them rightly, they must be compared with the remains of other cities, known to be of the same or of earlier date. Such are Tusculum, and the Sabine town, Varia, which have well-defined walls, left in considerable masses, of *Opus quadratum*, consisting of large stones, rudely fitted, and without any mortar. Similar structures are found, as was said, in Etrurian cities; thus at Fiesole, close to Florence, there is a wall built of split tufa-stone, closely corresponding with that of Romulus. Such buildings are classed as Etruscan in style, and this is admitted to be a right nomenclature; it was Etruscan influence that brought in this early architecture, and caused it to be widely distributed over the fortified places of ancient Italy.

Such, then, was the first wall of Roma Quadrata. When it is considered how small a portion of the whole hill was thus enclosed at first, and that all very old towns in similar positions were surrounded with exceedingly strong and massive stoneworks, many of which still exist, and that effectual ramparts were a first necessary condition of existence, we can find nothing incredible in the statement that, from the first, Rome's citadel was made a strong place of arms. The tradition says this, and the examination on the spot of what must be, from their nature, primitive structures, confirms the tradition.

It has been noticed that it was usual to construct round the hill-towns of old Italy a kind of ledge, or terrace, or more than one such, out of the earth, which was thrown down the face of the slope in the process of scarping the cliff, with the design of making the upper part of it vertical. This ledge against the western side of the Palatine, called Germalus, was at about half the height of the hill. It was usual also to make a zig-zag roadway up an inclined slope of the hill, so as to render the ascent more easy. All the hills of Rome had these zig-zag approaches formerly; traces of them exist, and that on the Palatine, opposite the Capitoline, may be still made out, and is still in use to some extent for carts. It has been ascertained that the distance between these two hills is short enough to allow a man to be struck down by missiles hurled from the opposite eminence: a Roman on the Palatine was not safe from being wounded by a stone shot from the Tarpeian rock. Therefore, it was necessary to make the defences on that side stronger than elsewhere, especially at the point where the northern angle of the hill juts out towards the Forum. When Rome was colonised, the Capitoline Hill, or Mons Saturnius, a very strong position, was already occupied by tenants of the Sabine race; and on the outbreak of wars, the natural fruit of such proximity, the legends say that the Romans thought it necessary to raise the walls of their fortress, and began to do so. Precisely at this point, where we should expect to find them, we do find a series of bastions built against the wall, to serve as buttresses, for raising the wall higher. These are of the same early construction as the other early walls, but they have been carried only to the height of ten or twelve feet from the ground, on the Germalus, and then are suddenly left unfinished. They have not been disturbed, but have been afterwards used as foundations for other buildings. It is evident that they belong to a design begun, but afterwards suddenly abandoned; and the reason of this was, according to the family legend, a sudden conclusion of peace. And when, through the intervention of the women, hostilities were suspended between Sabine and Roman, and the fusion of the two peoples into one took place, the contemplated addition to the fortifications on that side was felt to be useless, and therefore was abandoned, especially when, according to the tradition, "the two hills were united into one city, and enclosed within one wall." There is a difference in the character of this piece of walling from the very earliest specimen farther to the south; for here, at the corner of Roma Quadrata, the joints are closer fitted, and the surface of the stones better dressed.

There is another evidence of the truth of these early relations between the settlers on the two hills in the discovery near the north-west corner of the Palatine of a large reservoir for rain-water, with a peculiar kind of well descending into it, having a hollow cone at the bottom. The Romans naturally drew their water from the copious spring in the cave, called Lupercal, under the north-east corner of the valley near the church of S. Anastasia and the Circus Maximus. Running down that face of the hill are primitive gigantic steps, leading straight to the spring: the women going to fetch water would go down those steps, but their steepness would hinder the return of the water-carriers with full pitchers on their heads. The way back to the hill-top would, therefore, lie along the zig-zag path that was cut from the terrace above the foss to the summit, and they would enter the Arx at the Porta Romana, close to the northern apex of the fortress. But this passage would expose them to danger from missiles off the Saturnian mount: the reservoir of rain-water was, therefore, a precaution for the Romans when at war with the Sabines, but would be useless at any other time. A singular confirmation of the tradition that Rome's founders came from Alba Longa is found in the fact, that there exists at that place another well similarly formed, and that these are the only two of the kind known to exist in Italy.

The Gates by which the fortress of the Palatine was entered, three in number, were named Porta Romana, or Romanula, Porta Mugonia, or Mugionis, and Porta Janualis. The first stood at the northern apex of the Palatine, where it projects towards the Forum, and two ways issued from it. One went down by the zig-zag descent to the Germalus, the terrace under the cliffs on the northwestern face, and from it to the bottom of the valley: this was a road for horses, and, as was stated, is still traceable and partly useable. The second way went down on the north-east face, turning the corner towards the Forum, and had a steep descent by steps for foot-passengers only. This was the Porta Romana, and stood at the foot of the road called Clivus Victoriæ, still existing, with its basaltic pavement, passing underneath the lofty remains of the palace attributed to Caligula. This Clivus was the highest portion of the road made by Augustus on the south side of the Forum, and called the Nova Via.

The Porta Mugonia is said by Varro to have been so named from the *mugitus*, lowing of the cattle in the pasture-grounds around the primitive town. It was on the Sub-Velia, and led out of the Via Sacra, at the top of the Clivus Sacer of that road, into the Palatine. It stood in the line of fortification on the north-eastern side of the city, and at about the middle point of that side, and in the great foss which formed the eastern boundary of Roma Quadrata, not far from the mouth of the foss-way, but distinctly within the gorge, where it would be more protected. Remains of what seems to have been this gateway are visible, with very old materials in the foundation. This is not far from the Arch of Titus, through which the continuation of the roads Via Sacra and Via Nova, when united, passed. This is the "old gate" mentioned by Livy, in his account of the vow of Romulus to rear a temple to Jupiter Stator, at the critical moment of his battle with the Sabines; and Ovid's guide (Trist. iii. 1. 31) says of this spot, "Inde petens dextram (i.e. out of the Via Sacra) Porta est ait ista Palati." In one MS. of Varro it is called Sacri Porta.

The third gate was the Porta Janualis, where Varro states the statue of Janus to have been; and probably it stood where the Arch of Janus still stands. Although reckoned by that writer among the gates of Roma Quadrata, it is not in the line of primitive fortifications on and under the hill itself, but at the lowest level between the Arx and the Tiber. It probably barred the way through the *mœnia*, or outer bank, running along the low land of the Velabrum, and, therefore, commanded access to the fortifications on the western side. This arch now stands over a stream of water which runs in the Cloaca Maxima, and always ran between the two hills, made into part of the Cloaca Maxima. Most probably there was originally a draw-bridge over this stream, in front of the gate. When the Romans on the Palatine, and the Sabines on the

Capitoline Hill, were at peace, the gate was left open, and the bridge was let down; when they were at war, the gate was closed, and the bridge drawn up. There are, or were recently, remains of a draw-bridge in front of a gate at Pæstum, which were seen and described, and drawn by Professor Donaldson. It was, therefore, a very ancient custom, as early as the foundation of Rome.

There was also a gate to the south-east, opposite the Cœlian, though not mentioned in Varro's list, nor is the name of it given, as far as has been ascertained, by any other writer; but the road exists, passing under a gateway of the Cæsars: probably it was not part of the ancient fortress. Festus says that all cities founded according to the Etruscan rite had necessarily three gates. But there were in addition flights of steps: one of these led down from the top to the site of the Arch of Constantine, where there are still steps; a second flight led off from the Porta Romana, as was said, to the Forum; and a third ran down towards the Circus, upon the western side of the hill, now passing under the church of S. Anastasia. Such steps would require to be closed with doors at the top, but these would not be usually called gates, although Plutarch mentions a gate with steps descending to the Circus. These last-mentioned steps are among the most interesting remains left of Roma Quadrata. They are of very great size, and are cut out of the natural Tufa rock, not inserted; and they are known as the steps of Cacus. An original Tufa wall runs parallel to the line of steps, and the two structures manifestly fit into each other, as being contemporaneously erected. They served as the most direct means of communication with the Murcian valley, the site of the Circus Maximus, at its north-western end, and past it, with the Tiber at the Pulchrum Littus; the river would naturally be the high road for conveying provisions to the garrison of the citadel. At the foot of these steps also was situated the spring which supplied the inhabitants of the Palatine with water. And at the top of the flight are the foundations, lately excavated, of a very small and massive temple, of the same early character, called Etruscan, and the only one of the kind in Rome. There are very strong reasons for believing this building to have been that temple which was dedicated by Romulus to Jupiter Feretrius, and in which he laid up the Spolia Opima, after triumphing over the Cæninenses, whose leader he had slain with his own hand. The construction of the walls of this temple, and of its Podium, or basement, is identical with that of the outer wall of fortification, being of the large squared stones of Opus quadratum, with the wide vertical joints, which are found scarcely anywhere else in Rome but at this north end of the Palatine hill. There is a manifest coincidence in style and age of all these remains of ancient stonework. But Livy states that this, the earliest temple in Rome, was reared *in Capitolio;* and this would be decisive against the supposition that we have here the very handiwork of Rome's founder. The question then arises, what was meant when, in the first years of Rome, a Capitol is spoken of. Some light is thrown on this by the express affirmation of Vitruvius, that the hut of Romulus was *in Capitolio;* yet all other authors describe it as being on the Palatine. On the Capitol of the Mons Saturnius, then in possession of the Sabines, it could not be; and a temple commemorating a victory in the very early years after Rome's foundation, could not possibly be there either. If Romulus lived *in Capitolio*, it was because at that time Roma Quadrata was the Capitolium, or keep of the city; and his first temple stood within that keep. His own dwelling is said by Solinus to be at the brow of the steps of Cacus; and the steps lead up to the temple; while the site of the house was on the platform lower down, now behind the church of S. Anastasia. If we accept the statement that the name Capitolium was applied strictly to the small temple which, according to the Etruscan rite, was always placed in the Arx, or citadel, as the most secure place in the fortress, or town, the difficulty of connecting a Capitol with the Palatine will disappear.

It was not merely a floating tradition that the Casa Romuli had been on the Palatine; the hut itself was preserved on its site as an object of veneration. Not only does Dionysius affirm that it existed in his day, but Seneca also speaks of it as a building known to every one, *humile tugurium;* and Vitruvius says that the sovereign people of the world still revered that cottage.

On the north-western face of the hill is another interesting religious relic in the form of a stone altar, with an inscription which is said to be quite unique. It runs thus, SEI DEO SEIVE DEIVÆ SACRUM. C. CALVINUS P. R. EX S. C. RESTITUIT. The present stone, according to the canon for Roman inscriptions, must be dated at least 124 years B.C. The form of the letter L occurs here as V, and this is decisive of a certain age. But the old altar thus replaced was of a very early date indeed, as is shewn by the dedication either to some god or to some goddess. Festus says that the religion of the early Romans made them careful and reverent in all things connected with the gods, and that they were fearful of offering them an unauthorized worship. Desiring to propitiate the tutelary deity when they took possession of a place, they made their offering with the guarded provision, **Sive Deus sive Dea.** Varro also affirms that it was the practice when any man wished, *conlucare lucum,* to effect a clearing in a forest (and all forests had their local deities), to do it thus according to the rule *Porco piaculum facito,* and then to add, *Sive Deus sive Diva,* with a prayer to the genius of the place.

From the fact that the Palatine was the most ancient seat of the settlement, that the great men of the city had their houses on it, and that the sovereigns of the Empire retained it as their place of residence, we see brought together in small compass the earliest remains of the infant community, and the splendid examples of imperial magnificence in the palaces of the Cæsars; while, lying between the two, we have the domestic architecture of the time of Augustus well illustrated. The student of Roman archæology must always come to take his first lessons on the Palatine Hill.

CHAPTER III.

THE CITY ON THE TWO HILLS.

THE next most important event after the foundation of Rome, was the incorporation of its fortress and people into one with the Sabine settlement on the neighbouring Capitoline Hill, anciently Mons Saturnius. The legend recording this has come down through one of the historians of Rome in these words: "Both those hills had been encompassed with one wall already" (Dionys. Hal., ii. 66); that is to say, by the time of Numa's accession. Of this wall we have some important remains; but these could not be expected to be equally prominent with the records of the first wall on the Palatine, which was never thrown into the body of the city, to be built over at pleasure, or removed as the wants of its inhabitants might require. The hill of Saturn lies nearly due north of the Palatine, inclining to the west, and is separated from it by a valley, anciently a marsh. The distance between the Porta Romana and the foot of the steps leading up to the Capitol is about 135 yards. Geologists say that the Capitoline was originally a promontory of the Quirinal: there was a depression between them, but this has been deepened by cutting a foss in it. It has two eminences: one to the south, the famous Tarpeian rock; and, separated from it by a natural depression or saddle, the northern one against the Quirinal.

Over the ridge on the north-western face the ground falls towards the Campus Martius: and below the ridge on the south-eastern face towards the Forum, rises an immense pile of massive buildings, the lowest portions of which are very ancient. These served as the municipal offices of old Rome, under the name Tabularium, and they are used for the same purpose in the modern city. The Tarpeian rock is of a much harder stone than the Palatine, being partly Tufa of a compact nature, and partly of the still more compact Peperino. Its great steepness made it a strong natural fortress, so that no mound or palisade was added to secure the edge of the cliff; of this neglect the Gauls took advantage, by scaling the height with ladders. Tacitus says that the Capitolium as well as the Forum Romanum was incorporated into the city by Titus Tatius; and Dionysius affirms that Romulus held the Palatine and the Cœlian (the latter for pasture-ground), Tatius the Capitoline, which he had first occupied, and the Quirinal.

The Mons Saturnius is the smallest in area of all the hills of Rome, not much larger than the site covered by Roma Quadrata: easily fortified, it became an excellent Arx for the occupants of the adjacent pastures. Thus the Roman and Sabine communities were in positions analogous to each other. When the two peoples were fused into one, their two citadels with the intervening space became one city, civilly and militarily, and enclosed within one wall. Dionysius says this was done when the Temple of Vesta was built; and when it had been done, the whole rock or hill of Saturn's mount became the Capitolium, the strongest fortified centre. The boundaries of this Arx were on the north, outside the foss and wall, a level plain on the bank of the Tiber, known as the Campus Martius, often flooded and left a swamp: on the east the valley, neither deep nor broad, separating it from the Quirinal; on the west the valley of the Tiber, and on the south the low marshy ground between it and the Palatine, with the market-places upon the level ground, in which was a wide and deep foss. In the eastern part of this foss the Forum Romanum was made: another, the cattle market, Forum Boarium, was placed at the south-western corner of the foss, outside the

Porta Janualis. The foss then turned northward, and in it a third market, Forum Olitorium, for vegetables stood. On the north side of this market stands the great semi-circular theatre of Marcellus, with its lower columns buried considerably by the raising of the old foss-way to the level of the street. The foss then turned to the east along the north side of the rock: part of the Ghetto, or Jews' quarter, is built in it; and the Porta Triumphalis of the Cæsars, now the porch of St. Angelo's church, was built across it. The foss then passed on to the modern S. Mark's-square, its northernmost point; and thence, towards the south, struck along under the east side of the rock in the narrow gorge between the Capitoline and Quirinal, which was afterwards widened to admit the Forum of Trajan: the Forum of Julius Cæsar was also made in it, uniting the Forum Romanum to that of Augustus.

Next, the wall of the united city on the two hills has also been traced out, and as it confirms the legend related by the historian, it is of high interest and importance. Dionysius says (lib. ii. c. 66), "Numa, after his election, did not remove the particular temples belonging to the Curiæ, but erected one temple common to them all between the Capitoline and Palatine hills. For both these had already been encompassed with one wall, the Forum in which the temple was built lying between them." Such was the tradition recorded by this writer only: but the tradition was true, and it accounts for the remains of this great wall as we now find them. Its line can be clearly made out. On the north side of the Capitoline the scarped cliffs were considered sufficient protection. The wall was joined on to its foot near the north-eastern corner, crossing the old foss described above. In that foss, as was usual, a road was made, which is still a street (Via di Marforio), and the wall crosses that street at its northern end, forming a ridge across it. Excavations made in it laid bare the tufa wall forming this ridge. The line of wall continues across the southern end of the Forum of Trajan under the houses in the street. It will be understood that, as much of old Rome lies buried and sometimes twice buried, it is only by burrowing among cellars and foundations of existing buildings that the remains of the old town are found: the archæologist finds them by patient search, and makes them intelligible to the scholar. The line of wall continued straight from west to east, and joined on to that part of the Quirinal which was afterwards scooped away to enlarge Trajan's Forum. It then turned to the right, or south, and here it still remains standing for a considerable distance, forming the eastern wall of the Forum of Augustus as far as the mediæval fortress Torre dei Conti, which stands upon the site of another very ancient fortress. Adjoining Augustus' Forum was that of Nerva, called also Forum Transitorium: the wall on its northern side is built of Travertine stone, the kind usually employed under the Empire, and this separates the two Fora. But it is inserted at a right angle into a tower of the great second wall or line of fortification, at about one-third of the latter's height. Half of the old tower is still visible behind the houses, a magnificent structure, fifty feet high and twelve thick, built of the usual great blocks of tufa.

On the south side of this Forum after leaving the tower, now dei Conti, the line of wall turns again at a right angle towards the west: it is not visible, but runs under the houses in the street, the backs of which stand upon the wall. At the corner of the next street, the conspicuous marble columns of the Altar of Pallas are built up against it, and the cornice is built upon it. Behind these columns is an ancient doorway, one of the entrances of the united city. At the easternmost point of the enclosure was the outlying or detached work, forming part of the defences of the Palatine, called the Velia: this was, in fact, the lower portion of the westernmost spur of the Esquiline, where it approaches most nearly to the Palatine. A great foss cut it off from the rest of the hill, which foss still exists in the street called the Via del Colosseo. Varro, however, states that it constituted part of the Palatine; and perhaps, considering the near proximity of the two hills, the Arx in the primitive occupation could not be safe unless this promontory were added to it as a wing. Traces of the second wall, after it had passed round the eastern side of the Velia, are found outside the so-called Temple of Venus and Rome, opposite the Colosseum. Thence the line continued onward perfectly straight, near the site of the Arch of Constantine, and past the whole south-eastern face of the Palatine; turning again to the north-west, some remains of it are visible in a garden behind the houses, and the line passes on to the fine masonry in the bases of the buried tower under the church of S. Anastasia.

This structure made a strong fort at the foot of the Palatine, just at the point where the wall, leaving the hill-side, would turn again westward and run across the valley, to the Pulchrum Littus on the bank of the Tiber, an important part of this second line of defence. This is a massive wall of tufa built against that river's bank for about half-a-mile, beginning at the Porta Trigemina and extending to the bridge on the island, or Pons Fabricius. For the most part it is concealed by the quantity of sand and soil thrown up against it by successive floods of the Tiber, but it is visible at intervals in several places. The mouth of the great sewer, Cloaca Maxima, with its triple concentric arch, is evidently inserted in it, that is, an aperture has been made in an earlier wall to introduce the mouth of the drain. This wall served a double purpose: first, to protect the foundations of buildings from being washed away in one of the great floods to which the Tiber is liable; in fact it kept the river out of that part of the city of the two hills which lay between the brink and the hills themselves. Secondly, it was a grand military rampart resting upon the river, as the other walls of the period usually rested against a cliff. Like others of the same kind and age, it is twelve feet thick and probably was fifty feet high, and it distinctly belongs to the second period of construction; for, while the blocks of Tufa composing it are of the same size as in the earliest wall, they are of fine-jointed masonry, not split off, but cut with the saw.

After running about half-a-mile upon the river's side until it arrived opposite the Capitoline Hill, it left the Tiber, and was carried across the plain, and joined on to the cliff on its western side. A fragment of an ancient tufa wall under the church of S. Angelo, at the foot of the hill, indicates its approach to the citadel. This line was long retained as the boundary of the city proper in that direction, and the Porta Triumphalis (now forming the porch of the church) was between the Porticus Octaviæ outside the city, and the Porticus Philippi within it. This grand triumphal entrance into the city continued to be used on state occasions; here the military processions were formed, and started to ascend the Capitol.

The remains of the wall of the second city thus traced have usually been attributed either to the original city, or to that of Servius Tullius. It is quite true that that prince made use of them, whenever they served his purpose, for the fortification of his enlarged city; but many parts of it, and some of the most conspicuous, as that against the Forum of Augustus, could not have formed part of his plan of circumvallation: they belong to a city of smaller area and of earlier date.

Festus speaks of the Fossæ **Quiritium**, works executed by the citizens of the united nationalities, when combined into one civil and military community. We have already seen how one great foss ran between the detached portion of the Esquiline, the Velia, and the parent hill; the two cliffs through which it cut are there still, with the modern street running between them twenty feet below their tops, while the vines growing above are visible over the walls which support the cliffs. The foss round the Capitol has been also traced, and to finish the work round the whole enclosure, there must have been a similar foss at the foot of the southern wall of the Palatine. On the side towards the Aventine was the low swampy ground called Vallis Murcia, through which the stream called the Almo runs; this communicates with the Tiber lower down than the great Cloaca, and the opening for it through the wall, Pulchrum Littus, bears evidence of being part of the original construction. And it is plain that by means of a flood-gate, when required, the water in that stream might be dammed up and made to flood the valley, thus adding another element of defence to the city on that side. The Capitol itself was deemed, from the steepness of its northern front, to need no wall to strengthen it; but in several places on the flat ground on the north side of that hill the earth slopes down on both sides towards a depression, implying the presence at some time of a considerable foss never quite filled up. There are evident traces again of a similar trench outside that part of the wall which was incorporated in the Forum of Augustus.

This eastern wall of the city on the two hills, which was necessary to connect them, is not generally understood, although there are considerable remains of it. Several market-places (*fora*) were made just within this wall. At the north end of this east wall was the Forum of Trajan;

this joined on to the north end of the Forum of Augustus, with the Temple of Mars Ultor built up against it.

The system of fosses, broad and deep, separating the city on the two hills from all the adjacent country, made it a strong fortress. This constituted the heart of Rome, to which as a centre the other mounts and hills were added one by one, as they were required to meet the increase of inhabitants, and of their substance in flocks and herds.

The names of three gates connected with this Arx of the second city have been preserved,—Porta Saturnia, Porta Flumentana, and Porta Carmentalis. The first, mentioned by Livy and Dionysius, was the entrance to the Capitol itself, on the slope of the clivus which led up from the Forum along the southern face of the mount: this Clivus was paved with basalt by the Censors, B.C. 174. Varro indicates its position, quoting old writers to shew that about the base of the hill, and facing the Forum, was the Temple of Saturn, and behind it the Porta Saturni, in the walls called *postici muri*, 'the postern walls;' the gate through these, therefore, at the back of the fortress, would properly be called the postern-gate. The Porta Flumentana, near the bank of the river on the western side of the hill, is frequently mentioned in connection with the damages caused by inundations of the Tiber: in time of flood the water ran through the gate. Cicero mentions it, but without indication as to site. It was probably placed across the street nearest the river, running parallel to it at a low level, and between the Fabrician bridge to the island and the Palatine bridge below the island. The Porta Carmentalis cannot be fixed with certainty, but Livy gives an account of a great fire which ravaged the quarter near that gate, and hence its site can be obtained approximately. On that occasion the Temples of Mater Matuta and Spes were burnt, one within and the other without the gate. This would make it nearer the foot of the Capitol than the Porta Flumentana, and just under its south-westernmost point. The name was derived from the altar of the goddess Carmenta close to the gate; it was also called Porta Scelerata, after the destruction of the 300 of the Fabia Gens at the river Cremera, who issued out of Rome by that gate on their ill-fated expedition.

We have no evidence that these two gates belonged to the second wall of Rome, but they were entrances into the city on the side of the Capitoline, and therefore are properly inserted in this place. Most probably they were rather the gates of the third wall of defence, the work of Servius Tullius connecting the seven hills together in one fortress.

CHAPTER IV.

The Fortifications on the other Five Hills, and on the Heights adjacent.

EACH of the seven eminences constituting the complete city was a separate fortress, and on nearly all of them there are remains of Tufa walls sufficiently indicating this fact. As was natural, they were added consecutively to enlarge the area of habitations, but they were not all included within one line of defence till the third wall was built in the time of Servius Tullius.

The Mons Aventinus lies south-west of the Palatine, separated from it by the Murcian valley, which composed the Circus Maximus. This intervening lowland was, till it was drained, a marsh or lake in rainy weather. On the north-western side of the hill runs the Tiber, with a very narrow strip of land between it and the steep face of the cliff. On the south and west sides the Aventine was strengthened by scarped cliffs and a wall. The area of the mount is larger than that of the Palatine, eighteen stadia in circumference, as Dionysius gives it. It is also divided into two portions by a natural depression, or Inter-montium; the smaller or south-eastern portion of which has been called by moderns Pseudo-Aventine, separated from the larger and higher eminence by a wide and deep foss made in the valley. In this foss runs still the modern road issuing out of the city in the direction of Ostia. The Pseudo-Aventine has monastic buildings at its two opposite ends, and these buildings stand on old fortifications, the sites of ancient fortresses which defended the approaches to the city in this part, by the Via Appia on **the north-east,** and by the Via Ostiensis and Via Ardeatina on the south-west. The Aventine was taken possession of at a very early date in the history of Rome, but as pasture-ground only, and therefore **was** only slightly fortified.

Dionysius says "it was covered with every kind of wood, **the** most numerous and most beautiful being the bay-trees, for which reason a certain part of it was called Lauretum by the Romans, but now it is quite full of houses. There, along with many others, a temple of Diana is erected." Livy and Dionysius both refer the permanent occupation of the hill as a dwelling-place to the removal of some conquered Latins to this spot. Ancus Martius took the Latin town Politorium, B.C. 630, and assigned **the hill** to its people; such imported inhabitants were admitted, not as slaves, but as part of the Plebs, or commoners of Rome, without political rights. It is to these Latins that the so-called Wall of the Latins on the Aventine has been attributed. But though the Aventine became essentially an integral portion of Rome, it was not included within the Pomœrium, or religious boundary, but remained outside it, not only after the third wall of the Kings was reared around all seven hills, but after the time of Sylla, and also of Julius Cæsar, both of whom could have exercised the right of extending the Pomœrium so as to include this hill. Nor was it done till the reign of Claudius Cæsar. But when first occupied as a place of permanent residence, it was of necessity fortified; then these walls of the Latins were built, and such remains of them as have lately been dug out answer very well to this period of the kingly history. The Aventine was not originally included in the Pomœrium, because it was separated from the other hills by the river Almo, then a considerable stream, and always liable to sudden floods.

Beginning at the Tiber, close to the Pons Sublicius, the ancient bridge of wood still discernible by its substructures in the bed of the Tiber in dry seasons, the edge of the hill was strongly protected by a wall against the cliffs, of which wall there are remains overhanging the Tiber under the monastery of S. Sabina, placed on the loftiest point of the hill. Other remains of the same wall face the cliff farther south, and near the corner where the scarped side turns round to the east. Nearer the Ostian gate, now that of S. Paul, a noble fragment of this great wall comes to view. This portion, with those before mentioned, is of rather different construction from the wall belonging to the agger of Servius Tullius; the edges of the stones are chamfered off as in rustic-work. The structure is in large blocks, partly of yellow tufa from the bed of the Cœlian, rudely hewn out of the rock and squared with the hatchet, and partly of the red variety of the same stone from the Aventine itself. There are several yards of this wall laid bare, fifty feet high and twelve feet thick, the usual dimensions of all the early walls.

After this fragment had been exposed for some time, farther excavations revealed a mass of concrete wall, and therefore of Republican date, behind the tufa, so that in this part the facing only is of the large blocks in the early style. Upon the top of this wall a wide arch of sawn stones, and a second and smaller one, have been inserted in later times, apparently to serve as embrasures for the discharge of missiles from a catapult and a balista. These arches command the southern slope of the hill, and the approaches to the gate on that side. A few yards farther on are other vestiges of exceedingly ancient wall-work, being almost identical in style with that of Roma Quadrata, with the vertical joints wide and repeated above each other. This was part of a fort commanding the approach to a gate; the rest of the structure shews the joints closely fitted.

There is another fort opposite to it under the monastery of S. Saba, on the Pseudo-Aventine, of similar character; and the pair of forts is placed, each at one angle of a gorge, at the narrowest point of which stood the gateway. Altogether it seems certain that **we have** here the original Latin wall of the time of the earlier Kings, and grafted upon it the work of Servius Tullius, who used the old fortifications wherever they suited his purpose. **It** will be seen in the next chapter **how the** position of such a gate as that here described corresponds with the design elsewhere adopted by the engineers in their enclosure of the whole city **on the** Seven Hills.

The Mons Cœlius lies south-east of the Palatine, and extends just as far to the south of it as does the larger or proper Aventine; the southern foot or spur of the Palatine strikes wedge-like between the other two. As the Aventine was surnamed Lauretum, and the valley of the Circus Maximus Murcia, from its myrtles, so the Cœlian was entitled Querquetulanus, from its growth of oaks. Varro **states** the origin of its name as follows:—"On the side of the region of the Subura the chief hill is the Cœlian (so called) from Cœlius Vibenna, a noble Tuscan chieftain, who is said to have given aid to Romulus against Tatius. After the death of Cœlius, because they occupied too strong a position and were not altogether trusted, the Tuscans were removed hence into the lower ground, and gave the name to the Vicus Tuscus." Dionysius assigns the same origin. Its formal occupation as part of the city is given as coinciding with the capture and destruction of Alba, whose inhabitants were transplanted hither and largely augmented the number of citizens, many of them being admitted into the patrician class. The addition of another mount to the city necessitated military engineering; but **Strabo**, the **geographer, assigns** military necessity as the cause rather than the effect **of occupation.** "Ancus Martius, when he took in the Cœlian and Aventine Hills, separated as they were from each other, and from the other fortifications of the city, acted from necessity in adding them. For neither was it expedient to leave such strong hills without the wall to serve as positions for attacking the **city** to any that wished it, nor was he **able** to complete the **whole wall as** far as the Quirinal," that is to say, to take in **the whole** seven hills.

The name of Cœlian Hill is given by some to the whole of the elevated land eastward, **as** far as the latest wall of Rome, where it encloses the south-easternmost angle of the **imperial and** modern city. Thus it would include the Lateran; but though now it seems all one hilly range, there is between the Lateran and Cœlian a valley and a foss cut in it at some very early period. Across this depression **has** been thrown up afterwards an agger, or bank, to carry the aqueduct and road, which makes the two heights seem continuous. At the very farthest point in this direction of the wall was another imperial fortress and palace, called Sessorium, belonging to the family of Verus, and the residence of Helena, mother of Constantine; this also is detached from the high ground of the Lateran by a foss, which is crossed by another bank of connection. So that these outlying spurs off the Cœlian were detached forts guarding the city proper, but outside it. All round the Cœlian, the sides have been scarped and evidently in very early days. The most prominent feature within its area, is a projection of the hill into the valley where the Colosseum stands, well defined to the eye as a nearly square mass. This was occupied in imperial times by the Claudium, consisting of a temple with its enclosure round it, with terraces built up against the cliff by the Emperor Claudius. These terraces have been nearly all destroyed, and the outline of the scarped cliff is therefore well seen. The Claudium is the northernmost portion of the mount; to the south-west of it the steep cliff formed the protection as far as the monastery of S. Gregory the Great, and there the wall begins, of which there is a fine piece close to the church. It consists partly of the usual large tufa blocks, partly it has been rebuilt of concrete, and is only faced with such stones.

Proceeding along the southern side of the hill is a modern villa, **the site of an ancient fort supported by** walls of mixed periods; but farther on eastward, where the cliff subsides, the outer wall disconnected with the hill seems to have been relied on for defence. **The present wall**, mainly the work of Aurelian, is built upon the old wall of the Kings in this part, **and has in its substructure** remains of tufa-work. There is also a water-course at the bottom of the slope, running to join the Almo **or Aqua** Crabra of the Murcian valley, which added to the means of defence hereabouts. **On** the north-eastern face of the Cœlian is a very strong ancient fortress now occupied as a monastery, in a commanding situation, with steep cliffs on three sides: it is joined on to the main body of the hill on the southern side only, and even here also is a small foss. Here is an example of the kind of precaution taken by Roman engineers in extending the military occupation of their city. To complete the circuit, at the east end opposite the Lateran, the cliff on the side of the valley is supported by a wall, and at the bottom of the hollow, as was said, is a foss also.

Roman writers mention also the Cœliolus or little Cœlian, which **as Varro** states was assigned to a section of the Tuscans who were **more to** be trusted than the rest. There is nearly at the southernmost point of the city a hill of small size, on which the Porta Latina stands, which is sometimes so called; but this hardly **bears out** the expression of Varro, "now joined to the Cœlian."

With greater probability the Lateran height seems to answer to the little Cœlian, being so close to the Cœlian proper, and **yet** naturally detached from it. In that case this colony was not included within the city: for on each side of the foss separating the eastern end of the Cœlian **from** the Lateran, stands **a tomb of the first** Christian century, **and this** is a certain indication **that** the Lateran at that date was not within the city of **Rome**, i.e. not within the precinct of the lines of Servius Tullius. Both the Sessorian and Lateran fortresses are within the wall of Aurelian, the latest line of enclosure.

The Quirinal, Viminal and Esquiline heights were called *colles*, elevated grounds, rather than *montes*, distinct and separate hills. The four mounts, the successive enclosures **of which** have been traced, rise out of low lands or valleys around them on every side. But the three remaining eminences are not in fact isolated, but connected: they are three promontories or tongues pushed forward from the high table-land, forming the whole north-eastern side of the city. If, therefore, Rome was to be enlarged in that direction, considerable artificial defences were required, so as to cut off the newly-enclosed ground from the unenclosed portion of the nearly level table-land. The western faces of these heights were naturally strong, and the whole eastern slope was weak for purposes of defence, and this defect was remedied, as will be seen, by the construction of the third great wall of the Kings. But at present we are following the indications remaining, to shew that each of these three elevated promontories had fortifications on them, independently of the great line of defence executed by the later kings. To begin with the Quirinal, the most northern of them, and lying nearest to the Capitoline. This Hill was sometimes called Agonalis; for *agon* is said to signify, in Sabine language, a small hillock. Now the Quirinal is a series of such small mounds; six of them can be counted upon it. It was also called early in Roman history Regio Collina, and still goes by the name Rione dei Monti, or the Region of the Hills. The Quirinal presents evidences in several distinct places of its early fortifications.

The King's palace, bearing the name of the hill, stands upon scarped cliffs of the ancient type, and in the garden attached to it are remains of tufa walling. A portion of a wall of kingly construction is visible under the cliff of this hill, upon its western face, in the gardens of the Colonna family. This piece is of very early character, the vertical joints being wider even than in Roma Quadrata; it may perhaps belong to the original fortification of the Sabines, when they held this hill, called also Capitolium Vetus. At the north-east angle of the Quirinal are distinct remains of a great horn-work, or detached fort, to defend that part of the line where it was naturally weak. This is close to the House of Sallust, who made the gardens and the circus bearing his name out of the wide and deep foss running at the foot of the cliff. Beneath a villa constructed on the western side of that circus, large stones, forming a wall of the Kings, can be seen against the cliff, behind the shrubbery. Past that point the cliff-line turns westward, with the same large foss between it and the Pincian Hill, which is another and more northerly spur or ridge of the high table-land, and running nearly to the Tiber. The cliff hereabouts has been faced everywhere with a wall of the Kings, and this wall has in most places been faced or rebuilt in the time of the Early Empire, and often again at later periods to support new buildings on the higher level.

But as an evidence of the original structure, a piece of the old kingly wall can be seen through a hole in an arcade of brick built up against it.

The Viminal ends in a short and narrow tongue of ground projected from the high table-land, between the Quirinal and Esquiline: this spur runs south-westerly, with its scarped cliffs very distinctly marked out. Between it and the south-eastern slope of the Quirinal is a well-defined valley, and on the north-western face of the Viminal above this valley, the cliff is supported for some distance by a wall of the kingly times, of the usual large tufa blocks, split with a wedge, not sawn, and put together without mortar, but of somewhat later character than the wall of the Palatine. On the south side, the great House of the Pudens family is built up against the cliff, and conceals it. At the west end, the cliff may be seen behind the houses, the back windows of which look right against the cliff and the wall supporting it.

The Esquiline Hill, south of the Viminal, upon a map properly shaded to shew high and low grounds, seems almost surrounded by three valleys, and to be connected with the great table-land by a very narrow neck. One derivation of its name assigned by Varro is "ab æsculetis," from the æsculus grown on it, a great forest-tree formerly common in Italy, but now supposed to be extinct. Its position made it easily defensible on all sides. On this hill the cliffs are mostly concealed by walls of the Empire built up against them, and there are fewer indications of early defences than on any other of the seven. The reason of this seems to be, that the Cæsars so largely occupied it with their vast structures, and thus either destroyed or effectually concealed pre-existing works. The great Golden House of Nero, the most ambitious of all imperial designs, extended from the Velia, which was considered part of the

Palatine, across the valley between the hills, and including the site of the Colosseum, occupied the largest portion of the Esquiline. The porticus or arcade in front of them was a mile long, and there are remains of it in **several** places. This palace, entirely on one level, **is now subter-** ranean, with many of its chambers still visible. Over these substructures were **afterwards** built the Thermæ of Titus and Trajan, occupying the central part of the hill. The key to the Esquiline as a separate fortress seems to have been at its north-western point, where stands the church **of S.** Peter ad Vincula. Here the cliff is very clearly visible, with a passage or steps cut through it, leading down from the high level at the church to that of the foss below, **now a street.** Again, there is a horn-work, or semi-detached fort, at the south-eastern angle of the hill, overlooking the valley between it and the Cœlian; it projects beyond the edge of the hill in a remarkable manner, and seems to have defended a gate placed in the bank thrown across the valley. The great agger of Servius Tullius broke off at the point where it touched the cliff of the Esquiline, on its eastern face. That was, therefore, an important portion of the ancient scarped cliff of the hill; but being long enclosed in the garden **of a nunnery,** this spot remained inaccessible **for** examination. A short agger across the valley, at the horn-work of the south-eastern angle, would **also connect the line of** defence with the strong out-post of the **Lateran.**

Each of these Seven Hills, in conformity with universal practice, had its own Arx or citadel, the strongest place within the enclosure. We have seen how Roma Quadrata on the Palatine was the citadel of the first colony, and how the Capitoline became the citadel of the city on the two hills. For the Aventine, the detached part, or Pseudo-Aventine, evidently had the citadel upon it. The monastery of S. Balbina stands on an old fort, upon the northeastern side, with scarped faces to the cliffs north and east very distinct, with walls also built up against them, and a foss on the western side. On the south side the cliff is concealed by masses of earth thrown up for garden cultivation. On the Cœlian the square fortress, afterwards the Claudium, was evidently the Arx. The scarped cliffs on three sides are quite visible, though later walls have been built against them; and on the fourth side, between it and the main body of the Cœlian, there is a deep fossway, on a steep slope, known as the Clivus Scauri.

For the Quirinal as a separate fortress, the citadel must have been on the site of the king's palace. There are cliffs all round it, steep and high, although the great papal edifices against them to a great extent conceal their form.

For the Viminal, the citadel extended from the part where the tufa walls remain opposite the Quirinal on one side, back to the House of Pudens, facing the Esquiline, on the other, where the cliffs can still be traced, with the houses built up against them.

For the Esquiline, its north-western angle at S. Peter ad Vincula was the site of the Arx.

There remain for examination the outlying eminences on both sides of the Tiber, which could not be neglected by the early Romans, although they formed no part of their habitable city. These are the Mons Janiculensis, Mons Vaticanus, and Mons Pincius. The Janiculum is, both by its position and its superior height, the most important outpost of Rome. This was perceived very early in its history, and accordingly both Livy and Dionysius refer its military occupation to the king, Ancus Martius, lest at any time it should become a fortress in the hands of a hostile force; it was, therefore, connected with the city by a bridge, and provided both with a wall and a ditch. The bridge was the Pons Sublicius, or bridge of wood, constructed without brass or iron, and so put together that a portion could be taken to pieces and removed in time of war. By the term 'wall' is to be understood not a line of masonry, but a bank, according to the account of Varro, who says that such a defence was called *murus*, and hence comes the term Pomœrium, the space *post murum*, behind the *murus* or outward rampart, and between it and the inner one.

The Janiculum is the key to the possession of Rome. Stretching along the western bank of the Tiber for more than 2000 yards, and at a much greater height than any of the seven hills, it completely commands the city. From the Porta Janiculensis at the southern end, the whole of Rome lies spread out like a map at the foot of the spectator. This important eminence has been strongly fortified in modern times, and has shewn itself capable of standing a regular siege. Early, again, in the times of the Republic, we read in Dionysius, "The Roman Consuls strengthened with more effectual fortifications the hill called Janiculum, which is a high mount near Rome, lying on the other side of the Tiber, and took care above all things that the enemy should not possess themselves of so convenient a post to annoy the city; and there they laid up their provisions for the war." But this fortress by no means included the whole range of hill; it occupied only the southern portion of it, in a line running up from the Tiber at the Porta Portuensis to the Porta Janiculensis, so as to take in the crest of the hill, and then running back easterly down to the river. The old foss of the Janiculum is distinctly visible in the vineyards on the slope of it. In the higher part, on the southern face, near the site of S. Pietro in Montorio, a battery was erected in the time of Pius IX., which destroyed the outline of the old earthworks; but below this, within the remains of the wall of Aurelian, it is discernible down the face of the hill, nearly as far as the monastery of S. Cosimato. Under S. Pietro also the ancient scarped cliffs can be seen; and upon the northern side, where the mills are placed upon the wall in the old towers, the foss is very evident on the outside of them, with a great difference of level between the inside and outside of the wall. There remains enough to shew clearly that the Arx of the fortress stood at this spot, which is naturally exceedingly strong. Remains of the towers and wall of Aurelian can also be seen built up against the scarped cliffs, serving as substructures to the mills. That foss goes quite down the hill to the Tiber, passing by the Porta Septimiana.

Near the northern end of the Janiculum is the Vatican Hill, and just to the south of the great Basilica of S. Peter's is another ancient fort very distinct, now partly occupied by the Villa Barberini. It is a natural rock, with steep cliffs fully fifty feet high all round it, and part of these have evidently been scarped by the hand of man. The western side of it lies outside the fortifications enclosing the modern town, or the Leonine City, but the eastern side is within that line, and the cliffs are behind the houses.

The Mons Pincius, the northernmost projecting tongue of high land in modern Rome, but not included in the ancient city till late in its history, was for centuries called the Garden Hill, and is still the recreation-ground for the people; but lying in such close proximity to the city, it never could be left unprotected. The northern portion of it was strongly fortified; a deep foss was cut, severing that part of it which is nearest to the Tiber from the continuous ridge outside the city, and in this foss the modern road at the foot of the lofty wall was made, and the wall is built against the cliff. This wall will be described in the latter part of the sixth chapter. All along the north-eastern face of the hill, which is a very narrow neck of high land, the cliffs were scarped steeply.

This survey of the circuit round the hilly lands of Rome on both sides of the river, shews clearly that the art of military engineering was understood by the early Romans; but a further development of sound principles of fortification was still required to make the Septimontium a secure enclosure. It will be seen in the next chapter how this was accomplished by earthworks of a very extended character, and by a very ingenious system of connecting neighbouring heights, and of making gates protected by forts in the connecting banks.

CHAPTER V.

THE CITY ON THE SEVEN HILLS WITHIN ONE ENCLOSURE.

HAVING traced the gradual increment of the town from the infant Roma Quadrata on one hill to the occupation of all seven hills, with lines of fortification round each of them, we now come to a most important work of the time of the Kings, namely, the completion by Servius Tullius of a continuous line of defence, so as to enclose the whole area into one place of arms. The statement is loosely made in books on ancient Rome, that this king built a wall six or seven miles long around the circuit of the seven hills; but it is certain that he did nothing so ambitious, for in the first place it would have been beyond his power; and secondly, it would have been unnecessary. What he did was to connect together the fortifications of two neighbouring hills wherever they were detached, and to rear one vast bank, supported by a wall with its foss, extending from end to end of the weakest part of the lines. He did, in fact, what any military engineer would do naturally, he made use of the previously-existing fortifications, consisting principally of the scarped cliffs of the hills, and he constructed a short agger or rampart across each valley from cliff to cliff, so as to unite the disconnected heights. In the agger he set a gate, and this was so high up the gorge in the valley as to be commanded by a fort upon each cliff; or it had a single flanking tower, as is seen in connection with the site of the celebrated Porta Capena, where the present mediæval structure is founded upon a square tufa tower of the Kings.

It is true, therefore, that Servius Tullius put or completed a girdle round the City on the Seven Hills, which, though severally protected by works of some sort, were up to his time disconnected, saving the conjoined group of Palatine and Capitoline. On the modern maps this girdle is traced out with very fair accuracy, and is called by the appropriate name of Recinto, or encircling compass. Then for the first time one continuous fortification encompassed the whole city; and though the suburbs were afterwards pushed beyond this boundary, no complete girdle of earthwork or masonry was subsequently made round the enlarged town till the reign of the Emperor Aurelian. The portion of this great work which was entirely original, namely, the agger and wall, is thus spoken of by writers on Rome. Dionysius says: "**The** Romans then, having mustered and armed their forces, stationed themselves on the girdle of the city, which was at that time of about the same extent as the Asty of Athens. On **one side it** depended on the hills and the scarped cliffs, on another side it was defended by the river Tiber. . . . . Another part of the city which was more easy of access, from the Porta Esquilina to the Porta Collina, has been made strong by art. In the first place, a foss has been excavated of such large dimensions that it is, at the least, one hundred feet wide and thirty feet deep; a wall is then built against this foss, and a large and high bank, which can neither be shaken by battering-rams, nor can the foundation be undermined. This part is in length about **seven stadia, and** in breadth fifty feet."

It may be properly noted here that the Cavaliere Fiorelli has excavated **this foss** and measured **it in** that part, at a place where it is now distinctly visible, and verified the exactness of the size of the trench **as** given above. Strabo, the geographer, says: "Servius supplied the omission by adding the Esquiline and Viminal Hills; but as these are easy of access from without, they dug a deep ditch, and threw up the earth on the inner side, and this agger or rampart on the inner face of the ditch they continued for a distance of six stadia, and raised against it a wall and towers from the Porta Esquilina as far as the Porta Collina." To estimate these passages rightly, we must endeavour to fix the position of the two gates mentioned by both authors. Neither of them exists now, because they were in the inner line of fortifications swept away long ago, after the city had become enlarged to its farthest eastern boundary, that is, the wall of Aurelian. Strabo says of the Porta Collina, "through it passes the Via Salaria;" this fixes the general direction in which to look for the gate. It was at the north end of the great agger of Servius, which, leaving suddenly its long course towards the north, turns to the west, and comes inwards to the House of Sallust. That house stood upon the hornwork, or semi-detached fort, before mentioned as part of the Quirinal defences. This latter was, no doubt, placed there for the protection of the gate. Here was the weakest part of the defences in the whole circuit of the city, for want of the outer wall left unfinished, exactly in this part between the Pretorian Camp and the Pincian Hill; it was the point most usually attacked, and was frequently burnt both during the Republic and under the Empire. Here the Gauls entered Rome; from this side Hannibal threatened it, and in the panic created by the appearance of his troops eight miles from the city, the Consular armies were ordered to encamp between the Colline and Esquiline gates. It was by the Porta Salaria, the entrance of the Via Salaria into Rome through Aurelian's wall, that the Goths forced the line of defence. Excavations made here reveal the foundation of a gate-house on the line with an aqueduct, along the horn-work, or bank of earth, to a reservoir under Sallust's house, about ten feet underground. The gate therefore stood near the modern street Via di Porta Pia, which traverses the whole north-western side of the Quirinal Hill, and its site was exactly in front of the church of S. Maria della Vittoria.

The Porta Esquilina, nearly at the southern end of the great agger, stood a little to the south-east of the great church of S. Maria Maggiore, at the spot where the road to the Porta Tiburtina, now S. Lorenzo, joins the street leading up to that church. Here stands the arch of Gallienus. But the same name was given to the outer gate in the *mœnia*, now the Porta Maggiore; for Frontinus says that the Aqua Marcia enters Rome at the Porta Esquilina, and the remains of that aqueduct are distinctly visible entering Rome through the exterior wall by the side of the Porta Maggiore. There was another gate in the agger called Porta Viminalis. Strabo says: "About the middle of the agger is a third gate of the same name as the Viminal Hill." Remains of the gate were found near the south-east corner of the great Thermæ of Diocletian, on the line of the old road which ran through the outer gate in the *mœnia*, called Porta Clausa or Chiusa, and passed along the south side of the Prætorian Camp. But in this case, as in the last, there must have been another gate in the outer line of defence bearing the same name; for Frontinus, the writer on the aqueducts and their superintendent, mentions such a gate, to which some of those works were brought to be distributed over the city. It appears strange at first sight that the same name should be given to two gates, one in the inner wall, the other in the outer line of defence. Yet such must have been the case in Rome, and it is confirmatory of this, that it is still the practice in the Leonine city, or Transtiberine quarter, where two gates in the same line of road, one in the inner and the other in the outer wall, are both called Porta Angelica.

The southern end of the agger of Servius ceases with its junction against the cliff of the Esquiline, where the natural defences become stronger through the greater abruptness of the ground, and facility for scarping the hillsides. The great bank, therefore, was a protection to all that north-eastern portion of the city lying upon the high table-land, from which the three Colles, Quirinal, Viminal, and Esquiline, jut out westwards into the heart of the city. Here the slope of the ground is so gradual, that a bank with its wide foss was the only resource of the engineer for protection.

This agger was cut through obliquely in making the railway into Rome, which enters the wall to the north of the Porta Tiburtina, and terminates opposite the south-eastern side of the Baths of Diocletian. On enlarging the station on the north side, the workmen came upon a considerable fragment of the wall supporting the agger, built of great squared stones, about twelve feet thick, and very well constructed, with finely-fitting joints, uncemented, but held together by iron clamps. It was immediately acknowledged to be that wall, and at first was treated carefully; every stone in it was numbered at once as soon as uncovered, in order that any removal of a portion might be immediately detected. Having stood exposed sufficiently long to convince any eye-witness of the solid and masterly style of construction displayed by Rome's early builders, it was swept away.

The great agger extended once, as we saw by fixing the gates at each end of it, from the cliff of the Quirinal to that of the Esquiline. Nearly the whole of it has been cleared away, in order to make room for the new quarter of the city upon the hilly ground: but what has been traced and measured of it, proves the truth of the traditions preserved in writers on Rome.

The next point of interest in the system of fortification adopted by Servius, is his method of connecting separate hill-fortresses, by throwing short aggers across the intervening valleys. Thus the Esquiline was connected with the Cœlian, by bridging the valley with a bank supported by a wall, and the passage through the bank was secured by placing a gate with its tower in the foss of the bank. Similarly, the Cœlian was connected with the Pseudo-Aventine; and the latter again with the greater Aventine, by the same process.

If we trace the line of the agger southward from the Esquiline gate, it is found to cease against the cliff of the Esquiline Hill on its eastern face, near the remarkable reservoir called by moderns Le Sette Sale, a massive building containing chambers for regulating the flow and pressure of water from an aqueduct belonging to the Thermæ of Titus. There are remains of the wall supporting the agger at intervals, from the site of the gate up to the cliff where the bank ended. The wall thence ran alone to the south-easternmost angle of the hill, where the semi-detached fort, before mentioned, projects into the lower ground. The nearest path across to the Cœlian would be from this fort. But that line is not taken, for the wall turns past the angle and keeps westerly till it almost touches the Thermæ, and then it makes a right angle to descend and cross over the valley to the opposite hill. By this process the position of the cross-bank is strengthened through being engaged more deeply in the gorge. At the point indicated, the church of S. Clement stands over the remains of a gate set in the foss belonging to the agger, and midway between the hills. Excavations made here revealed first the older church or crypt of S. Clement beneath the present one, and beneath it again the original wall of the gate, the masonry of which is in the same style as the portion of the wall of Servius at the railway station; and the great depth at which it lies, being literally twice buried, proves that the fort of which it is a part stood in the bottom of the deep foss-way. The gateway thus discovered was that called Porta Querquetulana, both the Esquiline and the Cœlian Hills having had oak woods on them.

After circling all round the Cœlian, in the manner described in the account of the several hills as separate fortresses, the line of defence reaches the south-western face, at the point where the Cœlian slope approaches most nearly that of the Pseudo-Aventine. This is a little way to the southward of the monastery of S. Gregory, and all this portion of the Cœlian is the vineyard of that institution. Here an agger about one hundred yards long crossed the valley from cliff to cliff, or from north-east to south-west; and on the eastern end of it, close to the Cœlian cliff, were discovered the remains of the Porta Capena, with its tower or fort flanking it, and guarding the entrance of the Via Appia into Rome. It is of great importance to fix this site, so celebrated and so much discussed, and fortunately it was possible by great exertions to do it. Under the Cœlian Hill stands a mediæval tower, now the house of the gardener of S. Gregory's, the foundation of which is built of tufa stones in the style of the walls of the Kings, and reveals the flanking-tower of the gateway. An aqueduct passes through it, and the specus, or channel for it, is cut in that tufa wall. In front of the tower is the wall again of Servius of the usual thickness, twelve feet, and buried about fifteen feet below the present surface of the ground. Against this wall are remains of two aqueducts, one above the other, as is usual in Rome, where a later channel follows the same course as an older one. The lower and earlier is the Aqua Appia, the higher Aqua Marcia. These are carried by arcades against the side of the agger of Servius, which connects the two hills; and the original pavement of the Via Appia, the earliest of the great roads from the capital to the provinces, runs underneath the agger and aqueducts at right-angles to them. Here, then, was the Porta Capena, made at first as an entrance through the foss of the agger, and fortified, and afterwards made to bear the water-courses over its head. But this was the custom in Rome, to carry aqueducts over gateway-arches previously existing, whereever it was convenient; and not only were the principal gates of the city made to convey water, but monumental arches also, as that of Dolabella and that of Drusus. Frontinus says of the Aqua Appia that its whole course was subterranean, except at one spot, where it was carried on visible substructures for sixty passus. In the course of ages it was allowed to fall into decay, so that in Juvenal's time the arches had become leaky, and the Porta Capena was a moist passage-way. Hence the "veteres arcus" and the "madida Capena" were at this one and the same spot, (Juv. Sat. iii. 11): and Martial also says, "Capena grandi porta qua pluit gutta." But this inconvenient highway was abandoned in the later Empire, and a new one made along the valley, at the same level as the present modern road.

The course of the structures of Servius, as traced both between the Esquiline and Cœlian under S. Clement's, and between the Cœlian and lesser Aventine at S. Gregory's, proves conclusively that the King did not build a continuous rampart all round Rome's seven hills, but connected them, where necessary, by short aggers across their intervening valleys, backing up the bank with a wall of stone. To put beyond all doubt the nature of this connecting structure, a series of seven pits was opened from the Cœlian over to the lesser Aventine, upon the line indicated by the arches at the Porta Capena. In every one of these the agger and wall were discernible; and one of them was left, and is kept open by the authorities at Rome, in order that scholars and antiquaries may be able to see for themselves an interesting relic of this celebrated work, which has had so much written about it on conjecture, and was till now so much misunderstood.

The same principle of joining hill to hill was applied to the passage across from one portion of the Aventine to the other. Here, again, the lines of circumvallation do not strike across the valley at the very mouth of it, but are first carried up higher in the gorge, till they converge and meet at the site of the ancient gateway, the Porta Ostiensis in the time of the Republic. When the Aventine was once reached, its scarped cliffs and the Tiber at the foot of the hill became adequate means of defence, and the enclosing operations came to an end.

It should be mentioned here, that during the time when the seven pits remained open, a survey was taken of the whole length of the agger and wall of Servius, and its course marked out by numbers placed at intervals along the walls, these numbers being within sight of each other, or within easy reach. The sites also of the gates were marked, and their names attached, as far as could be gathered from Latin writers. This could never be done again, and a final farewell has been taken of nearly the whole of Rome's third wall of defence. When contemplated as a whole, and its line followed on a good map constructed upon actual discovery, such a series of connecting and enclosing works seems to have been skilfully conceived and admirably carried out. Their great solidity, and the excellence of the materials used, made them virtually imperishable, and only the hand of man could undo them again.

CHAPTER VI.

The Agger of Tarquinius the Second.

IT has always been, and is still matter of wonder, that so small a state as kingly Rome could have reared such mighty monuments. But the traditions, backed by the remains, are too strong for the incredulity of scholars; and it has been acknowledged by Niebuhr that the great works, undeniably executed, attest a political body of no mean power. The legends attributed the system of drainage below the Palatine, issuing in the Cloaca Maxima, to the first Tarquin; also the permanent structures for the spectators of the Circus Maximus, and the Mamertine Prison. Of these, the first was really a considerable undertaking; and there seems no reason to doubt Pliny's statement, that great oppression was used in compelling the lower classes of the people to labour upon it; and consequently, suicide was a thing of common occurrence among them, as a refuge from their troubles. Of this king, Dio Cassius also says,—" He began the building of the sewers, —a wonderful work, exceeding description. And in my opinion the three most magnificent works in Rome, are the aqueducts, the paved roads, and the sewers." The extensive lines of Servius must have exacted still greater and more prolonged toil in stone and earthwork. Thirdly came an additional enlargement of military defences, attributed to the last of the Kings.

We are bound to see, in the oppression used by these rulers towards their people, indications of foreign domination, and of forced labour under it. Such a power, not of home growth, must of course have been Etruscan. Of the last prince of that line Pliny says,—" It (the city) is bounded upon the eastern side by the agger of Tarquinius Superbus, a work of surpassing grandeur; for he raised it so high, as to be on a level with the wall on the side of which the city lay most exposed to attack from the neighbouring plains." Dionysius says of this work,—"That part of the circuit of Rome by which you go to Gabii, was fortified by him (Tarquin). A large number of people were employed in making an agger, and excavating a great foss, raising the wall higher, and occupying the place with thicker towers; because in this part the city appeared less strong, whereas in all the rest of the circuit it was very secure, and difficult of access." These quotations testify the belief of the writers as to the magnitude of these works.

This additional rampart was added as the usual complement to an entrenched town, which had its outer as well as inner line of circumvallation. The tradition affirmed that this last great agger was never finished, proving too great for the patience of the people, and failing under its own weight; in fact, it seems to have been broken off at both extremities.

But great difficulties have arisen about the agger of Tarquin, and no satisfactory solution has yet been given. In despair of finding any work answering to this description, the passage of Dionysius has been usually interpreted by scholars to apply to the work of Servius. But it would seem hardly possible for that author to say of that king's wall that it lay on the side of Gabii, lying as it does altogether too far to the north. The Esquiline gate, the southernmost in his line of defence, led out into quite another direction of the country. And it is at least three-quarters of a mile from the gate leading to Gabii to the agger of Servius, that is the Porta Prænestina. We are not to seek for the work of the last king in any re-arrangement of the older works; but in a rampart of larger circuit, lying outside the former one, and nearer the edge of the plain from which attack was most to be feared. And there are reasons for believing that this rampart coincides with the present wall of Rome, which is Aurelian's. At the south-easternmost angle of the city is the site of the palace called Sessorium, anciently a fortress, and subsequently an imperial residence. Frontinus, the chief authority on Roman aqueducts, states that they enter Rome at this angle in the palace garden, and thence are carried forward upon the *high bank*. To interpret this, it should be understood that the channels were not necessarily brought straight away, after entering the city, into the streets for distribution. Sometimes they divided into branches, of which one struck immediately into the heart of the town, and another ran along the outer rampart for more than a mile before it quitted the wall.

Now the aqueducts which enter at the Sessorium do, in fact, run upon an agger northward to the Castra Prætoria, which form the other great angle in the fortifications of Rome, at the north end of the eastern line of defence. Three aqueducts, the Aqua Marcia, Tepula, and Julia, are traced from the Sessorium to the Porta Tiburtina, now S. Lorenzo. From that point the Marcian is carried all along a high bank to the camp, and runs round three sides of its square. Upon this part of the agger there are villas built, the outer faces of which stand twenty feet above the level of the road outside; and on the inner side the bank slopes away, and is laid out in gardens. It is by paying close attention to these indications of old works, that the topography of such a city as Rome becomes intelligible. This bank is evidently an ancient agger, and there are still remains of the old wall against it at intervals. And it is also plain that the Wall of **Aurelian,** the latest girdle put round Rome, was in many places built up against the old agger. Putting these facts together, we have a reasonable solution of the questions where the great agger of Tarquin ran, and what became of it in aftertimes. It began at the Sessorium, and ended at the Castra Prætoria, a distance of at least 2,600 yards, and the traces of it still exist; but everywhere either carrying other structures upon its top, or built against with high walls. Whether the old earthwork upon which that camp stands was a portion, but unfinished portion of Tarquin's work, cannot be determined. It must have been his design to carry on his outer defences right round the table-land on the east, till they should unite with the strong line of the older agger and forts at the north-easternmost point of the Quirinal Hill. Had the junction been made perfect to the Pincian cliffs, it would have rendered Rome virtually impregnable. This was not done, and thus a long gap was left, which proved a weak and dangerous interval. There is no reason to doubt the tradition which points to the excessive tasks exacted in the formation of these works, as the chief cause why the people rose in rebellion, and expelling foreign domination, put an end to their state of slavery. The legend coincides with the manifest fact, that the rampart was broken off while incomplete; and though the defences of the city were thus left insecure, it was unlikely that the attempt to renew them should be made, with the memories of so much oppression attached to them.

This great rampart, stretching along the whole of one side of the City, must have been pierced with gates at intervals, and these furnished the "thicker towers" assigned by the historian to the outer enclosure of Tarquin. There are strong reasons for believing that these gates were the doubles of those in the inner circle of Servius. There were two such gates, the Porta Esquilina and Porta Viminalis, and those names were repeated in the new structure; for Frontinus speaks of the Marcian aqueduct coming into the City at the Porta Esquilina. It could not enter at the Esquiline Gate of Servius, but its remains are distinctly visible entering through the outer wall, by the side of the gate now called Porta Maggiore, and by Frontinus Esquilina, as leading into the Esquiliæ—that space which lay between the city proper of Servius and the outer fortification, and long used as a burial-ground. This Porta Esquilina is also known as the Porta Prænestina and Porta Labicana, because the roads to Præneste and Labicum respectively diverged from that gate, and passengers from those terminal places would name the gate according to their line of march. The same holds good of the middle gate also of Servius, the Porta Viminalis; the space between it and the outer rampart, consisting of meadows and gardens, was called Campus Viminalis. This gate also had two names, being called Porta Tiburtina by those going out to Tivoli, and Viminalis by those entering Rome through it.

LATER FORTIFICATIONS.

No additional space seems to have been enclosed, either by walls or earthworks, from the time of the last king until the dictatorship of Sylla. During this long interval the defences of the western side of Rome ended with the Pulchrum Littus, the lofty Wall of the Kings along the Tiber. Sylla extended that line of wall farther northward, along the edge of the Campus Martius. This large area was never part of the town in ancient times, although the greater part of modern Rome lies upon it, and hence is very liable to inundations; while, on the other hand, the larger portion of the seven hills is now not built over, but was occupied principally with villas and gardens[a]. Meanwhile, the great Campus was studded with public buildings. Here were the vast Septa, or polling-places of the Roman people, in their Comitia Centuriata, which by law must be held without the pomœrium, or religious boundary; and beside the great military and recreation grounds, there were temples, thermæ, mausolea, and monuments. Sylla's work consisted in carrying on the wall upon the Tiber's edge, and furnishing it at intervals with towers, after the plan of the kingly structure. These are discernible still to a spectator in a boat, or from the opposite bank, when the water is low; just as the outlines of Aurelian's towers are to be seen by an experienced eye, as substructures for later buildings, in the bed of the river. They are built of the rough concreted stonework usual under the late Republic, similar to the walls of the Emporium. Mediæval castles and dwelling-houses have been grafted upon them as foundations, and thus they have been preserved. From the Tiber eastward to the Porta Flaminia, the northernmost point of Rome, a distance of 300 yards, there are no indications of Sylla's hand in the present wall-work. But eastward of the gate it continues again, where, close to the gate, the cliff of the Pincian Hill rises abruptly from the low ground. There is every reason to believe that Sylla erected his new principal fortress or palace on this hill, which we find mentioned in after history as the Pincian Palace. Belisarius, during the siege of Rome by the Goths, occupied it as his head-quarters.

The northern boundary of the cliff here is formed by the celebrated Muro Torto, or distorted wall, the peculiar form of which arose in this manner. When the wall had been built flat against the face of the cliff, the pressure of earth

[a] The new City, begun in 1872 on the chess-board plan, is partly built, or building, on the high hill now called the Esquiline.

against it was found too great for the foundations; the lateral thrust caused the wall to bulge and lean over, as it now does. But when the architect found that it gave way no farther, he considered it safe to resume the building of the upper portion. Still, taught by the danger, he constructed it not as a flat surface, but in semicircular recesses or niches of wide span, and these remain. The upper part is perfectly perpendicular; the flat wall below leans over. (Unfortunately, this very interesting specimen of reticulated-work has been blocked up by a tasteless modern wall in front of it.) Having learnt the wisdom of this precaution, the builders reared the rest of the high wall on the east side in niches of two tiers, one above the other.

The student in Roman architecture will observe that Agrippa's vestibule or dome, commonly called Pantheon, has its very lofty casing of outer wall constructed in arched brickwork, the semicircles being built so as to resemble an arcade, but being in fact entirely solid; this adds great strength to the structure. The character of the whole work along the face of the Pincian is that of Sylla's time. The central mass of the interior is solid concrete; the front of the wall was composed of small blocks of tufa, rather larger than modern English bricks. This accounts for the admirable preservation of an exposed front of masonry for nineteen hundred years. The work of Sylla terminated probably at the sharp angle in the wall, where the Belvedere, built by the Medici family, stands; the line which had been south-east turns north-east, and here there is evidently a joint in the construction, indicating an interval in its progress. The wall, however, is still built against a scarped cliff as far as the Porta Pinciana, an ancient gateway still remaining, but closed; after which the ground on both sides is more nearly level, and traces of a wall with square stone towers of this period are visible beneath the brick wall of Aurelian, which is erected upon them. The wall of this part of the rampart is neither a mere concrete foundation, nor is it a finished wall intended to be seen. It was, no doubt, originally covered with earth to some height, and is so still in places where it has not been disturbed. The stonework is visible in the garden of the Villa Ludovisi, where it is ten or twelve feet above the level of the soil, standing on a bank, with the foss very distinct inside, some ten feet deep. From the point where Sylla's work breaks off, the fresh stage of continuation seems to be the work of Julius Cæsar. That great man had formed plans on a large scale for enlarging the boundaries of the City by turning the course of the Tiber under the Vatican Mount, and making a new Campus Martius in the meadows at the foot of it; but his premature death put an end to this and other designs for improving the suburbs of Rome. He seems to have only carried onwards the defences along the north side of the Pincian, and past it eastward as far as the Porta Salaria. It is not possible to distinguish the work of his time from that of his successor; they would be similar in construction, and both have been built over and refaced by the later labours of Aurelian. In all probability, Augustus completed the work of Julius Cæsar where left unfinished, and continued the line at least as far as the Porta Tiburtina, now S. Lorenzo. Here the gateway of his period remains, bearing an inscription with his name, which records the restoration of the three aqueducts conducted over the arch.

Beyond this gate southward ran the great agger bearing the aqueducts, and there was also the fortification of the Sessorium: these had no imperial additions made to them, being deemed sufficient protection.

The next reign, that of Tiberius, produced the Castra Prætoria, designed by Sejanus, minister of that prince: it is a projection from the line of fortification, built upon an old earthwork; and it was calculated to hold twelve thousand men of that formidable body of troops who afterwards so often made and unmade Emperors. The materials of which it is built are very various, the north wall being of that finest brickwork which distinguishes the first century; that of the south wall is chiefly of the large split stones of the times of the Kings, evidently taken from some other place and used again, but not likely to have been carried far on account of their weight. The eastern wall between these was for the most part rebuilt some time in the fourth century, after the fortifications had been dismantled by Constantine in consequence of a mutiny among the guards; but what remains of the older work agrees with the rest of Tiberius' time.

When we arrive at the next gate belonging to the Sessorium, namely the Porta Prænestina or Esquilina of Frontinus, the works of the Aqua Claudia, or aqueduct of the Emperor Claudius, are seen to form an important function in the fortifications. From the tower on the north side of this gateway, along both sides of the angle made by the wall on the south side, the lofty structure runs, and fills up the distance between the gate and the Sessorian fortress. There were, however, older defences than his at this point, for in the repaired Wall of Aurelian near it, there are remains of ancient structures in the kingly style discernible. The military amphitheatre, which is half enclosed by the wall of the city, and belonged to this Sessorian Palace, is of brickwork, and of the time of the Claudian Emperors.

We have now turned the south-easternmost angle of the city's wall, and move along its southern face westward. There are stone towers occurring in this line which may be of Claudius's reign, or earlier. The walls of the Lateran Palace itself, which was in old times without the city proper, formed an important addition to the fortifications when these were extended to this outer boundary. These towers occur along the defences as far as the Porta Metronia, a gate no longer existing[b]. The line then makes a sharp angle, and takes a great sweep to the south, enclosing a long promontory standing off from the foot of the Cœlian Hill; and here are the Porta Latina and Porta Appia. The addition of this promontory is attributable to Augustus. Having rounded part of it, and arrived on the southern side of the Pseudo-Aventine, here again we fall in with portions of the old line of regal work. Claudius, in advancing the line of the Pomœrium so as to include the Aventine, seems to have taken in the considerable space on the flat ground outside the Aventine. Hitherto, the Emporium and large commercial store-houses had been outside the walls. The wall of Claudius, which is traceable hereabouts, was, like that of Sylla and of Augustus, made use of by Aurelian for a substructure as far as it was available. Where the wall of Aurelian ceases, that of Claudius is still to be seen, when the water of the Tiber is low, extending along the eastern bank of the river. It seems to have gone up the stream to the Emporium, and no farther; this is a distance of over half-a-mile. We have now made the passage round the whole line of enclosure on the eastern bank of the Tiber, and stand facing the Transtiberine quarter. The Janiculan had been very early occupied as a military post, but it never was included within the city in any sense till the time of Augustus. That prince had re-organized the municipal divisions of the city, which from four in the time of Servius became fourteen under him. These divisions, answering to our wards, were known by their numbers, and the

---

[b] The arch of the gate remains in the tufa wall on the bridge over the southern slope, which was at that angle.

Transtiberine quarter was Regio XIV. Thus it was regularly incorporated into the town as an integral part of it; and it seems tolerably certain that it was walled in. We cannot, indeed, find the same evidence upon this side of the water that Aurelian's wall stood upon an older one, because the remains of that fortification, though traceable, are so meagre here, in comparison with the grand long line around Rome on the eastern bank. This want is owing to the destruction wreaked upon the fortifications by the Goths, who occupied the Janiculan side. They were known to have a special hatred of all military enclosures, and when they once were masters of the city itself, these works, with their gateways, very narrowly escaped total ruin.

The evidence as to the enlargement of the area of the Urbs proper from time to time is gathered from the Cippi, or boundary-stones, used to mark out the Pomœrium. The space within those Cippi was the Urbs for the time being. Of course, the Pomœrium had long ceased, under the late Republic and the Empire, to have any connection with the idea of fortification; it had come to signify the boundary of privilege or jurisdiction attached to the city. Much in the same way, the limits of the city of London, at first extending to the western foss at Lud-gate, were afterwards enlarged farther westward to Temple Bar, without reference to any foss or defence. At Rome, no officer of the State was allowed the honour of extending the Pomœrium, unless he had augmented the dominion of his country. There are preserved Cippi of Sylla restored by Augustus, of Augustus himself, of Claudius, Vespasian, and Titus, and also some which record the restoration of older boundaries by Hadrian. The last-mentioned Emperor had not enlarged the boundaries of the Empire, but had rather reduced them. Although in the long course of Republican victories many great generals had earned this right of extension, none it seems exercised it till Sylla, as undisputed master, ventured to imitate the ambition of the Kings. A Cippus of Augustus from the northern side of Rome, and one of Claudius from the southern side, shew by the positions in which they were found that the limits of Rome in the first century were nearly the same as under Aurelian. With the important exception of the extension of the boundary so as to formally include the Aventine, the changes mentioned in imperial times concern small alterations in the line of the Pomœrium; an act which, though it had lost its original importance, was still attended by the observance of ceremonies, and was registered in the public records. The conclusion seems to be safely drawn, that the limits of Rome were not materially different in the time of Claudius from what they were under Aurelian. The length of line within the Pomœrium of Vespasian's time is given in a well-known passage of Pliny, and is found to approximate closely to the measurements of Aurelian's wall.

It may be interesting to mention, that the last instance of the use of the word Pomœrium is probably that by Apollinaris Sidonius, who wrote an account of his journey to Rome, A.D. 467, shortly before the final extinction of the Empire of the West. He relates that he visited the shrine of S. Peter's before entering the Pomœrium; in other words, he entered Rome from the side of the Vatican, and on crossing the bridge came within the precincts of the city.

CHAPTER VII.

THE WALLS OF AURELIAN AND HONORIUS.

ABOUT the middle of the third Christian century the Roman state had already been made to tremble before the barbarian hosts from the north, which had invaded its choicest European provinces, and even Italy itself. Rome was felt to be insecure when Ravenna was surrounded by Alemanni, and some flying parties of that nation had, as Gibbon says, displayed their victorious banners almost in sight of the Capitol. These incursions of northern tribes, coupled with the weak government of such princes as Valerian and Gallienus, gave so much encouragement to the barbarians, that serious fears were entertained of a combined attack upon Rome. The reigns of Claudius II. and Aurelian restored the balance of military power; the latter of these captains was victorious over both Goths and Germans, as well as over the formidable monarchy in the East which Zenobia had reared upon the ruins of Roman provinces. The suppression also of a pretender to the Empire afforded an interval of comparative rest, and this was employed upon the construction of a new line of defence round the city. Aurelian determined to rear a much stronger wall, and of uniform character throughout. The plan was conceived on a grand scale, and being taken in hand upon the Emperor's return to Rome, after granting peace to the Vandals, A.D. 271, was partly carried out in his reign. It was finished by his successor, Probus, A.D. 280. The accounts of this work given by several historians are somewhat varied, and not easy to reconcile with the statements of other writers, as interpreted by the existing remains.

Five authors agree that Aurelian built new walls; three mention their greater strength; two the increased extent; one says these were the first walls built round Rome. But, rightly understood, all these statements may be justified. Of their strength there is no question; that they did in some places depart somewhat from the old line, and take in fresh ground, is also certain from some singular arrangements in respect of buildings previously existing. The last statement may also be explained, by considering that these later writers would not use *murus* in the same sense as that formerly attached to it. The word which in the older language of fortification meant earthwork, had come to stand for walls properly so called, of solid stone or brick. And it was also true that there had been no entire line of defence of uniform construction hitherto put round the whole city.

The previous defences were more or less of patchwork, partly earth and partly stone. Now there was a magnificent rampart of one height, nearly fifty feet, and of equal strength, encircling Rome on every side. It was furnished throughout with square towers at regular intervals, and was battlemented along the whole line. It was pierced with large windows and small windows, and other openings for shooting out rubbish. The great distinguishing feature in it was the corridor, or arcaded passage, running between tower and tower on the inner side of the wall, thus affording a continuous and protected communication, by which sentinels could traverse the whole distance in safety from one end to the other. These arches are often mistaken for the arcaded substructures of aqueducts; this is especially the case between the Amphitheatrum Castrense and the Porta Asinaria, or S. Giovanni, where the outer wall has been destroyed, and the arcade of the corridor stands in clear relief against the sky, so as to closely resemble an aqueduct. It is observable, however, that where the wall includes the old agger, there the arcades break off as superfluous, **the passage** from tower to tower being supplied by the bank of earth. The finest part of the corridor is near the Porta S. Sebastiano, the old Porta Appia, on both sides of which it is for about half-a-mile perfect. Only one tower in the whole course remains uninjured; **but across the** Tiber, in the gardens of the Vatican Palace, some towers remain nearly perfect. The whole structure throughout is of brick, but is always stately in appearance.

A peculiar feature in the plan of this great wall is, that it takes no count of existing structures found standing in the line which **it was most** convenient to adopt for it. It does not **cut through the** impediment and half-destroy it, but **adopts and** imbeds it, as it were, in its own body. Thus **near the Porta** S. Paolo, the Ostian Gate, it encounters the huge **pyramid** known as the monument of Caius Cestius, which is more than twice as high as the wall, and half of the pyramid stands within the line of the wall, and half projects outside **of its face.** At the Porta Salaria, on the northern side of the city, the wall has enclosed the tombs. This was discovered in removing the gate in recent times. A similar arrangement occurred at the Porta Prænestina. Such a position of a burial-place at the entrance of the city is an illustration of the usage, commonly followed by the Romans, of lining the public roads with tombs, and the gates of the city were favourite places for them.

As the power of Rome gradually declined after Aurelian's time, while the hordes of various barbarian stocks kept pressing more closely round her, it was felt that the city itself had to trust more and more to its fortifications, in proportion to the weakness of her arms in the field. The gateways in the line of defence were considered deficient in strength, and consequently Honorius, son of Theodosius, who reigned A.D. 395—425, added gatehouses or gateway-fortresses to all the principal entrances, not destroying the old works, but adding towers to them, so that each became a complete castle in itself. A good illustration of the nature of these additions might till very lately have been seen at the Porta Tiburtina, where the arch and gate of Augustus were walled in by the towers of the later additions. The foss-way leading through the Arch of Augustus having been filled-up in the interval between these Emperors, the bases of the piers of the later gate stand at the present level of the soil; those of the older gate, which were originally at the level of the roadway in the bottom of the foss, are now deeply buried. Inscriptions exist which shew that a great deal of rebuilding took place in the time of Honorius, and of his brother Arcadius. These record that immense repairs and additions along the line of walls, gates, and towers, were effected by those princes, and that Stilicho, their celebrated general, had proposed in the Senate the erection of that inscription in their honour. Hence it is concluded that such alterations were carried out not later than A.D. 400. The work of this period is usually distinguishable by the lighter or yellow colour of the bricks; that of Aurelian is red, and often dark red.

All these precautions, however, failed to render the city secure, which was forced at its weakest point, the Porta Salaria, by Alaric, King of the Visigoths, in 409. On this occasion all that part of the town was burnt, including the house of Sallust the historian, which had been restored in the time of the early Emperors, after its destruction by fire. In 455 Rome was again captured by the Vandals, under their king Genseric, and though there is no precise mention of the walls in the sacking and burning of the city, it is scarcely possible that they should have escaped. Our next record is one of restoration by the hands of Theodoric the Ostrogoth, about the year A.D. 500. That enlightened king, the benefactor of Italy, shewed himself the patron of Rome especially. In the seventh year of his reign he personally visited the old capital of the world, the public works of which attracted his highest admiration. And anxious that the Gothic kings should not be charged with the destruction of ancient glories, he at once took active measures for their preservation. The king's instructions are preserved, in which a professed architect, an annual sum of two hundred pounds in gold, and the customs from the Lucrine port, are assigned for ordinary repairs. The Senators and Prefects of the city are charged, as we learn from Cassiodorus, that nothing is more seriously fitting than the expenditure of money on the buildings of Rome. The "fabric of the wall" is mentioned, and the "guarding against the necessities of war;" and the Prefect is ordered to see that the money sent for the buildings in Rome, which was of large amount, be properly applied to the walls of Rome, and no frauds permitted.

Theodoric also, as it seems, re-constructed some of the gate-fortresses, the style of which resembles the brickwork of that period at Ravenna, the capital of the Gothic kings in Italy. The towers of these gateways are chiefly round, and battlemented. An example of his work is the present structure of the Porta Appia, now S. Sebastiano; this has been attributed also to the Exarchs of Ravenna, who, after the suppression of the Gothic monarchy, were the lieutenants of the Emperors of the East in Italy. But we have evidence of Theodoric's handiwork in that gate, agreeing with some instructions of his which are preserved. For in a letter to the Comes Suna, or Sura, the king directs him to have the squared marble, then lying neglected, employed for the fabric of the wall. And in this Appian gateway the lower stages of the two flanking towers are built of large blocks of marble, apparently taken from some other building, and turned inside out. These stages are square, while the upper portions of the towers are round, and are built of brick, very much in the style of the round belfry-towers of Ravenna.

Another very fine gateway of the same date, and exhibiting the same handiwork, is the Porta Ostiensis, now Porta S. Paolo. Here the towers are wholly round, and are of good brick throughout; in the upper stages they are pierced with wide semicircular arches. An ornamental string-course, now much defaced, ran round the towers and along the flat face of the gateway at one level.

The third gate of Theodoric's restoration is the Porta Pinciana, the closed gate on the north side of the Pincian Hill. The brickwork is good, but the flat wall of the gateway itself is of modern stone. Both towers are round, and have not been pierced. On both these gates the battlements are preserved.

Resuming historical notices of the outer wall of Rome, we find that Belisarius, commander of Justinian's army, having marched from the south of Italy to the gates of the city, compelled the forces of the Goths, under their king Vitiges, to evacuate the place, A.D. 536. Having taken possession of it, he found the walls in great need of repair, which were hastily executed in the weakest portions. During the interval between the evacuation and the return of the enemy in the spring of 537, Belisarius employed the labours of the citizens and soldiers alike in incessant labour on the fortifications. The foss outside the rampart was renewed, the repaired gates were put each under the charge of one of the lieutenants of the general, and the Mausoleum of Hadrian was occupied as a fortress. These repairs and precautions enabled the Romans to withstand a prolonged siege. The Goths, who spread themselves round the north and east sides of Rome, from the Flaminian to the Prænestine Gate, occupied six separate camps on the east bank of the Tiber, and a seventh on the west, in the flat land at the **Pons Milvius**, which commanded the approach to Rome from the north. The sites of all these camps, which were fortified, are still visible.

Nine years after this deliverance, the city was again occupied by the Goths, whose king, Totila, meditated the razing of the whole of its defences to the ground, and so far carried out his purpose, that about one-third of the circuit was thrown down, not continuously, but in detached portions. Upon the temporary retreat of the Gothic army, Belisarius again undertook the defence of the city. He planted his standard on the Capitol, and summoning the inhabitants to return to their deserted homes, set himself to the work of closing up the breaches of the wall. The account of Procopius the historian is as follows: "But as he (Belisarius) was not able to rebuild in a short time as much of the wall as Totila had destroyed, he adopted this plan; collecting all the stones which happened to be near, he laid them on one another, without order and with nothing between, since he had no mortar at hand; but in order that the mere appearance of building might be preserved, he placed on the outside a great abundance of stakes. He happened also before (in 537) to have dug deep ditches round the whole circuit of the walls, and as the whole army worked with zeal during twenty-five days, all the wall that had been destroyed was in this way completed." And again, "As soon as Totila heard this, he broke up his camp with all his army, and reached the city before the former had been able to fit the gates to the walls. For Totila had destroyed all of them, and Belisarius, from want of workmen, was not able to get the start in constructing them."

Of the hasty repairs performed on these different occasions there are evident traces to be seen. Thus, in the wall of the Pincian Hill, on the east side, this work is recognised by the rough mixture of concrete and stone usually prevailing at that period. On the west side of the Sessorium is a piece of bad walling of the type of the sixth century, built across a foss. Then farther south, after a good strip of Aurelian's wall, comes another piece much damaged and badly repaired. And also after turning the south-eastern angle of the city, there is a piece of very rude bad wall-work across the foss of the Lateran Palace, about a hundred feet in length.

With respect to the actual gates themselves, which moved to open or to bar the roadways, there is reason to believe that, beside the doors swinging upon hinges, there was in addition the *porte-coulis*, or sliding framework, so well known in mediæval times; for the grooves of these slides remain in the stonework of several of the gates of Rome. Such port-cullis grooves were at the Porta Salaria, Tiburtina, Prænestina, Latina, Appia, and Ostiensis. But the use of this form of gates belongs to a still earlier period, as they occur at Pompeii also, which was buried in the first century.

Two centuries later the Lombards attacked the city, and greatly injured its buildings during three several attempts to capture it, between A.D. 730 and 754. They never succeeded in making themselves masters of it, but the fact that seven churches in the region of the Aventine and Pseudo-Aventine were all rebuilt after the sieges, shews that they must have penetrated the walls and inflicted much damage. Finally, delivered from these enemies by the overthrow of the Lombard kingdom in 774, Rome passed into the hands of the Popes as its natural protectors, and in the latter part of that and in the next century the restoration of the old Imperial walls was vigorously carried on by different pontiffs. Hadrian II., succeeding in 772, found these defences in a very bad state, many parts in ruins, and towers thrown down; he collected a large body of labourers from the towns of Tuscany, as well as from Rome itself and the country adjacent, and devoted the whole of the ecclesiastical revenues to this object; and as he reigned twenty-three years, he was enabled to effect very great repairs upon the walls. The work was continued by Leo IV. in the middle of the ninth century; he is said "to have visited the works continually in person, both on foot and on horseback, and to have allowed no delay in them; to have rebuilt fifteen of the towers from the ground, and to have repaired the gatehouses, and fortified them with new wooden doors strong enough to resist an enemy." This account is by a contemporary writer.

But this Pope executed also another great undertaking, the memory of which is preserved in the name of the Leonine City. The Saracens had four years previously invaded and spoiled the suburb of the Vatican and S. Peter's church, but they had desisted from attacking Rome itself: its walls were still capable of defence. In addition to the buildings around the shrine of the Apostles at the Vatican, a large and populous suburb had grown up, composed chiefly of settlers of northern and western nations; but the whole area was undefended. Leo, therefore, by very great efforts enclosed this Transtiberine quarter with a continuous wall, and in four years completed his new city. The new defences were connected by a covered way with the strong fortress of the Castle of S. Angelo, as the Mausoleum of Hadrian was now called; but they were not united with the Janiculan fortress, or with the Wall of Aurelian on that side of the Tiber. This was not done till the seventeenth century, when the whole of the city on the western bank was enclosed in a new wall on modern principles of fortification.

The notices of active restoration of the old Imperial walls account for the description given of them by an eye-witness in the ninth century, when the whole circuit seems to have been complete. The author, a Swiss ecclesiastic, gives in his work, known as the "Itinerary of Einsiedeln," a precise record of what he saw: he had evidently walked round the whole circuit on both sides of the river, and he reckons all the component parts of the structure, as they occur between gate and gate, towers, battlements, posterns, corbels, and windows. He begins his survey at the north-western angle, where the Tiber, close to the Mausoleum of Hadrian, makes a great horseshoe curve; and at this point was a gate called by him the gate of S. Peter, the same to which Procopius gives the name Porta Aurelia[a]. From this gate he ascends the eastern bank to the Porta Flaminia, and thence along the Pincian Hill he passes east and then south, and so on till he reaches the Tiber, crosses the river, climbs the Janiculan, descends north-easterly to the Tiber again, crosses it by the Pons Janiculensis, and pursuing the wall on the eastern bank again, arrives at the gate from which he

[a] There is some doubt about which gate bore the name of Aurelia. Procopius seems to make it the same as S. Peter's, the gate that led to that great church at the end of the bridge of Hadrian, now called of S. Angelo. The Itinerary seems to make it the same as S. Pancrazio on the Janiculum. The explanation probably is, that it was at the end of the Porta Triumphalis, on the line of the Via Triumphalis, and near to S. Peter's. In the Itinerary both the Porta S. Pancrazio on the Janiculum, and the Porta Septimiana at the foot of it, are omitted, as if this suburb on the other side of the Tiber was not then considered part of the city; there were probably four gates to that suburb, which would agree with Pliny's number of eighteen, instead of the fourteen of the Itinerary, or perhaps Pliny included the Porta Lateranensis, which was closed at the time of the Itinerary. This would give three gates to the suburb called Trastevere, in addition to the Portuensis, which is mentioned.

started. He concludes his enumeration by summing up in the whole 383 towers, 7020 battlements, 6 posterns, 106 corbels, and 2066 large windows.

Procopius numbers fourteen gates in the circuit of the city, but unfortunately he gives the names of a few only, and the same number is given by the Einsiedeln chronicler three hundred years afterwards, who names them all in the following order: 1. **Porta** Flaminia; 2. Pinciana; 3. Salaria; 4. Nomentana; 5. Tiburtina; 6. Prænestina; 7. Asinaria; 8. Metronia; 9. Latina; 10. Appia: 11. Ostiensis; 12. Portuensis; 13. Aurelia; 14. S. Peter's. Procopius, however, calls 13 the gate of Pancratius, now S. Pancrazio. From this list are omitted the Porta Ardeatina, the starting-point of the Via of that name, which is still standing between the Porta Appia and Ostiensis, though long closed; also the Porta Lateranensis, existing and traceable, though much walled up; and thirdly, the Porta Chiusa, of which the true name is unknown, against the Prætorian Camp. All these had been long disused and closed, and were therefore omitted in the Itinerary. These would bring the total number of the gates up to seventeen, and if we add Porta Septimiana on the Transtiberine side (for there must have been a gate in Regio XIV. communicating between it and the country to the north), we have the whole number of eighteen gates, which in Pliny's time formed the entrances into the city.

In the modern circuit of wall the gates open and in use are as follows: 1. **Porta** del Popolo, very near the site of Porta Flaminia; the latter was not, it seems, on the flat ground, but on the slope of the hill rising above the Campus Martius, and therefore a little to the east of the present gate. II. **Porta** Salaria, identical with No. 3. III. **Porta Pia, a modern gate,** a little to the north-west of the ancient **Porta Nomentana.** IV. Porta S. Lorenzo, identical with

Porta Tiburtina, No. 5. V. **Porta** Maggiore, identical with **Porta** Prænestina, Labicana, and Esquilina, No. 6. VI. Porta S. Giovanni, modern, a little to the east of the Porta Asinaria. VII. **Porta** Metronia; a new **gate** has been made here by the side of the ancient No. 8. VIII. Porta Latina, long closed, identical with the old No. 9. IX. Porta S. Sebastiano, identical with Porta Appia, No. 10. X. **Porta S. Paolo,** identical with Porta Ostiensis, No. 11. On the Transtiberine side, XI. Porta Portense, about three **hundred** yards farther north, or inside of the old Porta Portuensis, No. 12. XII. Porta S. Pancrazio, identical with Porta Janiculensis, No. 13. In addition there are now five gates under and about the Vatican, and all of mediæval or post-mediæval construction. Those on the west side, through the line of fortification, are called Porta Cavalleggieri, Porta Fabbrica, and Porta Pertusa; and the two on **the north side, through the line of wall** which connects the Vatican with the Castle of S. Angelo, are the Porta Angelica and Porta Castello. In the original Leonine City three gates were built, and these are believed to have remained till the return of the Popes from Avignon, when new streets grew up, and new gates were provided.

Some well-informed antiquaries are of opinion that **the gate** known by the name of Porta Chiusa, or the closed gate (because, when the gates were named in the sixteenth century, the name of this could not be agreed upon), is really the *old* Porta Tiburtina, on the most direct road to Tibur, or Tivoli; and the ancient road called Via Cupa, which is cut through **the tufa** rock for about a quarter-of-a-mile, leads from this gate, and joins the present road near the church of S. Lorenzo f. m., which gives the name to the present gate.

CHAPTER VIII.

THE STREETS AND ROADS.

A CONSIDERATION of these naturally follows that of the Walls and Gates, through which they issued. The great Viæ Stratæ, leading from the city to the provinces, and reckoned with justice by Strabo and other writers among the wonders of construction achieved by the Romans, are highly celebrated; and as the names of the chief among them occur frequently in history, they have become familiar to us. Everybody knows the direction of the Via Appia, Flaminia, or Æmilia; and there are so many of these Roman streets, as they are called, left in Britain, as in other countries permanently held by that people, that a general idea of the nature of their roads is quite common. Directness, solidity, durability, were their special features; and these are strongly impressed on us when we find not merely the line of street, but the very pavement itself unaltered, and virtually unaffected by the traffic of centuries. The material used in Rome, and wherever such stone could be had, was black basaltic lava, laid in polygonal blocks; and interesting examples of such paved work exist still, especially in the most ancient portions of the city.

The method of street construction was of necessity entirely different from that adopted in modern cities, which are laid out in lines of buildings with adequate roadways between them. But Rome was, as we have seen, only an aggregation of hill-fortresses, gradually brought within one connected line of defence. Between the several hills were natural valleys, and these were trenched out so as to become wide and deep fosses, for defence at the foot of each height. Then there must have been a foss by the side of each agger that was thrown up to connect two adjacent hills. There was also the great eastern agger of the City on the Seven Hills, with its double foss; and in each of these there would be a road as a matter of course, according to the almost universal practice in the early times, when these fortifications were constructed. Such roads at first were probably nothing more than track-ways upon the soil, and as time went on some harder material was added; but the elaborate Via Strata was a much later invention. These ways, therefore, were the first means of communication within the city. And in the time of the Republic and of the Empire each of these roads in the trenches became streets in our sense of the word, by building houses against the bank, often cutting away part of the bank to admit the back of the house. This arrangement was distinctly shewn in the excavations made near the railway station, after the great agger of Servius had been cut through. The houses on one side of a street, in the style of the first century, were brought to light, built into that bank. The railway itself runs for a short distance on the site of the old roadway, about twenty feet above its level. There was a similar street on the outer side of the bank, and in one of the houses in this line paintings on the walls were found. It is plain from this example that the old banks, being no longer cared for as defences, were built into or built over as might be convenient, and that along the line of their fosses rows of houses were planted. And it is found usually that the streets within the city occupying the old foss-ways lay about twenty feet below the ordinary surface of the ground. In some places two pavements have been found, at different levels; and there is good reason for believing that those on the higher stage were added in the second century.

The old streets, sunk so deeply, were not calculated for the passage of carriages, for they were frequently only about three yards wide. In consequence of their inconvenience for carriage-traffic, and of the unwillingness in Republican times to incur the expense and annoyance of making new streets in an old city, the authorities sought to meet the difficulty by issuing edict after edict against the use of carriages in the streets. This state of things continued till about the middle of the second century of the Christian era, when these edicts ceased, and new streets were made by bringing up the level of the ancient foss-ways to a convenient height. Upon the hill sides the streets were open cuttings, ascending the incline in zigzag fashion; and from the deep hollow ways steps led up to the top of the banks. Not only within the area of the city of Servius, but in other parts of Rome, there are indications of these paved ways, and at great depths. A buried street was found in the Transtiberine region, near the palace of the Anicii, thirty feet below the present surface, indicating one of the sunken foss-ways leading from the Janiculum to the city, at the time when the former was a separate fortress, connected with Rome by such deep foss-ways only.

The earliest distinct notice about the streets within the city is believed to be when Augustus placed the gilt column called Milliarium Aureum in the Forum Romanum, which he intended to be the central point from which all the roads should be measured throughout Italy; it was also called Umbilicus Urbis. But it seems that this plan was never carried out; the roads continued to be measured from the gates, as they had been before. The streets within the city were measured from this starting-point, as is plain from the passage in Pliny, where he calculates the aggregate length of all the ways in Rome from it in a direct line to the gates.

He there states the number of the Compita, which are supposed to mean the cross-streets intersecting the main lines, at 265. On the fragments of the Marble Plan of Rome, which was found on the back wall of the Temple of Roma, and is of the date of the third century, the work of Septimius Severus, numerous lines of streets are given. Some of these streets, and those best known in history, are traceable from the central milestone of Augustus; a **round base** of brick, standing on the western side of **the Arch of Septimius Severus, is believed to represent the exact site of this column.** From it the remains of an ancient paved street may be seen ascending to the Capitol; it passes between two blocks of tufa stone which formed the jambs of a gate to the citadel above it. At this point the street divides into two parts, **going** in different directions; the right-hand branch, which is **seven yards and a-half** wide, passed between the column of Phocas, still standing, and **the great building called the** Basilica Julia, and thus separated the latter from the eastern side of the Forum Romanum. Further to the south it touched the base of the Temple of the Dioscuri, to which belongs the group **of** the three celebrated columns still standing; here it bifurcated, **the** right-hand branch turning off to the Forum Boarium, through the Arch of Janus Quadrifrons, under which it passed. One branch went along the north-east side of the Circus Maximus, and part of it may still be seen under the church of S. Anastasia, originally under the lower gallery of the **Circus.** This branch, keeping in the low ground of the valley, **was** called **Infima** Nova Via. The left-hand branch also divided, one branch to the right ascending up a steep incline to the Palatine, where the pavement **remains** well preserved under the portico of the palace usually assigned to **Caligula,** on the Clivus Victoriæ.

We now return to the second street, issuing from the gate

of the Capitol on the left-hand, or towards the south-east: it passed under the Arch of Septimius Severus, where the ancient pavement is visible, and ran in a straight line along the edge of the Forum Romanum in front of the Temple of Antoninus and Faustina, A.D. 165, at the same level as under the arch. The bases of the columns of that temple have been excavated, and are left visible; they stand at the top of a flight of steps which led down into an ancient street. The difference of level between the old Forum and the modern streets is brought out very clearly here, and there is no denying that the Forum was at the level of the old foss-ways. A branch then leaves the straight line in an easterly direction, or to the left, but the main street, or Via Sacra, continues from the Temple of Antoninus and Faustina to the Temple of Romulus, now the church of SS. Cosmas and Damian, then up the Clivus Sacer, past the great Basilica of Constantine and the Arch of Titus, on to the Summa Sacra Via. The ground here forms a large level platform on the Sub-Velia, beyond which it slopes downwards again towards the Colosseum.

To return to the other, or left-hand branch of the road, called Nova Via, which we left near the temple, the three columns of which are still standing, it passed along the right-hand, or south-west side of the Forum, and under the cliff of the Palatine, and so onwards to the Arch of Titus: at its highest elevation it was called Summa Nova Via, and it then formed the clivus or sloping road from that arch to the Colosseum; and branching off to the right, a continuation of it descended to the valley between the Palatine and the Cœlian, passing under the Arch of Constantine, and proceeded to the Circus Maximus on the right and the Porta Capena on the left. The formation of the Nova Via is attributed to Augustus, but there must have been a roadway on both sides of the Forum previous to his time. He therefore probably restored and improved it, but it is not mentioned in the catalogue of his public works engraved upon the tablet called Monumentum Ancyranum.

From the streets within the walls we pass on to those Viæ leading to the provinces, which began their course from the gates of Rome. No works produced by the Romans were more celebrated than their long roads, by which they could communicate with all the principal cities in the world as then known; so that it became a true proverb, that "All roads lead to Rome." The mere inspection of their remains sufficiently shews that there is no exaggeration in the statements of foreigners like Strabo and Dionysius, in expressing their admiration of these great undertakings. Vitruvius the architect gives minute details of the method of constructing a regular paved road. Where there was no natural foundation of rock, an artificial one was formed in three several layers, and uppermost of all was laid the course of basalt in polygonal blocks, most nicely fitted in and smoothed on the surface. Such paved roads still exist, and are used daily in Italy, which have not been touched by the hand of man, because they needed no repairs, for far over a thousand years. In enumerating the roads we begin at the north end, and pass round eastward, marking the point of issue of each from the walls, so as to connect the topography of the city with the geography of the provinces.

The Via Flaminia, or great north road, was commenced by C. Flaminius in his censorship, B.C. 220, the same who built the Circus Flaminius. It left the city of Servius by the Porta Ratumena, which stood on the agger connecting the Capitoline with the Quirinal, just within the spot where still stands the tomb of Bibulus in the modern street. In its course across the Campus **Martius** it passed by the Mausoleum of Augustus, and reaching the outer line of defence, issued by the **Porta** Flaminia. Running nearly due north from the walls, it crossed over the Tiber by the Pons Mulvius, or Milvius, celebrated in Belisarius' sallies against the Goths, who had a camp there. Near the bridge the Via Cassia turned off from the Flaminia to the left, and ran through Etruria from south to north. The Via Clodia, or Claudia, also branched from the Cassia, and keeping to the south of it, went to the Lacus Sabatinus. Cicero describes the journey to **Mutina**, or Modena, as open to his choice by any of the three roads, Flaminia, Cassia, or Aurelia. After leaving the shore of the Adriatic, the Flaminian was continued under the name of Via Æmilia, and went to Milan, and so on throughout Gallia Cisalpina, with numerous branches, as far east as Aquileia on the Adriatic, and west as the Graian Alps.

The Via Salaria, the next road eastward, issued from the city of Servius by the Porta Collina, at the northernmost end of that king's agger, and passed through the outer line of defence at the Porta Salaria. It led out to the old town of Antemnæ, and crossing the Anio by the fine Ponte Salaro, blown up by the Pontifical army in fear of Garibaldi, but now restored to use, went north-easterly, and is still to be recognised in the old road to Monte Rotondo; ultimately it crossed to the coast of the Adriatic at Ancona.

The Via Nomentana left the city of the Kings by the same Colline Gate, and passed out of the Imperial wall by the Porta Nomentana, still traceable on the outside of that wall. It went to Nomentum of the Sabines in the direction of the Mons Lucretilis. It crossed the Anio, two miles from Rome, by the picturesque bridge, Ponte Nomentano, still visible. Its pavement also may be seen at six miles from the city. Beyond Nomentum it joined the Via Salaria.

The Via Tiburtina began at the Porta Esquilina of the Kings, and passed through the outer wall by the Porta Tiburtina. Another branch of the same road passed out by the closed gate on the south side of the Prætorian Camp. Before its juncture with the first road, it goes through a deep cutting near the wall, where it is called Via Cupa, the hollow way. To this sunk road, and to others to the right and left of it, the passage in Livy, lib. xxvi., has been referred, relating that the Consuls concealed a body of deserters in ambush in the Viæ Cavæ, between the Anio and the walls, to defend the city against Hannibal. After passing Tibur, or Tivoli, it continued northeast across the Apennines to the Adriatic, as the Via Valeria; and another branch, Via Sublacensis, continued up the valley of the Anio to Sublaqueum, Subiaco, the region of the sources of the great aqueducts.

The Via Prænestina is the next road on the eastern side. It also left the kingly city by the Porta Esquilina; and issuing through the outer wall by the Porta Prænestina, the modern Porta Maggiore, led to Præneste, now Palestrina. But the first portion of this road was originally the Via Gabina. Gabii is eleven miles from Rome, and is interesting as shewing a good deal of its ancient fortifications, and illustrating very well the idea of a primitive walled hill-town. From the same gate went the Via Labicana to Labicum, now La Colonna. Both these roads fell afterwards into the important Via Latina. At a little over eight miles from the gate, on the Via Gabina, is a very fine ancient bridge, 320 feet long, called the Ponte di Nono. It has **seven arches** of large squared blocks of Lapis Gabinus or Sperone **stone**, and of red tufa, with great buttresses and pilasters. The pavement is of polygonal basaltic stone, and is twenty-one feet wide.

At the third mile from Rome upon this Via Prænestina,

another, the Collatina, branches off to the left for Collatia, now Lunghezza, along which are seen the respirators or ventilators of the Aqua Virgo, an underground aqueduct of great celebrity, and which has always been fully maintained, still supplying all **the lower part** of the modern city.

The Via Latina diverged from the Via Appia inside the walls, near the Thermæ of Caracalla, and issued by the Porta Latina, near which the old pavement exists: the gate has been long closed. The line of road outside the wall is marked by many tombs of the time of the Empire; and about three miles from Rome are the celebrated "painted tombs" of the Latin Way. It ran to Tusculum, the modern Frascati; and after receiving the Via Præ-nestina, and traversing Latium and Campania, entered Samnium, and at Beneventum fell into the Via Appia.

A few hundred yards south-west of the last-mentioned gate stood the Porta Appia, through which issued the celebrated Via Appia, the great southern coast-road. This gate is still the principal entrance to **the city** from the south, under the name Porta S. Sebastiano. Just inside it is the monumental Arch of Drusus, disfigured, as so many other architectural ornaments of Rome, by bearing on its back the aqueduct built by Antoninus Caracalla, to convey water to his baths. This, the earliest of all the great Viæ Stratæ, was constructed by Appius Claudius Cæcus, the Censor, A.U.C. 441, B.C. 312. As has been already said, the Porta Capena in the Wall of Servius was its true starting-point, and in that part of the **wall which** crossed the valley between the Cœlian and Aventine upon the cross agger. At the gateway it is only three yards wide; but this is in accordance with the **Laws** of the Twelve Tables; **and** the width of the paved way of the Porta della Marina at Pompeii is of the same dimensions. The usual width of the pavement otherwise than at a gate was four yards, exclusive of the raised footpath, or crepido, for foot-passengers.

When Domitian rebuilt the Porta Capena, A.D. 90, the level of the gateway and road was raised several feet. Just outside the Porta S. Sebastiano, and on the right hand, the first milestone of the Appian Way was found, the spot being exactly one Roman mile from the site of the Porta Capena, in the vineyard of the monastery of S. Gregory; the milestone is in the museum of the Capitol. Several portions of the pavement have been found within the outer line of wall. This great road, the first constructed on regular principles of engineering, and of considerable length, ran through Latium, passing by Aricia, Forum Appii, and across the Pontine marsh to Anxur or Tarracina on the sea-coast: past Mintumæ, and through Sinnessa; on entering Campania it left the coast, and struck inland to Capua, its termination. It was afterwards prolonged by Caudium, through Samnium to Beneventum. Traversing the Apennine chain it entered Apulia; and touching Venusia and Tarentum, finally dipped to the Adriatic at Brundusium. Whether considered in its great length, or the admirable manner in which it overcame very formidable difficulties in construction through marshes and in the mountains, it deserved the title which the poet Statius bestowed on it, "Queen of long roads." As the great thoroughfare out of the city, it was lined for miles with sepulchral monuments, of which the great circular tomb of Cæcilia Metella, in travertine stone, is the most conspicuous.

The Via Ardeatina lay next to the Appia on the west, issuing from the outer wall by the gate of that name, which is of the age of Nero, and equals in the excellency of its brickwork any building of that material in Rome. It ran into the Appia, and can be traced from the walls to its junction. The polygonal paving-stones are left on the line in many places; and the foundations of a bridge are visible by the side of a water-mill near the Appia. It ran to Ardea, nearly due south from Rome; it may be traced, and used, though in a bad state: the indications of its course are more distinct near Ardea.

The Via Laurentina issued out of the wall by the same gate as the last mentioned; and the way inside the wall common to both, must have come out of the city of the Kings by the old gate, supposed to have been the Porta Raudusculana, which stood in the gorge half-way between the churches of S. Sabba and S. Balbina on the Aventine. Those buildings were originally forts to defend the gateway. Laurentum, the termination of this road, was on the coast of Latium, five or six miles south-east of the Tiber's mouth.

The Via Ostiensis began at the Porta Trigemina, the gateway of the Kings, situated on the narrow strip of land between the Aventine and the Tiber. It passed by the Navalia, or docks on the river, and the Emporium, and wound away from the bank to the pyramid of C. Cestius. At this spot the original pavement can be seen, sunk at a lower level than the modern road, and on the opposite side of the monument. Ostia, at the mouth of the Tiber, fifteen miles from Rome, was one of its earliest colonies, having been founded by Ancus Martius. About nine miles from the city, at Malafede, there is the ancient bridge by which the road crossed the Decimo; it is built of large tufa blocks, and has eleven arches to allow passage for floodwater: these are all buried, but the ancient pavement is still visible here.

Via Portuensis: on crossing the Tiber to the Janiculan side, the old road nearest the river is that which led out to Portus, through the Porta Portuensis, a gateway in the wall of Aurelian. The modern gate, Porta Portese, is not in the line of the ancient fortification, but lies some distance within it. From the city proper the road lay across the Pons Sublicius into the Transtiberine quarter, and on reaching the right bank ran in nearly a straight line to the outer wall. The gateway of Aurelian was destroyed by Pope Urban VIII., but the inscription on it recording the name of Honorius, who rebuilt it, has been preserved. This Via became important on the construction of Portus Augusti, the new harbour and city, now Porto, at the Tiber's mouth, and on the northern or right bank. These works were projected by Augustus, and carried out by Claudius, for the double purpose of remedying the silted-up condition of the natural port of Ostia, and of providing a straighter and deeper course for the waters of the river, which, being held back by the bar at its mouth, aggravated the frequent floods at Rome. The process of silting, however, proceeds so rapidly in the Tiber, owing to the quantity of sand washed down from the hills, that by the time of Trajan it was necessary to form both a new harbour and a new channel. The site of the Claudian works has become completely solid land, while the port of Trajan, which is hexagonal in form and about 2400 yards in circuit, still exists, with a depth of about ten feet of water. The canal communicating with this port is still open, and is the only navigable channel into the river. Porto itself is now two miles from the sea.

Branching off from the Via Portuensis, and to the right-hand, about a mile and a-half from the gate, ran a second road, the Via Campana, upon which, before reaching Magliana, the Prædium Manlianum, a favourite villa of the Popes, and about five miles from Rome, inscriptions belonging to the Fratres Arvales were found. Their sacred grove was here, and the buildings belonging to the fraternity are visible.

The Via Aurelia, the great coast-road to the north through Etruria, passed out of the Transtiberine quarter by the Porta Janiculensis, or Porta S. Pancrazio, on the highest point of the hill. The road is called in some inscriptions Aurelia Vetus, because there was a Via Aurelia Nova, passing under the Janiculan heights, which united with the older road at three miles and a-half from the walls. Each of these threw off a branch: from the old Aurelian the Via Vitellia diverged near the church of S. Pancrazio, and ran direct to the sea. The Via Cornelia left the new Aurelian at two miles from Rome, and turning to the right, ran between the Viæ Clodia and Aurelia into the heart of Etruria. The Aurelian Way commenced properly at the Porta Aurelia, an inner gate close to the Pons Ælius, under the Mausoleum of Hadrian. It ran to the sea, striking it at Alsium, and it forms the modern road to Civita Vecchia, the Portus Trajanus. Like the other great thoroughfares from the city, it was lined with splendid tombs; some of these are still preserved in the garden of the Corsini, near the gate. Along the coast of the Mare Inferum the road went to Pisa at first, and was afterwards prolonged into Liguria, passing by Genoa, and as far as Forum Julii in Transalpine Gaul, a colony of Julius Cæsar's, and represented by the modern Frejus.

This review completes the circle of all the Viæ which took their origin from the gates of Rome: thence the threads of communication ramified through all the provinces, and it was through this means that the Romans provided for the passage of their legions, by which they kept firm command over every corner of their immense dominions. To make them as short as possible, they were carried in straight lines over heights and dales, with the crests of the hills lowered by deep cuttings, or they were conducted across valleys upon high viaducts, and along morasses upon long embankments when necessary, as may still be seen. For these great works are never wholly effaced, but bear continual witness to the grandeur of their construction.

In the time of the Emperors the principal Viæ were made regular post-roads, by establishing stations at every stage of from four to six miles, each of which posts was provided with forty horses; and by the help of these it was easy to travel a hundred miles in the day. Gibbon relates that in the time of Theodosius a journey was made by a magistrate from Antioch to Constantinople, 665 English miles, in about five days and a-half. And in estimating the distance traversable by these roads within the Empire's boundaries, he calculates that from the Wall of Antoninus in Britain to Rome, and from Rome to Jerusalem, the great chain of communication was drawn out from north-west to south-east to the length of four thousand and eighty Roman miles. To make the system perfect the milestone was added, a Cippus or Milliarium being erected at every mile, with the number upon it; this was due to Caius Gracchus, B.C. 123. Raised causeways, margines or crepidines, on each side of the main street, provided for the safety and comfort of foot-passengers; and lastly, mounting-stones were fixed at the roadside for the convenience of horsemen to regain their seats.

CHAPTER IX.

THE AQUEDUCTS.

WE have now to describe the system of Aqueducts connected with the City. While it is true that no remains of antiquity that have survived to modern times are more worthy of admiration than these monuments of Roman skill and boldness, it is also true that it is impossible to understand the material history of Rome without studying them. They form a constituent portion not only of the useful and architectural features of the place, but also of its defensive works: for on its eastern side they form a long line of rampart in connection with the Wall of Aurelian, and they have borne an important part in various sieges of the city. It has required a close and patient study to unravel the great network of conduits, which partly above and partly underground carried water sufficient to supply the Thermæ, Naumachiæ, and countless fountains. But this has been done, and we are able to give an account of all the known aqueducts formerly entering the walls, with the exception, perhaps, of a branch from one of them to the Thermæ of Diocletian. Most of them have been traced from the source downwards, and a chart on a large scale, the result of actual investigation, shews where each ran as far as to the walls of the city, while the most important ramifications within the walls are shewn on separate diagrams. The spot also where most of the older water-courses finally discharged themselves has been discovered.

Fortunately we have a trustworthy guide to the history of the Aqueducts in Sextus Julius Frontinus, who was Governor of Britain under Vespasian, and was appointed Curator Aquarum, Superintendent of Aqueducts, A.D. 97.

He tells us not only what was effected during his own administration, but also gives an historical account of the advances made from time to time in the means of supplying water to the city, so as to keep pace with the growing wealth and population. At the time of his death these works had probably reached perfection, and were justly the admiration and surprise of all travellers. He states in his fourth chapter that for 441 years after the building of the city, i.e. till B.C. 312, the people were content with the water which they drew from the Tiber or from wells and springs. At the time of writing his treatise, he says there now flow into the city :—

I. Aqua Appia.
II. Anio Vetus.
III. Aqua Marcia.
IV. —— Tepula.
V. —— Julia.
VI. Aqua Virgo.
VII. —— Alsietina, or Augusta.
VIII. —— Claudia.
IX. Anio Novus.

In describing these nine aqueducts in order, he gives particulars as to the source of water to each, the quantity, and the distribution. In later times seven others were successively added, namely,—

X. Aqua Sabatina, now Paola.
XI. —— Trajana, or Hadriana.
XII. —— Aurelia.
XIII. Aqua Severiana.
XIV. —— Antoniniana.
XV. —— Alexandrina.
XVI. —— Algentiana.

These are all that are known belonging to the times called classical. In addition, there was one added, or rather restored to use from the old sources, in the twelfth century, one in the sixteenth, and one in the third quarter of the nineteenth. Procopius gives the number existing in his time as fourteen.

The channel of an aqueduct was called Specus, and was

built of stone carefully cemented: after the time of Claudius the specus of concrete was faced with brickwork. The floor was laid with the kind of concrete called Opus Signinum, modernly Coccio Pesto, made of broken pottery and Pozzolana sand mixed with fresh lime, forming a coating impervious to water. The specus was closed in above to exclude impurities, and also the sun's heat, so that the water might come down as cool as possible: this covering was in some cases an angular roof coming to a ridge at the top, in some it was square, in some arched. The two earliest, Aqua Appia and Anio Vetus, were ridge-roofed; the third, Aqua Marcia, is square-headed; the first that was arched is the Aqua Virgo, of the time of Augustus; and all three forms were repeated in subsequent structures. It is observable that no two aqueducts shew the same section across; for it was necessary to distinguish them, so that the workmen, who were called Aquarii, might always know to which of them each channel belonged at the points where they cross each other, and thus, in the process of repairing or cleansing an obstructed specus, might without error follow up the course required. The channels varied also very much in dimensions as well as in form. The Aqua Marcia may be taken as a typical representative of size, being five feet high by two and a-half in breadth, and the thickness of the wall on each side is one foot. The Claudia and the Anio Novus were considerably larger; the area of the channel of the Virgo was just half that of the Claudia.

At the source of each aqueduct a filtering-pool, Piscina Limosa, or Limaria, was constructed to catch the impurities held in suspension by the water, before it was led away into the specus. These were repeated at intervals, and were usually connected with the structure called Castellum Aquæ, or reservoir. The force of the water running in a strong current from such great distances required to be broken frequently, and this was effected by turning the course at a sharp angle, and then allowing it to resume its former direction by another angle. It is observable also that the base of the channel is often broken by inequalities or dips, as if purposely introduced to agitate the fluid in its course, and thus to make it combine with a larger quantity of atmospheric air; and these inequalities would tend to check the passage of heavy earthy matter held in the water. In addition, there were ventilating-shafts at proper intervals, which were used also as wells to let down buckets for drawing water, and on the sides of these shafts steps were cut for the workmen to descend into the specus and remove obstructions. In directing how the levels should be taken for carrying water through the valleys, Vitruvius says that there should be standing or upright pipes, Columnaria, as respirators, to let off the confined air, and thus reduce pressure. The sharp angles spoken of just above were made useful for carrying the later and higher aqueducts over the older courses. This arrangement is admirably seen at the building called Torre Fiscale, three miles out of Rome on the east side, and also at the Porta Maggiore. At the former, five aqueducts are carried through the same tower, three in one arcade, and two in another, at right angles to them; and the Aqua Felice runs at the foot of the tower. The same six pass at the gateway, Porta Maggiore, the Claudia and Anio Novus over it, and the Marcia, Tepula, and Julia on the northern side of it, and the Felice also over it; the three continue onwards to the Porta S. Lorenzo, and over it, with the Felice also. There was, as it were, a pressing and multiplying of water-channels against the south-eastern portion of the city wall, where the roads from Præneste and Labicum come in towards the Esquiline Hill. After the engineers had brought the waters down from the valley of the

Anio and across the Campagna, they led them to that point as the most favourable for preserving such a level as to allow them to flow naturally over the highest ground in the city. The great art lay in keeping the right gradient of inclination in the bed of the channel, so as to conduct the water by the sole force of gravity from its source to the capital, neither too swiftly nor too slowly: Pliny calls this balancing of forces, Libramentum Aquæ. The general basis of result may be taken as a stream of water from four to five feet deep, and two and a-half wide, running at an average speed of six miles in the hour. The chart of the aqueducts will shew plainly to the **eye how the** principal aqueducts, Anio Vetus, Marcia, Claudia, Anio Novus, were brought down very gradually from the edge of the mountainous gorge near Tivoli, not in a direct line towards Rome, but in a great sweep to the south. By keeping this course along the higher ground, they avoided the many small valleys of the streams which run from the hilly ground on the south down toward the Anio, and in fact wound round the heads of those valleys in order to retain the level, till **the** Campagna was fairly reached. It **is** after turning again northward, below Tusculum, **that the** long ranges of arcades begin, which before reaching Rome cross and recross each other.

The Claudian and Marcian, both of solid stone, **are** on an average fifty and thirty feet high respectively. Before these aqueducts, and those carried with them on the same arches, rise from the plain, they pass through the Piscinæ **mentioned by** Frontinus, which are large subterranean reservoirs, or filtering-places; these are between six and seven miles from the city, and are still traceable by the earthy mounds, or tumuli, **reared** over **them.**

It is to be observed that the period of the construction of the nine principal aqueducts described by Frontinus, embraces about four centuries of years. And that author points out how the order of level of the eight upon the east side of the Tiber follows the order of construction in time, with the exception of the Virgo, in a short underground channel; the level was raised as each new water was added. The height of these above the sea, as they enter Rome by the Porta Prænestina, is as follows:—Aqua Appia, 121 feet; Anio Vetus, 149; Aqua Marcia, 173; Julia, 191; (the Tepula between these two last;) Claudia, 203; Anio Novus, 212. The two last were designed to carry water to the very highest points of the city, which are as follows:—Esquiline Hill, 187; Palatine, 170; Viminal, 170; Cœlian, 168; Capitoline, northern ridge, 159; Quirinal, 157; Aventine, 155.

Every aqueduct was brought down to its own principal terminus within the outer wall of the city, where there was a final receiving reservoir, also called Castellum Aquæ; and from it the distribution of water began for the Regions supplied from that source. This was constructed in some cases very much after the fashion of the larger ornamental fountains in modern Rome. It was at this chief reservoir that the measurement of the quantity of water was calculated. From it the other Castella were supplied; and the total number of these connected with the eight aqueducts, was in the time of Frontinus, 247. It was also arranged that in the supply of water to the smaller cisterns and fountains fed from the Castella, some of the aqueducts could be interchanged. A network was established, so that where one channel, from whatever cause, failed, another could supply its place. But as the water from some sources was liable to become muddy, and unfit for drinking purposes, as was notably the case with the Anio Vetus and Anio Novus, care was taken under the curatorship of Frontinus to rectify the evils arising from unskilfully mingling the products of these with the purer waters.

In the treatise on the aqueducts, the details of distribution are given under three heads,—Imperial, Public, Private. After the palaces and gardens of the Cæsars had been served, the Public Service was divided under four heads :—Castra, the soldiers' barracks, of which there were 19; Public Establishments, 95; Theatres, and places of entertainment, 39; Public open reservoirs, called Lacus, for the service of all comers, free of charge, 591. These last would resemble what we commonly speak of as fountains, in the streets and open places, upon which the poorer classes depended entirely for their water. The more wealthy had their own private reservoirs in the courts of their dwellings, very much as is the usage in the modern city, and paid the State for the quantity supplied. About one-third of the whole was expended under this head.

If the whole of the water measured at the head of each of the nine aqueducts were put together, it has been calculated that it would represent a stream twenty feet wide, by six feet deep, constantly flowing at an inclination six times as rapid as that of the Thames. And taking some additional aqueducts into account, made between the time of Trajan and Aurelian, it has been computed that there flowed into Rome daily about 333 millions of gallons.

Frontinus gives an account of all the aqueducts constructed up to his own time. I. The Aqua Appia, dated B.C. 312, rises in the Lucullan fields on the Via Prænestina, between the seventh and eighth milestone. The channel from its source to the Salinæ, which is near the Porta Trigemina, measures 11 miles, 190 paces. For 11 miles, 130 paces, it runs underground; and for 60 paces (about 100 yards) it is carried above ground, on a substructure and arcade. A branch was added to it by Augustus, whence it received the name of Gemellos. At the point of juncture the depth of the water was five feet; and width, one foot nine inches. Outside the city the specus was seen by Frontinus buried fifty feet deep. The stream having been conducted underneath the Cœlian and Aventine Hills, came to light, and was distributed at the foot of the Clivus Publicii, which was a zigzag slanting road leading from the Tiber up to the top of the Aventine, and at this spot stood the Porta Trigemina.

The sources of the Aqua Appia are still to be seen in different very ancient stone-quarries or caves; from these the waters are collected at first into a stone specus open at the top, and cut in the rock. It then enters the ground by a tunnel, where there is a Castellum, or reservoir, and continues a subterranean course the whole way into Rome. And as it had no Piscinæ, or filtering-places, it flowed in an uninterrupted channel to the point of its distribution. Having its origin in a clay soil, and being also unfiltered, this aqueduct was very liable to obstructions; and the choked condition in which it was found wherever it has been examined, is thus accounted for. It entered the outer wall near the Porta Prænestina, between which and the Cœlian it is used to carry the leaden pipes of a modern aqueduct, Aqua Felice; from the surface, where one of the shafts of the latter is situated, to the bottom is a depth of twenty-five feet. The direction of the channel after it enters the city happens to be well seen aboveground, as it is identical with that of the fine arches of the Neronian branch from the Claudian aqueduct, as far as the Arch of Dolabella, on the Cœlian. From that hill it is carried over the Porta Capena, across the intervening valley to the Aventine, upon the agger of Servius Tullius. Here, and here alone, throughout its whole course was it raised, according to the statement of Frontinus, upon a substructure and arches, for a distance of a hundred yards. Thence it ran underground beneath the Aventine, and came out in a cave-reservoir at the level of the wharf called Marmorata on the Tiber, and between it and the Salinæ, or salt warehouses, close to the Pons Sublicius and the Porta Trigemina.

II. The Anio Vetus, B.C. 272. **This aqueduct** was constructed, according to Frontinus, 40 years after the Appian, by Marcus Curius Dentatus, when Censor; who contracted to bring into the city the water of the Anio from the spoils taken of Pyrrhus. It takes its rise, says that author, beyond Tibur, outside the gate, at the **twentieth milestone**. Its course, in consequence of the difficulties caused by the levels, is 43 miles **in length**. Of this, for 42 miles and 779 paces, the stream is underground, and **for 222 paces on a** substructure aboveground: it **holds the** sixth place **in** height.

The **Anio** rises above Sublaqueum, Subiaco, in high mountains, **on which** snow lies for a great part **of** the year; and being liable to sudden floods, which bring down much mud, great precautions were necessary for filtering it. Accordingly, Frontinus specially mentions Piscinæ as connected **with this** aqueduct; but notwithstanding the care taken to purify its water, it was very inferior to other aqueducts for drinking-purposes. It can be usually distinguished from the other **aqueducts** connected with the **same system,** or group, **as** itself, **by** being half underground, or very near the surface. In general, its course was the same as that of the Aqua Marcia downwards from Tivoli, the Anio Vetus being at the foot of the piers of the arcade of the other. It has also both **its specus** and castella faced with Opus Reticulatum, wherever they are found. A good example of its style and degree of elevation is seen at the Tor Fiscale, the tower through which five aqueducts pass above; while the Anio Vetus is half underground, at the foot of the Claudian arcade. It enters Rome at the usual place, at the foot of the Marcian arcade, close to the Porta Maggiore; and here it is almost level with the ground. It passes through the city wall there, and is visible on the other side of it in the wall of a garden. Here it forked off; one important branch went northward, carried along the bank of the Kings, on which the Wall of Aurelian was afterwards built; this specus is not visible in this part again till it reaches the Prætorian Camp. A portion of it, excavated under the Porta Chiusa against the camp, was found to be built of large stones of tufa. It may then be traced all round the three sides of the camp, and is distinctly visible upon the north side, where the Wall of Tiberius remains perfect, standing upon the old specus which is faced with reticulated-work. From near the Porta Chiusa another branch went off to the left, crossing the agger and foss, towards the Thermæ of Diocletian. In constructing the railroad, which enters Rome hereabouts, the specus itself was found, and two Cippi with inscriptions, naming this aqueduct the Anio. The other main branch struck off westward into the bank on which the arches of Nero stand, near the Lateran; and in fact followed the course of the Aqua Appia downwards, and along the line of the Cœlian, to the valley between that hill and the Aventine.

III. The Aqua Marcia, B.C. 145. Frontinus says, 127 years later, the conduits of the Appian and Anio being much decayed by age, the business of repairing them was entrusted by the Senate to Q. Marcius Rex, then acting as Prætor. And because the increase of the population of the city seemed to demand a more ample supply of water, instructions were given him by the Senate that he should carefully examine how far there were other streams which he might be able to bring into the city. He therefore restored the two old conduits, and introduced a third, which he caused to be erected with squared stones, and larger channels, and carried through them the water which he had obtained for the public service. Hence it received the name of Marcian from himself, as the author of it. The Marcia has its origin on the Via Valeria, at the thirty-sixth milestone, three miles off in the cross-road on the right-hand in going from Rome, and at the thirty-eighth milestone on the road to Sublaqueum; for the space of two hundred paces, on the left-hand, the water lies like a pond, bubbling up in innumerable springs from the stony hollows, and is very green in colour. The length of its course from its head to the city is 61 miles 710 paces: by an underground channel, 54 miles 247 paces; on structure aboveground, 7 miles 463 paces. Out of this it is carried in parts away from the city, in the upper part of the valleys, on arched substructure for 473 paces; nearer the city, from the seventh milestone, on a substructure for 538 paces; in the rest of the work it is carried on an arcade for 6 miles 472 paces. The Marcian ranks fifth in height, and is at its head even in level with the Claudian. In the year B.C. 34, Agrippa repaired the three aqueducts, Appian, Anio Vetus, and Marcian. In the reign of Nerva, A.D. 96, the Marcian having been enlarged, was carried across from the Cœlian to the Aventine.

The principal source of it, as described by Frontinus, is called Acqua Serena, a beautiful spring gushing out of the hill, seven miles and a-half below Subiaco, very clear and abundant, on the right bank of the Anio. The specus is carried in the valley, and crosses the river near Varia (Vico-Varo); at Tivoli it leaves the Anio and turns southward, so as to preserve a gradual descent, while the river descends in cascades. It crosses several ravines, one by the bridge of S. Antonio, in company with the Anio Vetus. At the bridge called Ponte S. Pietro the specus of the Marcian is again visible, but alone; and at the Ponte Lupo, together with the Anio Novus and Claudia, and the Anio Vetus again. Thence it continues, chiefly underground, to the Piscinæ before mentioned, where, Frontinus says, the aqueducts, as though breathing again after their course, deposit mud. For the rest of the way it was carried on its stone arcade to the city wall. Within the wall it divided, the branch to the north, parallel to the wall, passing underground for some distance, and then running into the bank against which that great wall is built. It emerges again near the Porta Tiburtina, where the ground becomes lower, and is reared on an arcade, one arch of which is made into the gateway. Here the specus lies quite open to view, on the southern side of the gate, with an opening into it, by which it is easily entered. There was a large reservoir for it near the Porta Chiusa, against the Prætorian Camp, and from this reservoir the water was taken westwards to the inner gate of the agger of Servius on the Viminal. Another division of the Marcian struck off westward: of this Frontinus says, "the Marcia after the Pallantian gardens (at the Sessorium) throws off part of its waters into a stream called the Herculanean; this conduit through the Cœlian, being of no use for the houses on the hill because at too low a level, comes to an end *above* the Porta Capena." There is a large reservoir of an aqueduct *in the* cliff of the Cœlian just above the remains of the Porta Capena; this was excavated for the British archæologists about 1870, and left open for students to see, by an agreement with the monks of S. Gregory, in whose vineyard it is situated.

The excellent qualities of this aqueduct were highly celebrated, and are frequently mentioned in Latin writers; and when it was found desirable, in modern times, to introduce a fresh supply of water, of the greatest purity attainable anywhere within reach of Rome, recourse was had again to the fountain-head of the Marcia.

IV. Aqua Tepula. B.C. 126, the Censors took care to bring into Rome the stream called the Tepulan, from the Tusculan fields. The Tepula has its source on the Via Latina, at the tenth milestone, two miles off to the right of those going into Rome.

V. Aqua Julia. Afterwards, continues Frontinus, B.C. 34, Marcus Agrippa collected the waters of another stream, at twelve miles from the city, on the Via Latina, and two miles off to the right, and so intercepted the Tepulan. To the newly-acquired water the name of Julia was given, from the finder of it: nevertheless the distribution was so divided that the name of Tepula was retained. The course of the Julia runs for the length of 15 miles 426 paces. In work above ground, 7 miles; from the seventh milestone it is carried on a substructure 528 paces, the rest on arched work for 6 miles 472 paces.

At the Piscinæ, he says, the Julia, Marcia, and Tepula meet: of these the Tepula, which had been intercepted by the Julia and joined to its stream, now receives from the reservoirs of the Julia its proper quantity, and flows out in its own channel, and under its own name. These three are carried from the reservoirs on the same arcade.

The sources of these two short aqueducts are in the valleys on either side of the promontory on which the town of Marino stands; that of the Julia is on the south side, and almost close under the crater, now the Alban Lake. As to the Tepula, ten miles on the Via Latina brings us near to Tusculum, Frascati, and two miles farther on a crossroad, before reaching Grotta Ferrata, are springs coming out under a cliff of the lava rock. The supply of water is small, and the specus of this aqueduct is the smallest of all the nine. Its roof is ridged.

The head-waters of the Julia are in some copious springs south-west from the Tepula, on the slope of Mons Algidus. The specus may be seen ten miles on the Via Latina, built of rough stone, faced with Opus Reticulatum, but of a rude kind. The vaulting of the roof is curved. Of the three aqueducts carried on the same arcade from the Piscinæ, the Tepula alone ran in a single channel without any branch. It supplied the Regiones in the northern part of the city only, and therefore it probably passed into the Castellum, the remains of which are still visible in the city wall near the Porta S. Lorenzo: adjoining this reservoir is a specus answering in form and dimensions to that of this aqueduct in other places. But the Julia, as Frontinus states, was divided at the usual spot within the walls, and the branch running westward from the gate was distributed in the Castella on the Cœlian Hill. It was third in point of height, ranking next below the Aqua Claudia.

VI. Aqua Virgo, B.C. 21. This aqueduct was made by M. Agrippa, to supply water to his Thermæ on the south side of the Pantheon, which was the entrance-hall to them. Frontinus says, the same, when he had been consul for the third time, thirteen years after he had brought down the Julia, brought the Virgo also, the water of which was collected in the Lucullan fields. It begins on the Via Collatina at the eighth milestone, in some marshy places, a cemented structure being placed round it to retain the bubbling waters. It comes for a length of 14 miles 105 paces: out of this by a subterranean stream 12 miles 865 paces; aboveground 1 mile 240 paces. It ends in the Campus Martius along the front of the Septa. The Virgo was the seventh in height as to level.

Near the ruins of Collatia there is a series of reservoirs just below the surface of the ground, the water from which is collected into a large central reservoir: from this the line of the specus may be traced onwards by the respirators at regular intervals of about a hundred yards. These are mostly round masses of concrete with round heads, but some are dwarf pyramids. The specus runs along the line of the old Via, which lies between the roads to Tibur and Præneste, and keeps westerly to a point about half-a-mile from the Porta Maggiore; when it turns and makes a great sweep to the north, and comes to the bank on which the Wall of Aurelian was afterwards built, near the Porta Salaria. It does not, however, enter the city there, but is continued upon or in that bank under the present wall for about a mile. Near the northernmost point of Rome it passes through the gardens of the Villa Borghese, and enters eventually through the Pincian Hill, a little to the north of the great flight of the Spanish steps. It then goes to the fountain of Trevi, the largest in Rome, passing along by the Via Nazzareno; and in a courtyard out of that street there is on the wall an inscription, dated A.D. 46, recording the fundamental restoration of the aqueduct by Claudius. A branch was taken off from it, which was found in a large leaden pipe two feet in diameter, enclosed in a casing of brickwork, laid down in the Via dei Condotti, or Conduit-street: this branch led to the Thermæ of Alexander Severus, north of the Pantheon. The original termination of the main line at the north end of the Septa, very near the Pantheon, was found. Remains also of the arcade of the Septa exist under the houses at the lower end of the Corso, the chief street in Rome, and which runs from one end to the other of the Campus Martius. This aqueduct still forms the chief supply of water to the fountains and houses in the lower city, representing the area of the Campus. It was always celebrated for its purity and coolness, and retains its character.

VII. Aqua Alsietina, A.D. 10. This water was brought in by Augustus, to supply his Naumachia in the Transtiberine Region, but being of bad quality, was of little use to the people, as Frontinus states. The fourteenth Region had its fountains supplied from the city by aqueducts crossing the river on the bridges, and it was only when the latter were under repair, that the Alsietina was used as a matter of necessity. It begins, says Frontinus, at the fourteenth milestone on the Via Claudia, and six miles and a-half more on the cross-road on the right hand. Its course is 22 miles 172 paces long, and over arched-work 358 paces. It is the lowest of all as regards the level, supplying only the Transtiberine Region and the places adjacent.

The Lacus Alsietinus, from which it was drawn, is situated in the hills on the north-western side of Rome, between the Via Aurelia and Via Claudia, and lies 679 feet above the sea-level. The aqueduct leaves the lake by a specus tunnelled through the rock. An additional supply was taken from the springs which supply the large Lacus Sabatinus, now Bracciano, close at hand. In the time of Trajan, owing to the complaints of Frontinus, great improvements were made, and the latter portion only of Augustus' work was restored. In 1611, Pope Paul V. renewed the whole structure, and introduced fresh water from purer sources, but using the channel of the Aqua Trajana, as may be collected from the inscription put up by him. This work, under the name of Acqua Paola, is still in full operation, and yields a large supply to the Leonine city. The fountain bearing the Pope's name, at which the water is delivered, is high up on the Janiculan Hill, and is one of the largest in Rome. Procopius expresses his amazement at the quantity of water thus brought to the top of that hill, and thence poured in torrents over the whole Transtiberine Region. This is still the case: the fountains in front of S. Peter's and in the Vatican gardens are supplied by this aqueduct, and the water is so abundant, that it is even brought over the bridge and feeds a fountain on the other side. The main branch, falling in a cascade down the face of the Janiculan, turns the wheels of three water-mills in its course, which are used to grind corn. This is also mentioned by Procopius, who states that the mills were destroyed by the Goths, but replaced by others in the channel of the Tiber by Belisarius.

VIII. and IX. Aqua Claudia and Anio Novus, A.D. 52. Frontinus says, Caius Cæsar (Caligula), who succeeded Tiberius, considered seven aqueducts scarcely sufficient for public purposes and private amusements, and began two new aqueducts in the second year of his reign, which work Claudius in a most splendid manner finished and dedicated. To one, which was brought from the springs Cæruleus and Curtius, the name Claudia was given: this one is next in order of excellence to the Marcia. The other, because two streams of the Anio had begun to flow into the city, so that they should be more easily distinguished by their names, began to be called Anio Novus; and to the former Anio the cognomen Vetus was added. The Anio Novus and Claudia are carried from the Piscinæ upon higher arches (than any other) the Anio being the higher of the two. Their arches come to an end after the Pallantian gardens, and thence they are carried down in pipes for the use of the city. But first of all the Claudia transfers part of its water on to the arches **which are called** the Neronian: these being continued in a direct line along **the Cœlian Hill, are terminated close to the** temple of Claudius. They disperse the quantity which **they had received** either **upon the Cœ**lian, or in the Palatine, in the Aventine, **and the** Transtiberine Region.

VIII. The Claudia begins on the Via Sublacensis, at the thirty-eighth milestone. There are two very large and beautiful springs,—one called Cæruleus from its blue tinge, **the other Curtius.** It receives also the spring called Albudinus, **of** such excellence, that when there is need of adding it to the Marcian, the latter loses none of its quality by the addition. The channel of the Claudia is 46 miles 406 paces in length: of this **36 miles** 230 paces is by a subterranean course; on work aboveground 10 miles 176 paces; and out of this on arched work **3** miles 76 paces, in the upper part; and near the city, 6 miles 491 paces on an arcade. The Claudian is the second in height as to level.

IX. The Anio Novus, at the forty-second milestone **on** the Via Sublacensis, is taken out of the river, which, since it has about it cultivated land in a rich territory, and such very loose banks, flows muddy and turbid even when uninfluenced by violent rains; and therefore at the very entrance of the channel is placed a reservoir for the mud (Piscina limaria), so that the water on its way from the river to the specus should settle and become clear. The length of the Anio Novus is 58 miles 700 paces: 49 miles 300 paces underground; **9 miles 400** paces visible, near the city, upon the same arcades as the Claudian. These are the highest arches, elevated in some places 109 feet.

Afterwards, Frontinus adds, it was **not** enough for our Emperor (Trajan) to have restored an abundant and pleasant supply of water in the other aqueducts, he thought he saw his way to getting rid of the bad qualities even of the

Anio Novus. He therefore ordered the sources to be changed from the river, and taken instead from the loch, in which the water was most pure, and which is situated above Nero's villa at Sublaqueum, i.e. Subiaco. This place is more than 2000 feet above the level of Rome, and derived its name from being below the lakes. The river Anio runs through a narrow ravine in the mountains, and in flood-time becomes very thick from the clayey soil washed down into it. To guard against this evil, Caligula or Claudius made these (*lacus*) lochs or pools, by building a massive wall across the stream to dam it up in the gorge. There were three such dams in succession, each forming a pool, the surface of which was at a great height above the natural bed, and each terminated in a great cascade. The bridge of S. Mauro, built upon the two ends of one of these dams, is 144 feet by measurement above the present level of the water, and the specus of the Anio Novus is nearly ten feet higher. It is about six feet high and only sixteen inches wide, and must have been cut by men standing sideways. The channel also is not exactly what we now call a tunnel, but is hewn in the rock of the cliff, with a few feet of stone only as an outer wall to it, and in this manner runs along the edge of the valley of the Anio, and on its left bank, for many miles. The Claudian came from springs upon the right bank, and ran on that side to the point where it crossed the river in company with the Marcia, half-way to Tivoli. At the bridge called Ponte Lupo, the Anio Novus seems first to have been united with the Claudian; from that point they continue one upon the other for the rest of their course, finishing upon the long arcade of solid stonework. This portion of the work, under two Emperors, was completed in fourteen years. Before reaching Rome the Claudian arcade crosses the Marcian at the Tor Fiscale, and re-crosses it again at the Porta Furba. The space enclosed within the intersecting lines was occupied by the Goths as one of their camps while they besieged Rome.

The arcade terminates at the Porta Maggiore, and here an inscription upon the face of the specus itself, over the archway, records that Claudius, son of Drusus, caused the water of the Claudian conduit from the Cerulean, or Curtian springs, to be brought into Rome from forty-five miles distance, and that of the Anio Novus from sixty-two miles. The length of the three lochs above Subiaco has to be added to that of the actual specus, as given by Frontinus, to make up the whole distance.

Within the city wall the water of the two aqueducts was united into one, in order to be carried upon the arcade of Nero. This lofty structure, of the finest brickwork, partly remains; it first crosses the foss of the Sessorium on a double row of arches, one above the other; then is carried on to the Lateran upon a high bank and as a single arcade, and on another bank across the old foss which divided the Lateran from the city, to the Cœlian, and on that hill to the Arch of Dolabella. This arch formed the principal entrance to that portion of the hill where the Claudium was situated. Over the arch are fine ruins of a large Castellum and Piscina, faced with the same excellent brickwork. As each successive aqueduct came to this point new reservoirs were needed, and at different levels; the highest, being that of Nero, was fifty feet from the ground. Thence the water was distributed in different directions; by one branch to the Claudium itself, and thence again northward to the Stagnum Neronis, at the site of the Colosseum, and afterwards retained under it for the exhibition of Naumachiæ. A second branch led to the Palatine, passing down the western side of the Cœlian by the slope called Clivus Scauri, and crossing the valley upon the arches attributed to Nero, but more properly to Domitian, who thus provided a supply of water for the Thermæ of the new Imperial palace on that hill. Part of this lofty structure still remains. The third branch was to the Aventine, but the plan for this was not carried out till the time of Trajan, when another lofty arcade was made across the valley to the Pseudo-Aventine; some of the brick piers of this work are still visible. On the Aventine itself remains of the aqueduct are seen in front of S. Prisca: the surprise of the people at seeing copious streams of water pouring over the heights and slopes of the Aventine is recorded by a contemporary author. There was also a branch from the Palatine to the Capitoline, of which two tall piers are standing; upon this, it seems, the aqueduct was conducted at the highest level, while at a lower level it served as a bridge, with a road for horses and passengers. We are unable to trace the course of these two great channels through the city otherwise than by the Neronian arcade; but we know that all the fourteen Regiones were supplied by them, and it is probable that, to convey their waters to the northern and western districts, the conduits of the older aqueducts were used.

It will be seen that of all the nine aqueducts up to the time of Frontinus only two remain in operation, the Virgo and Trajana. The additional modern supply is from the Aqua Felice and the revived Aqua Marcia. The first-named, which is partly the same as the Aqua Hadriana, was brought from Labicum (La Colonna), by Felice Perretti, Pope Sixtus V. (1585), and runs upon the piers sometimes of the Claudian, sometimes of the Marcian, as best suited the engineer's purposes, and sometimes on its own separate arcade. From the Porta Maggiore it is taken off to the west in underground pipes laid in the old channels, and goes to the Lateran, thence descending to the lower parts of the city, and supplying water to the Ghetto, or Jews' quarter, and the streets along the Tiber. The main channel follows the line of Aurelian's wall, in company with the Marcia, Tepula, and Julia, to the Porta S. Lorenzo, where its arcade turns westward, and goes on to the high plateau of the Viminal, and round three sides of the Thermæ of Diocletian. It yields a copious supply, the Specus being three feet wide and usually from three to four feet deep, and the water flowing with a current of five miles an hour. The different reservoirs and fountains of the upper town are fed by this aqueduct. It is not, however, of good drinking quality.

The newest aqueduct, introduced under Pius IX. (1870), in order to provide more water and of the purest kind for the eastern districts, in which a new town is now springing up, brought in again the waters of the Marcian from their true fountain-heads. These form a small lake in the valley, and when the surface of this was lowered by draining for the new works, the old specus was laid open. The course as far as Tivoli is in a stone specus upon the old Roman principle, but on reaching the lower ground it is taken in cast-iron pipes, passing beneath the bed of the Anio by a great syphon. The use of these enabled the constructors to carry the work in a more direct line, and to preserve the fresh qualities of the springs. Within the city its distribution begins on the high plateau of the Viminal, opposite the Thermæ of Diocletian, where it issues in a magnificent fountain and basin.

CHAPTER X.

THE THERMÆ.

CLOSELY connected with the Aqueducts are the Thermæ, the great bathing establishments of the citizens of Rome. The earliest bath constructed for their use in common was the Piscina Publica, in the valley between the Cœlian and Aventine, and close under the cliff of the latter. It was of very large dimensions, being intended as a swimming-bath for the whole people: the outline of it can be traced for about a quarter of a mile, from the northern corner of the hill on which S. Balbina stands to the north end of the Thermæ of Caracalla. This pool was fed by the Aqua Appia which crossed the valley here: from its main line, after passing over the Porta Capena, a branch has been traced turning off to the left, and running into the subterranean chambers of the Piscina. It is obvious that the flat ground between those two hills offered the first eligible site within the walls for receiving so large a body of water. With this earliest bathing-place were connected gymnastic entertainments, as we learn from Festus, who also says that, though the Piscina itself no longer existed in his time, the name was still retained; and in fact the twelfth Regio of the city was named after it. This seems to have been the only provision of the kind during the whole period of the Republic, and in it no warming-apparatus was used. The hot bath was introduced into the private houses of great men before the Empire, but only on a small scale. Seneca describes those of earlier times as narrow and dark, and the bath-chamber of Scipio Africanus, in his villa at Liternum, he says, was lighted only by small slits in the stone wall.

The first of the Thermæ (hot-air and hot-water baths) constructed in Rome, were those of Marcus Agrippa, who led his aqueduct, the Virgo, to the spot now marked by the great circular building with the lofty flattened dome, called by Roman writers the Pantheum. The inscription on the portico fixes the date, B.C. 27; but this was not part of the original structure, though most probably added during Agrippa's lifetime. It is agreed by the best authorities, that this Rotonda, as it is now called, was the entrance-chamber to the Thermæ; and not, as has been supposed, one of the divisions of the baths themselves,—either the Laconicum, the hot-air compartment, or the Tepidarium, the tepid-water bath. The great bronze doors, which work on pivots instead of hinges, are undoubtedly original, and evidently formed the chief entrance to a great public building. This façade fronts the north; and upon the opposite or south side are remains of walls, shewing that the round hall did not stand alone. There are also traces of the thermæ attached to it, in the cellars and in the walls of the houses between the Pantheum and the Capitoline, shewing that they covered a large area; and in places the old walls are higher than the modern houses. The position of this celebrated building is about the centre of the Campus Martius.

The next Thermæ were those of Titus, upon the Esquiline, A.D. 79, occupying a large portion of the western side of that hill towards the Colosseum and Palatine. They were constructed out of the great buildings planned, and partly carried out by Nero, but left unfinished at his death. Suetonius tells us what that Emperor aimed at; it was to erect a palace which should extend from the Palatine to the Esquiliæ; this he called at first Domus Transitoria; then, after it had been burnt and restored, Domus Aurea. So large was the space included, that it had a triple arcade a mile long, and a reservoir in size like a sea (the Stagnum at the Colosseum). As some atonement for the wrong done by Nero, who had driven the inhabitants from their homes to make way for his pleasures, Titus converted a portion of these structures to the use and benefit of the people; and although he reigned only a little over two years, he was enabled to leave a portion of the Thermæ opened, and at work. But it remained for his successors to complete them, and they were not finished till the time of Trajan; they are called in the Catalogue of the fourth Regio, Thermæ of Titus and Trajan; and on an inscription of the fifth century by Trajan's name only. That the latter Emperor made extensive additions to the baths, is proved by the brick-stamps found in the walls with his name. Notwithstanding their ruined condition, the remains still preserve the outline of a plan; and there are visible the apses, or exedræ, for semicircular ranges of seats projecting beyond the straight lines of wall, the largest on the south side overlooking the Colosseum, and a smaller one on each of the three other sides.

The water-supply to these thermæ was derived from the extensive reservoirs known by the name of Sette Sale, from the seven vaulted halls into which it is divided, and situated on the eastern side of the Esquiline Hill, at a higher level than the baths. Connected with these are two other chambers, one at each end, which were piscinæ, or filtering-places. After serving the thermæ the water passed out underneath the great exedra on the southern side, and went to feed the Stagnum of the Colosseum.

The magnificence of the House of Nero, as well as of the baths, is attested by the great abundance of fine works of art found at different times under all parts of these extensive buildings. Titus is said by Pliny to have adorned his palace with the finest statuary; the group of the Laocoon was placed there, and was discovered in a vineyard between the Sette Sale and the church of S. Lucia, on the north side of the hill.

The next Thermæ were those of the Emperors Commodus and Septimius Severus, which were situated in the southernmost part of the city, between the Porta Latina and Porta Metronia. There is nothing left of them visible aboveground, but large subterranean chambers, similar to those below the Thermæ of Titus and of Caracalla, have been excavated under the small hill called Monte d'Oro, due south of the Cœlian. Two of the later aqueducts were brought in to feed these thermæ; first the Aqua Aurelia, so named from Marcus Aurelius, father of Commodus, who constructed it originally to supply his villa on the Via Appia. His son prolonged the Specus into Rome past the Porta Latina. Septimius Severus finished the works begun by Commodus, and introduced the second aqueduct, called Severiana, which had, like the other, a reservoir still traceable just outside the Latin Gate.

After these came the great Thermæ of Caracalla, son of Septimius Severus, often called of the Antonines, because the name Antoninus was given as an honorary title to that prince, as well as to Elagabalus, by the Senate. The latter commenced the great portico or arcade of two storeys on the eastern side; and his successor, Alexander Severus, finished it (A.D. 222). They are situated in the low ground between the Cœlian and Pseudo-Aventine, covering a very large area, and are amongst the most magnificent of all Roman buildings. The walls are sufficiently perfect to allow the outline to be made out; they exhibit the plan of a square of 1100 feet on each side. The front of the central building is 720 feet long, the width across 375 feet; and from this, in the centre of the western side, the calidarium, or hot-air chamber, circular in form, pro-

jects 150 feet. The walls of this last are all hollow, with
hot-air flues, heated by the hypocaust in the underground
chamber. But the apparatus for bathing occupied only
a portion of the enclosed space; provision was made for
athletic exercises and games, which required an arena;
and part of the ground was planted so as to afford shady
walks. Against the western external wall are the remains
of the great reservoir of water, and of the aqueduct, the
latter covered over with tiers of seats; and immediately
below them is a space which is considered to have been
a Stadium. The aqueduct supplying these thermæ enters
Rome at the south-east corner, near the Gate of S. Sebastian
(Porta Appia), and then immediately passes over the Arch
of Drusus. It is called the Aqua Antoniniana, but it is
not of the same magnitude as the older works of this
description, having been taken off from one of the higher
aqueducts in the main line; and the chronicler of Einsiedeln states that this one was the Marcian.

The Thermæ of Diocletian, on the high platform of the
Viminal, were the largest of all, and these are the only
buildings of the kind left which are not wholly or almost in
ruins. Begun by that Emperor, they were finished by Con-
stantius and Galerius in A.D. 305. Inscriptions connected
with them shew that they occupied fully twenty years in
building. The enormous scale of these baths may be estimated from the fact, that they accommodated double the
number that any other establishment of the kind could receive, even that of Caracalla; this would make the places
for bathers amount to 3200. Although a large proportion
of the whole has been swept away, enough of the central
mass remains to shew the magnificent dimensions. Two
monasteries with their gardens, and several large public
buildings, have been made out of the original structure. In
the centre is the Certosa, or Charterhouse, the church of

which is principally constructed out of the largest bath-chamber, the calidarium. This hall was 200 feet long and 100 feet wide; it retains the ancient vaulted roof and granite columns, and is in its converted state one of the noblest churches in the city. Fronting this church, and on the western side, is a great semicircular projection beyond the flat line of wall, which composed a vast exedra, or raised flight of seats for spectators, looking down upon the arena or stadium; and at each end of this line was a circular hall, one of which, at the northern angle, is also converted into a church.

The water-supply to these baths came by the Aqua Jovis, a branch from the Marcian: great reservoirs connected with it have been found on the eastern side, at the site of the Railway-station, and in the gardens of the Massimo family. Altogether these Imperial Thermæ covered thirty acres.

About twenty years afterwards the Emperor Constantine added his Thermæ, over the southern portion of the Quirinal Hill. Though very extensive, reaching from the Colonna gardens in the valley west of that hill, completely across it, to its eastern slope facing the Viminal, their area has been so much built over, that the remains of them are not to be compared with the conspicuous masses of the other thermæ. Like most of the grand buildings of old Rome, these also were destroyed to provide materials for modern palaces. One celebrated ornament of these thermæ still survives in the group of bronze horses which stands upon the crest of the Quirinal, called from that group Monte Cavallo, and which therefore properly belongs to that site. They represent the Dioscuri reining in their horses: one pair is ascribed to Phidias, and the other to Praxiteles. But though in Greek style, they belong to the revival of art under the Early Empire.

Constantine was the last prince who added to the public architecture of the old capital of the Empire. In the list called the Regionary Catalogue of the fourth century, eleven Thermæ are named, as follows: 1. Trajanæ; 2. Titianæ; 3. Agrippinæ; 4. Suranæ; 5. **Commodianæ**; 6. Severianæ; 7. **Alexandrinæ**; 8. Antoninianæ; 9. **Decianæ**; 10. Diocletianæ; 11. Constantinianæ. **Of these, the baths of** Sura, a relative of Trajan, and those of the Emperor Decius, were on the Aventine, supplied by Trajan's aqueduct. Those of **Alexander Severus (7) were in** the flat ground not far from **the Pantheum, but more to the** north. There is also mention in the catalogue of a Nymphæum of **this prince upon** the Esquiline, which **seems to** have been an entrance-hall to baths for women, as the **Pantheon** was to those for men.

CHAPTER XI.

Forum Romanum.

THE Forum occupied the flat ground between the Capitoline and Palatine Hills, running from north-west to south-east [a], and filling an irregular area, which is 671 feet long by 202 at its broadest end near the Capitol, and only 117 feet at the opposite end under the cliff of the Palatine. The valley receives the waters of three natural springs, which anciently formed a swamp, pool, or *lacus*, with which the legend of Curtius is connected; but this was effectually drained by the great Cloacæ, and the site of it seems to have been marked in later times as a spot to be venerated, by a well or some enclosure, into which on certain occasions offerings in money were thrown.

Properly speaking, the Forum began outside the wall of the original Sabine fortress on the Mons Saturni, or Capitoline Hill, which was entered by the Porta Saturni; but this wall of partition having been destroyed after the union of the two hills into one city, the buildings immediately under the south-eastern face of the Capitoline, and reared against it, are understood to be included in the Forum. The whole of that front towards the Palatine is occupied by the high and massive structure called the Tabularium, or Public Record Office, with which was connected the Ærarium, or Treasury, under it, and the Senate-house behind it.

At its base are the remains of three buildings, filling up the whole space along its wall: that to the east, or extreme right in the plan, is the Temple of Concord, the central one the Temple of Saturn, and the third the Porticus of the Dei Consentes, with the Schola Xantha underneath it. Of

---

[a] In assigning the points of the compass in the Forum, it is assumed that the Tabularium stands at the north end, looking from which the eastern side is on the left hand and the western on the right.

the first temple there is nothing remaining but the Podium or basement, about fifteen feet high; it was twice rebuilt between its foundation, B.C. 303, and A.D. 11, and there are traces of all three periods in the masonry. This edifice was undoubtedly connected with the Senate-house, and it would seem that the Senate actually met in it sometimes, since Cicero in the second Philippic Oration implies that he was addressing that assembly in the cella of the temple. But the area is too confined to have allowed the Senate to meet in force; and it appears from the life of Pertinax, that on being kept waiting for the key of the Senate-house, he sat down meanwhile in the Temple of Concord. It seems probable that the temple was a kind of vestibule standing before the Senate-house, which latter was a large hall in the same block of buildings as the Tabularium, and stood, as is collected from Varro, at a higher level than the temple [b]. From the steps of this temple the decrees of the Senate were publicly read. The ambassadors of foreign nations assembled in the building called Græcostasis, on the right-hand, or north-east of this temple, while waiting to be received in audience by the Senate. Next to that of Concord stood the Temple of Saturn, to the west of it: of this there remain the basement and three columns, with their entablature, on which are inscribed some letters connected with the restoration of the fabric.

The Ærarium, or Treasury, is stated by several authors to have been joined to the Temple of Saturn, so that no distinction is made between them. In the basement of the Tabularium, at the back of the temple, is a series of square chambers of very massive architecture, and the old doorway by which access was gained to them from the side of the temple is traceable. These must have been the vaults in

[b] The whole of this great block of building stands on the steep slope of the southern side of the Capitoline Hill.

which the treasure was kept, and they were connected with the office of the Treasury in the upper storey by a very steep flight of steps, still preserved, communicating with the doorway below the podium of the temple. This entrance was walled up when the temple was rebuilt by Septimius Severus, and another entrance was made to the money-chambers.

Beyond the Temple of Saturn, on the left-hand in the plan, or west side of it, is the third range of buildings at the foot of the Tabularium, consisting of the Schola Xantha and Porticus of the Dei Consentes. The first formed a row of chambers with square-headed openings, resembling shops; these were built, as an inscription belonging to them states, for the use of the copyists of books, and the criers or trumpeters of the Curule Ædiles, and were restored and beautified by A. F. Xanthus and his colleague: they were faced with marble, and had Doric pilasters. The other is on the higher level, or upper storey, and the remains consist of eight small columns of the Corinthian order, not however standing in a straight line, but forming an obtuse angle. An inscription, of the date A.D. 367, records the placing of the images of the twelve Dei Consentes, which were of gilt bronze, between the pillars of the colonnade. The portion of this work now standing is a modern restoration out of fragments found in the ruins; the ancient bases of the columns, having been preserved, served to mark the position of the original shafts.

To the south of these three edifices, nearest the Tabularium, runs the pavement of the road called Clivus Capitolinus, which wound up from the Arch of Septimius Severus at the level of the Forum, in front of the Capitolium. On the southern side of that street is another temple, with eight columns of the Ionic order, and a considerable portion of its basement well defined. This is the Temple of Vespasian, or as it is called in the Catalogue, of Vespasian and Titus, as joint Emperors. The relative position of this and the central one of the three first temples is usually reversed, the name of Saturn being given to that with the eight columns, and the name of Vespasian to that with the three. But as it is now certain that no treasure-chambers existed beneath this one, and there could have been no communication between it and the public offices in the Capitolium, the names are rightly assigned as here given. The original structure was reared by Domitian in honour of his father and brother, and restored by Septimius Severus.

A little below this temple, eastward from it, and between it and the Arch of Severus, are the remains of the Rostra, from which orators addressed the people. There were two such stages or pulpits in the Forum, and this one was distinguished as the Rostra Vetera. From the remains of the stonework forming the foundations, it would seem that the shape of these raised platforms was the segment of a circle, the orator being free to move within the enclosed space, and to turn himself in speaking either to the flat or the curved side.

Northward from the Rostra, and close under the western side of the Arch of S. Severus, is a round brick pedestal, which is taken to be the interior mass of the Milliarium Aureum, placed by Augustus, B.C. 28, as the central milestone of all the Viæ issuing from the city, as has been already stated. It is mentioned frequently by writers under the Early Empire, by some as beneath the Temple of Saturn, by Pliny as "In Capite Fori Romani," and as the point to which all the streets leading to the thirty-seven gates of Rome converged.

The marble Arch of S. Severus and his sons Caracalla and Geta stands on the low level of the Forum Romanum, and, as is supposed, on the site previously occupied by the Arch of Tiberius, which was destroyed, or so much injured by the great fire in the Forum, as to require rebuilding shortly before the time of Severus. The structure consists of a lofty central arch and two smaller lateral ones, and over the southern front the inscription states that it was erected in honour of the Emperor and his two sons, Caracalla and Geta, after their victorious campaign against the Parthians and Persians; the name of Geta having been erased, and replaced by titles of the other two princes. Caracalla, having murdered his younger brother, caused his name to be obliterated from all public memorials. The date of this triumphal arch is A.D. 203. On both fronts are panels, with sculptures representing scenes and incidents relating to the wars in the east; and on the top there stood originally a chariot with six horses abreast.

To the south of the arch the modern road crosses the Forum at a high level, but underneath that road runs a subterranean passage connecting the arch with the area of the Forum beyond, the whole of which has been excavated. Close to the mouth of this passage stands the column of Phocas, usurper of the imperial throne of East and West, to whom it was erected by Smaragdus, Exarch of Ravenna, A.D. 603. The name of Phocas was erased by Heraclius, his successor, the last Emperor that visited Rome. The shaft is simply a marble pillar taken from some older building, and apparently matches those remaining of the Temple of Saturn. The base is very rudely constructed of heterogeneous fragments, and shews the decadence of art in the seventh century.

The space in the Forum devoted to the assemblies of the citizens in their Comitia Curiata was itself called Comitium. Just beyond the monument of Phocas are remains of two marble partition-walls in the Comitium, covered with fine sculpture on both sides; they are replaced upon the old stone bases of the time of the Republic, and stand ten feet apart. The purpose of these walls originally was to keep

off the pressure of the crowd in going up to vote by their
Curiæ. They were at first of wood, but when rebuilt in
the time of the Empire, were of marble highly ornamented.
On the inner side of each screen are figures of the three
animals prepared for sacrifice, the boar, ram and bull, hung
with garlands, composing the offering called Suovetaurilia,
which was a special feature of the ceremonies observed in
taking the census at the end of every Lustrum, or period of
five years. One of the outer sides represents a procession
of persons carrying tablets, and throwing them into a heap
to be burnt: this is to commemorate an act of the Emperor
Marcus Aurelius in remitting taxes due from the people,
and burning the records of the debt, in imitation of a similar act of Hadrian. The remaining side shews two subjects, one, on the left, of an Emperor addressing the people
from a raised platform, with coins dropping from his hand
into that of one of the foremost of the populace, who holds
out five fingers, while the next figure holds out three, to
make the number of eight gold pieces, which they demanded
and obtained, as is recorded by Dion Cassius; the other,
on the right, of the same on his throne of state, with attendant officers.

Farther to the south, on the same or eastern side of the
Forum, is the basement of a gigantic equestrian statue,
commonly said to be of Domitian; but it may have been
afterwards that of the horse of Constantine, which is mentioned in the Catalogue of the Regiones as existing in
Regio VIII., while it omits any monument to Domitian.
The brickwork forming its base indicates a rather late
period of the Empire; it seems from remains close to it
to have been cased with a variety of yellow marble, which
was highly esteemed.

Along the western side of this division of the Forum
stands a row of square chambers in brickwork, which were

considered to be the bases of enormous columns crowned with images, such as are represented in a sculptured panel on the Arch of Constantine, with the screens of the Comitia and part of the Forum in the background. But further observation has shewn that this is a mistake, they are wine-shops, and there is a doorway in each. To the south, again, are fragments of the second Rostra, called **Nova**, assigned to Julius Cæsar, and behind it again are the foundations of the Temple of Julius Cæsar.

An ancient paved roadway runs through the middle of the Forum, dividing it into an eastern and a western section. Crossing from the eastern, which we have been describing, over this roadway, we come to the great structure called Basilica Julia, the hall originally constructed by Julius Cæsar, but damaged by fire before it was completed, and subsequently added to and finished by Augustus. The remains of the older building occupy only the north-western end of the area; the walls belonging to it are of travertine stone, and would, if continued, cross the north end from west to east. It was so much enlarged by Augustus that what had been the length became the breadth, and it occupies a very large portion of the western side of the Forum. The raised platform of the centre, as rebuilt, is all laid open, and of this there were three divisions; the sides were of arched work, and a portion of this exists at the north end, but contains much brickwork of an inferior character, having been rebuilt under Diocletian. Under the south end of this Basilica passes the Cloaca Maxima, and hereabouts must have been the site of the **Curtian lake**. The entrance to it is kept open for inspection; there are two arches visible over the channel; that in the foreground, in brick, is of the time of the Empire, and the one behind is part of the original vaulting, built of large blocks of tufa of the time of the Kings. The latter agrees in construction with the subterranean passage connected with the Mamertine Prison, which is also attributed by the legend to the kingly period. Past the Basilica the great drain ran very near the north-west angle of the Palatine, and so through the Forum Boarium towards the Tiber. The Basilica of Julius Cæsar extended the whole way to the Temple of Castor and Pollux, represented by the three celebrated columns still standing; the Monumentum Ancyranum mentions these two buildings as contiguous.

This temple to the Dioscuri was of early date; the first notice we have of it being A.U.C. 256. It was rebuilt by Augustus, and dedicated by Tiberius, and to this period the columns belong; but the original foundations still exist and are visible, of large tufa blocks. A little to the south of the temple are the outlines of a small oval basin, the Lacus Juturnæ, which is frequently mentioned as near to it: it was in the spring supplying this basin that the twin deities, according to the tradition, washed themselves after taking part with the Roman army against the Latins.

Farther to the south again, and just beyond this basin stood the Temple of Vesta, the circular basement of which is laid bare, shewing by its rude construction that it belongs to the time of the kings. Dionysius says that Numa erected a temple common to all the citizens of the State considered as a family, between the Capitoline and Palatine Hills, the Forum in which the temple was built lying between them; and ordained that the keeping of the holy things should be committed to Virgins. Horace speaks of the great flood of the Tiber in his time extending to the monument of the kings (the Regia) and the shrine of Vesta. It is possible that this very temple was intended, for in a great inundation in 1870 the waters from the river backed up over the low ground of the Forum as far as this structure. Coins represent a temple of this goddess as a

K

very small circular building, which would exactly suit the remains as they are on this spot.

With respect to the site of the Regia greater uncertainty exists, but it undoubtedly stood close to Vesta. This important historical building owed its name to its having been the residence of king Numa Pompilius, who first lived on the Quirinal, and afterwards in the palace at the foot of the Palatine. In the time of the Republic it became the house assigned to the Pontifex Maximus, which usage lasted till the death of Julius Cæsar. But Augustus on assuming that dignity, as all subsequent emperors did, being unwilling to abandon his own residence on the Palatine (the House of Hortensius), gave up the Regia to the Vestal Virgins, because it adjoined their temple. There is strong evidence to shew that the site of the Regia corresponds with the church of S. Maria Liberatrice, which stands just under the north-west corner of the Palatine, westward from the circular temple, because, when that church was built, inscriptions were found with the names of Vestal Virgins on what had evidently been the bases of statues.

A line drawn from the temple of Antoninus and Faustina in a westerly direction, so as to include that of Vesta, defines the southern limit of the Forum Romanum: within that line, and as far as the base of the buildings which are erected against the Capitoline, the whole area has been excavated, except where a modern road runs, necessary for keeping up the communications. Thus the Forum has been traced out in its greatest length from north to south, and all the buildings within the limits of the excavations have been here mentioned: the eastern side is still buried under the modern road and the buildings lining it, which includes two churches of mediæval date, S. Maria or S. Martina, and S. Hadrian. In old writers both these are described as being *in tribus Foris*, from their vicinity to the three

Fora, Romanum, of Julius Cæsar, and that of Augustus. It will be convenient to add in this place what is known of these and of the others, all added by later emperors.

Regio VIII. was called Forum Romanum Magnum, that is, the district which contained these various places of business; it extended to the Tiber, and included the Forum Boarium, the others lying on its eastern side. The Forum of Julius Cæsar was the one next adjoining the Forum Romanum, and stood north-east of it. It is mentioned that Cæsar consecrated his Forum and the Temple of Venus Genitrix in it, B.C. 45: the ground in this part of Rome was so valuable, that the site cost him eight hundred thousand pounds sterling. It must have commenced on the eastern side of the Mamertine Prison, where there are remains of an arcade or porticus, the arches of which are of tufa resting upon blocks of travertine stone. This seems to have formed the western side of the Forum, and is the only vestige of it remaining. Not far from this spot, which is a little courtyard in a thickly-populated district, was found the statue of Julius Cæsar, now in the Capitoline Museum.

The Forum of Augustus stood again to the eastward of the last, and joined on to it. Of it the eastern wall remains, which is part of the fortifications of the second period, after the two hills had been made into one city, but it has been partly rebuilt of the old materials. On the inner side of the wall, where rebuilt, are niches for statues of illustrious men, with records of their deeds: and there was also in this Forum a monumental chariot with four horses, an offering from the Senate in honour of Augustus, under which was inscribed the title Pater Patriæ, as we learn from himself in the Ancyran Marbles. The great ornament of it was the Temple of Mars Ultor, which occupied the middle space on the east side; this, and the Forum itself, Augustus tells us, was reared from spoils taken in war, the ground being his private property, that is to say, probably purchased by him from the same resources. The portico of Mars had eight columns, of which four are visible, the substructures and bases of the rest being concealed in the cellars of a nunnery. Its cornice rests upon the old wall at the back, shewing that the wall was standing there when the temple was built. In this Forum also stood the triumphal arches decreed by the Senate in honour of Germanicus and Drusus, alongside of the Temple of Mars, together with the effigies of those princes. The temple itself is stated by Suetonius to have been vowed by Augustus to Mars Ultor, in acknowledgment of his victory at Philippi over the authors of Julius Cæsar's death.

The Forum of Nerva joined on to that of Augustus on its south side, and is separated from it by a wall of travertine stone, built into the ancient tufa wall, but much lower than it. Properly speaking, it was begun by Domitian and completed by Nerva. It went also by the names Forum Transitorium and Forum Palladium, the latter from the figure of Pallas still existing over the site of an altar dedicated to her. This stood at the entrance into the Forum from an open area called *Atrium Minervæ*, lying between it and the Forum Romanum. The old tufa wall bounding the Forum of Nerva was cased with marble, and had marble columns in front of it, three of which remain with the fine cornice and the effigy of Pallas, or Minerva, being at one side of the *Atrium Minervæ*. Under this figure was an inscription carved in marble, with the name of the Emperor Nerva, removed in the seventeenth century, together with a large quantity of marble casing, which was employed in the adornment of the great fountain on the Janiculan, bearing the name of Pope Paul V.

The Forum Boarium, or cattle-market, was space lying nearly due west of the Palatine, ing to the Tiber, approached from the side Romanum through the Arch of Janus Quadrifrons, and that of the Argentarii behind it. The latter was erected in honour of Septimius Severus and his sons, in this part of Rome called the Velabrum, as the inscription upon it states, by the Argentarii or guild of silversmiths, and the merchants residing in the Boarium beyond it. As on the Arch of Severus before mentioned, the name of Geta has been erased here also. It is in this Forum that the circular temple stands, close to the Tiber, usually attributed to Vesta, but more properly to Hercules. Livy mentions the "Chapel of Patrician Chastity, which stands in the cattle-market, near the round temple of Hercules." On the south-eastern side of the open area, and opposite that building, is an interesting example of the conversion of two temples into a Christian church, S. Maria in Cosmedin.

The Forum of Trajan was built on the north-eastern side of the Capitoline, with the Forum of Augustus abutting on it to the south-east, and that of Julius Cæsar to the south-west. The level space naturally extending to the foot of the Quirinal not being sufficient to admit all the structures which composed the Emperor's magnificent design, it was enlarged on the eastern side by cutting away as much as was necessary of the rock from the face of the Quirinal Hill. It is recorded in the inscription on the base of Trajan's column that the rock was cut away to a depth equal to the height of the column, and we see the medieval round tower, the Tor delle Milizie, standing now on the natural level of the mount above. At that, the eastern end of the Forum is an apse or semicircular termination, with a triple row of shops rising in stages one above the other behind it; one of these being on the level of the Forum, the old pavement of which remains in front of them; the next on a ledge of the rock behind and above them, and the third row on the top of the cliff. The buildings belonging to this Forum were the temple, basilica, column, and arches. The Temple of Trajan stood farthest to the north of this group: it is shewn on a medal of Hadrian, in whose reign it was finished, as a portico with eight Corinthian pillars, and flanked on each side with a colonnade lower in height: there are three steps up to it from the level area, and in front of the portico is the altar. Attached to the temple was a library in two divisions, of Greek and Latin authors respectively; it is mentioned by the name Bibliotheca Ulpia, Trajan's name having been Marcus Ulpius. To the south of the temple stood the great Basilica Ulpia, the remains of which are visible in the form of a large number of broken shafts, replaced on their bases. Among the fragments are prostrate columns of the largest diameter to be found in Rome, fully six feet. The whole scene conveys an impression of the greatest magnificence, and this is fully borne out by the representations of some of the chief structures on coins. One of these is of the basilica, shewing its façade as solid, with a row of columns supporting a massive entablature covered with sculptures of figures on foot and horseback. Between the temple and this great hall came the celebrated column of Trajan, still standing and perfect, the only change being in the replacement of the Emperor's statue by that of an apostle, and the loss of the two gigantic eagles on either side of the pedestal. It is entirely of white marble, in enormous blocks, and measures $127\frac{1}{2}$ feet in height. The interior is occupied with a winding staircase of 185 steps, and lighted by 45 loop-holes. Both the base and the shaft are covered completely with sculptures, those on the column winding upwards in a spiral curve, and representing scenes in the campaigns of the Emperor in the Dacian war.

The arch connecting this Forum with that of Augustus is, as represented on the coins, a large triumphal archway, with a flat top and solid sides, and three columns on either side of it with niches containing figures between, the whole surmounted by a figure of the **Emperor drawn by** six horses abreast, with attendants and **trophies.** Another coin shews a second arch of a similar character, with a raised centre, on which is the triumphal chariot. This is said to have stood between the column and the basilica. **On the** Arch of Constantine, between the Palatine and Cœlian, are four panels of oval form, which were taken from one of these arches of Trajan when destroyed **in the fourth** century; they are of the same high **character of art as the** sculptures on the column. Roman **architecture reached its** highest perfection under this Emperor. On the western side of the Forum was a second apse, corresponding to that under the **Quirinal** cliff, the foundations of which are slightly traceable in the substructions of the houses built on the curve. **The architect** of these great buildings **was Apollodorus of Damascus.** Besides the cluster of Fora in Regio VIII. connected with each other, and close to the Forum Romanum, there was a fifth, of Vespasian, which, though not properly within that Regio, was practically joined on to the rest. It is called also Forum Pacis, because, as Procopius states, the Templum Pacis was in it. **Regio IV. was** named after that temple. There **are no** remains of this Forum aboveground, but its direction has been in part traced, **and it** seems to have **stood** against the Forum of Nerva, in that part where the image of Pallas is preserved, the wall which **supports the** image being the boundary between the two. Extending southward from thence, it went to the cliff of the Velia, detached by the great foss from the Esquiline, and westward in the direction of the Forum Romanum up to the back of the Temple of Antoninus and Faustina, and the great Temple of Rome, the same which had the Marble Plan of the city attached to its wall. Thus it is seen that all these different Fora of the Emperors were congregated together in the same district of the city, lying near to the Forum Romanum, forming a continuous line of open spaces magnificently adorned, and opening successively into each other.

The Forum Pacis was the largest market-place in Rome, and the Temple of Roma stood at the south-west corner of it; under the lofty porch of this temple plans of the principal buildings in Rome, engraved on marble slabs, were placed against a brick wall of the third century. This wall is still standing, and has at regular intervals the remains of the metal hooks by which those slabs were attached to the wall. It was at the foot of this wall that all the fragments of the Marble Plan that have been found were brought to light at a considerable depth, by excavations made in the seventeenth century, as recorded by eye-witnesses; and again in the nineteenth. All these fragments that have been preserved are now fixed against the wall of the staircase of the Capitoline Museum, and the passage at the foot of it. These plans are on three different scales, to allow for the distance at which they are placed from the eye of the spectator. They never could have formed a complete plan of the city of Rome; the wall on which they were fixed is not a tenth part large enough for that purpose; the object evidently was, to display the magnificence of Rome to strangers, not to serve as a plan of the city.

CHAPTER XII.

The Mamertine Prison.

THE Prison of the Kings, commonly called the Mamertine Prison, placed, as Livy describes it, in the middle of the city of the early Kings, and close to the Forum, can to a certain extent be traced by its remains. The name is connected with Mamers, or Mamertus, the Oscan form of Mars, and there was a statue of that god placed opposite the entrance to the building, on the side of the Forum; but it is usually derived from Ancus Martius, the first founder of the prison. The existing portion nearest the Forum stands not far from the Arch of Septimius Severus, to the right-hand, and beyond it to one looking towards the Capitol, or northward from the arch: there is a second portion detached farther to the north-east. Of these the first is under a modern church, which is separated from the Temple of Concord, abutting against the Tabularium, by the flight of steps leading up the ascent to the Capitol from the Forum. There are two chambers, usually called the Prison of S. Peter, from the legend that the Apostles Peter and Paul were confined here; they are not on the same level, but one stands over the other, with a vault between. The lowest of them is circular, and is partly cut out of the tufa rock, and lined on one side with slabs of travertine; another side is built of the large blocks of tufa used in the kingly times, and the roof, or vault between the two chambers, which is flat, is also of travertine. In the centre of this vault is an opening from the upper chamber, to give air to the lower chamber. On the cornice in front of this chamber is an inscription, which fixes the date of rebuilding by the names of the Consuls under Tiberius, A.D. 22.

These two small compartments cannot possibly have constituted the whole chief public prison of Rome, and researches made further to the north-east of the " Prison of S. Peter," shew a series of much larger chambers, which evidently formed part of the great Mamertine dungeons. These are situated westward of the wall which is taken to be the western limit of the Forum of Julius Cæsar, as mentioned in the notice of that Forum, and begin at the distance of about a hundred-and-twenty feet from the small prison just described. There are six chambers, now cellars under the houses, those of them that remain perfect being forty feet long by fourteen in width, and twenty in height, and though much divided and mixed up with later additions, the large blocks of tufa clearly distinguish the original walls. They are vaulted with brickwork of the time of the Empire, and, as in the vestibule, there is an opening in the centre for letting down the prisoners. It is evident that the floor has been raised since the original construction about six feet, as shewn by the bed of plaster now covering it; and this was done probably when the prison was partly rebuilt under Tiberius, in order to raise it above the reach of ordinary floods in the Tiber: a very high flood brings the water into these dungeons still. As it seems extremely improbable that there should have been two distinct prisons so near each other, the solution is that the smaller of them was a vestibule and guard-room to the rest on the western side of the quadrangle formed by the whole block of buildings, the southern side being open to the Forum, the main body of the prison occupying the north side, and another wing the east, of which last the six chambers are a portion.

Between the two divisions of the prison a communication exists in a subterranean passage, which has underneath it a drain. Out of this long sub-way a short branch turns at right angles up to the lower chamber in "S. Peter's Prison," and there are other cross-ways from it, evidently communicating with the different substructures of the buildings. The main passage has been followed downwards along the whole front of the Tabularium and beneath the Forum, and is found to terminate in a branch of the Cloaca Maxima. It is of exceedingly early construction, being quite Etruscan in character, of massive squared stones, and identical in style and form with the original parts of the great Cloaca of the Kings. One object of this passage was to enable the Aquarii to gain access to the drain beneath, for the purpose of removing obstructions; and another use of it probably was to carry along it the bodies of strangled prisoners, and throw them into the Cloaca, the copious stream of water which runs through this would carry them into the Tiber through its mouth in the Forum Boarium. The most northern of these cells has one wall of the time of Servius Tullius, and was part of the *Robur Tullianum;* the rest of that appears to have been destroyed. The walls of that king are known to have been built of the usual large blocks of tufa, connected by iron clamps, the holes for which remain at the edges of each stone.

CHAPTER XIII.

THE MAUSOLEA AND TOMBS OF ROME.

THE magnificence displayed in the public buildings of the Romans, was extended in full measure to their sepulchral monuments; in grandeur of dimensions, excellence of materials, and beauty of ornamentation, such structures equalled the other architectural works of that people. This chapter aims at giving a notice of the more remarkable among the remains of Roman tombs within and without the present walls.

It will be remembered that the ancient law of the Republic, contained in the XII. Tables, forbade interment within the city; and this regulation was closely observed. But it must be understood that the term City is to be taken very strictly as signifying the area of the Seven Hills enclosed by the third Wall of the Kings, that of Servius Tullius. It is important to observe this, which enables us to understand how the Esquiliæ was for centuries a great burying-place for the people, outside the limits of the city proper, but within the external line of fortification. In like manner, the Campus Martius, being without the inner wall, was used for the interment of the higher classes, and was studded with their tombs. The position of a tomb enables us in certain instances to determine the limits of the city; as, for instance, in the case of the Lateran fortress, the existence of a monument between it and the Cœlian Hill, shews that it was an outwork, not included in inner Rome; and that this distinction was maintained in early Imperial times, and in fact till the reign of Aurelian.

MAUSOLEUM OF AUGUSTUS.—The site of the remains of

this great structure answers to the position assigned to it by Suetonius, as lying between the Via Flaminia and the Tiber. That road, corresponding to the modern street, the Corso, ran nearly due north through the Campus Martius, which is bounded by the Tiber on the west. Strabo's account of this great burial-place, reared by Augustus for himself and others of the family of the Cæsars, is as follows:—" The most remarkable of all the tombs in the Campus is that called the Mausoleum, which consists of a huge mound of earth, raised upon a lofty base of white marble, near the river-bank, and planted to the summit with evergreen trees. Upon the top is a bronze statue of Cæsar Augustus; and under the mound are the burial-places of Augustus, his family, and friends; while behind it is a spacious wood containing admirably-designed walks. In the middle of the Campus is the enclosure made by Augustus for burning the corpses, also of white marble, surrounded by an iron railing, and planted with poplar-trees." The mound had become a vineyard in the fifteenth century, and still went by the name of Augusta; but in the next century had disappeared.

The gardens behind stood northward from the Mausoleum, the principal entrance to which from the side of the city faced the south: here there was a vestibule flanked by two obelisks, one of which stands before the Quirinal Palace, and the other in the square of S. Maria Maggiore. In the vestibule were fastened the bronze plates engraved with the Gesta Augusti, of which the Monumentum Ancyranum is a copy in marble. The main body of the building was circular, about 220 feet in external diameter: the interior consists of a great central vault, 130 feet in diameter, for Augustus himself; and thirteen smaller cells arranged round it for the members of the family; each of these cells measures 35 feet by 20.

The material used is concrete, faced with reticulated-work; and the walls are of immense thickness. The first person buried in the Mausoleum was M. Claudius Marcellus, the favourite nephew of Augustus, and intended for his successor, who died B.C. 23, at the age of 20; and the last was Nerva, A.D. 98. Cippi of other Cæsars interred here, with inscriptions, have been found; amongst them of Agrippina, wife of Germanicus, of three of their sons, and one daughter; and of a son of Drusus. The inscription to the Emperor Nerva was thus briefly expressed: HÆC . SUNT . OSSA . ET . CINIS . NERVÆ . IMPERATORIS: with his burial the Mausoleum was full. Trajan, his successor, was buried beneath the triumphal column in his Forum; and the next Emperor, Hadrian, reared the second great Mausoleum, bearing his name.

THE HADRIANUM, OR MOLES HADRIANI.—This vast structure stands in the Transtiberine region, near the river, in a position corresponding to that of the work of Augustus on the opposite bank. It is a circular building, nearly 1000 feet in circumference, and standing on a square basement. Begun by Hadrian about A.D. 130, at the same time as the new bridge bearing the name Pons Ælius, after that of the family of the Emperor, it was carried on and finished by one of the Antonines, probably Commodus, to whom an inscription was placed upon the wall of the Mausoleum. As usual, the main core of the building is of concrete, faced with large blocks of peperino stone; but originally it was cased with Parian marble, and crowned at the top with statues in the same material, of men and horses; such is the account of Procopius, who saw it before it was despoiled. In the centre of the interior is the sepulchral chamber in the form of a Greek cross; and here the remains of the Emperors, from Hadrian to Septimius Severus, were interred. In later times, when Rome

itself became the object of attack, the great strength and
height of the building naturally caused it to be occupied
as a fortified castle; and it has ever-since remained the
fortress of the Popes. There is an easy road for animals
made in the wall, winding round up to the top, and this
seems to indicate that it was intended to be used as a fortress in case of need. A covered-way connected it with
the Vatican, so that it became their place of refuge when
the pontifical residence was threatened. This was made
on the top of the wall of the Leonine city, but not until
the fifteenth century; the passage remained open until the
time of Pius IX., when the end joining the Vatican was
closed.

THE MAUSOLEUM OF THE EMPEROR ALEXANDER SEVERUS
was wholly outside the walls, nearly on the line of the
Via Latina, and about two miles from Rome. This was
another example of a circular structure of masonry, vaulted
over, and covered with a tumulus of earth. The mound
covering it is visible, and has trees on it, like the Mausoleum of Augustus. In the interior is a large chamber
which contained the sarcophagus of the Emperor, and in
this case the material of construction is brick; once this
was overlaid with a costly facing, and richly decorated.

Just within the Porta Appia, or Porta S. Sebastiano, are
three tombs of the first century, shewing how provision was
made in the time of the Early Empire for economising
space in burial-places, in contrast to those great structures
which were intended to receive but a few persons of the
highest rank. Such resting-places were called Columbaria,
from the resemblance to the arrangement of pigeon-holes
in dove-cotes, the walls within the vaulted chamber below
the ground being pierced all round with niches, usually of
semicircular shape. In these niches the *ollæ* were placed,
jars or urns of earthenware covered with a lid, which con-

tained the ashes of the deceased; some of them also had
busts. Inscriptions are added sometimes on the urn itself,
other times on the flat stone below the opening, and also
below the busts. In one Columbarium there are nine tiers
of niches in parallel lines on the principal wall, and each
niche was intended to receive two cinerary urns. By such
close arrangement, a chamber 25 feet long, 18 wide, and
20 high, contained not far below one thousand ollæ. This
particular Columbarium is shewn, by the inscriptions still
remaining, to have been assigned to freedmen and slaves
of the Imperial household; many of them have the title or
office of domestic service held by the deceased added to
his name. As freedmen assumed the name of their masters
in addition to their servile name, we find a record in this
place of such attendants upon the Court, from the time of
Augustus to Hadrian. And as, besides this sepulchre, two
or three others of similar character in or near Rome have
been examined, which were chiefly devoted to interments
from the Palace, we have in this way a mass of evidence
to shew how very numerous the various offices were in
"Cæsar's household." Another interesting fact is, that several of the names engraved on the stones in these Columbaria coincide with those mentioned by S. Paul in the last
chapter of his Epistle to the Romans, such as Amplias,
Urbanus, Stachys, Apelles, Tryphæna, Tryphusa, Rufus,
Hermes, Hermas, Patrugas, Philologus, Julia, Nereus; Pudens also occurs, and Claudia.

The plan of such sepulchres is not confined to the
chamber-form; there is on the Via Labicana a spot called
Cento Celle, from the great number of cells excavated
around it. Here occurs an example of a cruciform tomb,
with the entrance at the end of the longer limb of the cross.
On each side of this passage the walls are pierced with
niches, as usual, in rows for the cinerary urns; but the

three other limbs terminate in an apse to each, in which there is a recess in the wall, with an arched opening over it. This arrangement was called an Arcosolium, and was adopted when the body was laid in a sarcophagus underneath the arch, instead of being reduced to ashes. It is common in the Christian Catacombs, and is sometimes taken to signify the presence of the remains of a **martyr**; the flat stone covering **the sarcophagus was in** that case used as an altar.

The tombs of wealthy Roman families were often highly decorated, and there are good examples of such still retaining their ornamentation in colours both within and without Rome. In the Esquiliæ, near the Porta Prænestina, is the tomb of T. Statilius Taurus, who is known as the constructor of the first stone amphitheatre, dated B.C. 28, and who was contemporary with Sylla, Julius Cæsar, and Augustus. We may therefore from this specimen **collect** evidence as to the state of the art of painting in the latter half of the last century before the Christian era. **The** building is arranged after the usual plan of other columbaria, but in addition to the niches for urns, it presents the earliest instance known of the use of the *loculus*, or place for a body, not cut in the rock, but built in the wall, so as just to contain the corpse wrapped round, without coffin of **any kind,** and sealed-up in front with a slab and cement. But these loculi occur only in the upper part of the building, which itself belongs to the time of the second century, and the use of them indicates that the custom of reducing the dead to ashes was going out of fashion about that time. This arrangement serves therefore **as a** kind of link between the usages of the Pagan tombs and the catacombs, the latter presenting the Christian practice of burying the body entire.

The chief interest of this tomb is in the decorative paintings of the wall, upon the spaces between the tiers of niches. They are executed in fresco, and represent various subjects in the legendary history of Rome, and more especially in the Æneid of Virgil, relating to the foundation of the first colony from Troy. As Statilius Taurus was contemporary with Virgil, and the tomb was prepared for him during his lifetime, and painted under his directions, there is no reason to doubt that these paintings were intended to illustrate the great national epic poem, then freshly published. They are considered to possess great merit, both as regards spirited conception and correctness of drawing. The tomb also exemplifies the usage of wealthy Romans in making a common place of sepulture for all members of the household; numerous inscriptions found in it shew the domestic employments of attendants on a great family, such as the Sarcinatrix, the sempstress; Lector, the reader; and there is one of the freedman who acted as door-keeper of the amphitheatre of Statilius Taurus in the Campus Martius.

The tomb of the Scipios is also within the walls of Aurelian, but both Livy and Cicero mention it as outside the Porta Capena, being situated near the point where the Via Latina and Via Appia diverge, and one of a great number of tombs in that quarter, which has hence obtained the name of the Necropolis of Rome. This is considered the earliest example known of a Roman place of burial, and is equally important as belonging to a family of the highest nobility and distinction. It seems to have consisted originally of two storeys, as was frequently the case, the upper chamber having been used for a family place of meeting upon solemn anniversaries. The remaining vault is entered by an arch of massive peperino stones, supported by columns half engaged, and there is a moulded cornice above, running along the face of the wall. It was upon this front that the three statues mentioned by Livy stood, which were believed to be those of Publius, and Lucius Scipio, and of the poet Ennius, who was the friend of Scipio Africanus, and was buried in the vault of this family. The interior contained recesses for bodies in coffins, and in one of them was found the celebrated sarcophagus, still preserved in the Vatican, of Publius Cornelius Scipio Barbatus. This is also of peperino, and though simple in design, shews genuine taste and grace in ornamentation. The date assigned to it is B.C. 303. The inscription upon it, together with that from the monument of Lucius Scipio, son of Barbatus, makes the earliest example of the Latin language preserved to us.

The tomb of Eurysaces the baker represents the type of monument belonging to one of the class of wealthy tradesmen. This very curious structure, standing just outside the Porta Prænestina, was found built-up in one of the round gateway-towers of Honorius, added by him to strengthen the wall of Aurelian. When the towers were removed in the present century, and the gate of Claudius became visible, this tomb was found in tolerable preservation. The inscription, which was repeated on all four sides, states it to be the monument of Marcus Vergilius Eurysaces, who was a contractor for the supply of bread to public offices of the State; a second inscription records the name of his wife, Atistia, and the deposition of her remains in a *panarium*, or bread-basket. The main structure of the building throws light on this expression, being composed in its principal storey of three tiers of hollow stone drums, representing kneading-troughs, enclosed by slabs of travertine. And on the frieze, supported at the angles by pilasters, are sculptures descriptive of the various operations of bread-making; so that the whole edifice is intended to be a memorial illustrative of the trade by which the founder gained his wealth. The effigies of the married pair have been placed against the wall by the road-side. It is collected from the style of workmanship and from the spelling of the Latin words, that the tomb belonged to the time of Julius Cæsar, or late Republican date. In any case it must have existed before Claudius reared his grand gateway as a monument of his great achievement in the aqueducts, and yet, though its position in front of one of the piers injured the architectural effect of the façade, it was not interfered with in any way by that Emperor.

Among all the sepulchral monuments on the chief lines of roads outside the city, that of Cæcilia Metella is most conspicuous, from its commanding position and its great proportions. It is situated on the Via Appia, two miles from the gate of that name, rising in a great circular tower constructed in the best style of the Republic. The base forms a square of about 100 feet, and this has been stripped of its casing of travertine, but the main body remains in its original condition. The chief mass is of concrete, and of immense thickness; and in the centre is the chamber for the sarcophagus, lined with brick, and approached by a passage, in which occurs a doorway also of travertine. A frieze of white marble, sculptured with festoons and bulls' heads alternately, runs round the whole, and above this is a simple cornice. The roof no longer exists, but it is proved by the inclination of the walls to have been in the form of a conical cap. From the ground to the cornice is a height of 42 feet, and to the apex of the roof was altogether 60 feet. On a marble tablet facing the Via Appia is the inscription, "Cæciliæ Q. Cretici F. Metellæ Crassi," that is to say, the noble lady interred here was Cæcilia, daughter of Quintus Cæcilius Metellus, whose agnomen was Creticus, from his capture of Crete, B.C. 67, and wife of Marcus Licinius Crassus, the triumvir with Pompey and Julius Cæsar, who was killed in the Parthian war, B.C. 53.

Such a massive structure in a commanding situation was sure to be made a military post in mediæval times, and accordingly it became the tower or citadel to the fortress of a powerful family, the Gaetani, which was extended on both sides of the Appian way, so as completely to control the approach to the city by the great road from the south.

A tomb offering features of unusual interest was discovered enclosed in the Porta Salaria, when the flanking towers added by Honorius to that gateway were pulled down in 1871. Among the monuments imbedded in this tower was one to Quintus Sulpicius Maximus, raised to a considerable height from the ground, so as to have been very conspicuous when first erected. It is in the form of a cippus, containing the effigy of the deceased in a central niche; the figure is draped in the toga, and holds a scroll in the left hand. Below is an inscription in Latin, stating that the monument is reared by the elder Maximus and his wife Licinia Januaria to their son, who died at the age of eleven years, after a successful competition against fifty-two composers in Greek verse, on the occasion of the third public contest of the kind, which had been instituted by Domitian, and was repeated every fourth year at the celebration of the Lustrum. Below the inscription are two epigrams in Greek elegiacs, not without merit, in praise of the youthful poet; and on each side of the figure are engraved the Greek hexameters to which the prize was adjudged. These, the inscription adds, are here recorded, lest the parents' estimate of their child should seem exaggerated. From the title placed at the head, "Καίριον of Sulpicius Maximus," it appears that the contest was for the production of a poem composed extempore upon a given subject, and on this occasion the subject proposed was, "What words would Jupiter use in rebuking Helios for entrusting his chariot to Phaethon?" The engraver, not allowing sufficiently for the length of the verses, was obliged to cram them towards the end into very narrow compass, and the concluding lines are finished upon the scroll held in the hand of the statue.

CHAPTER XIV.

The Colosseum, or Flavian Amphitheatre.

NONE of the great Roman buildings has had more light thrown upon it in recent times than the Colosseum: the whole of it having been thoroughly laid open, we are better able to understand the history and mode of its construction. It is here proposed, not to give a general description of it, because that is sufficiently found in our school-books, but to supply such notices, gathered from the excavations, as may enable us to form a judgment as to its rise and progress, and to clear up difficulties hitherto felt with regard to the substructures and certain of the spectacles exhibited.

The current tradition has been, that this vast edifice was all reared in ten years by the Emperors of the Flavian family; but this is not borne out by the examination of its parts, and especially those parts which hitherto were buried. Suetonius indeed mentions it among the works of Vespasian, but the author of the idea, he says, was Augustus. Julius Cæsar had accustomed the Roman people to spectacles in the Circus Maximus on a large scale, including the hunting of wild beasts and naval fights. For the latter of these exhibitions, Augustus made separate provision by the construction of his naumachia in the Transtiberine region; and he meditated also the building of an amphitheatre in the middle of the city. It was not, however, till the reign of Nero that the combination of athletic exhibitions with sea-fights could be carried out in such a position. The prolongation of the Claudian aqueduct across the Cœlian first furnished the supply of water to the site of the Colosseum, and from his reservoir on that hill the Stagnum

Neronis was filled. We are told that this prince made a gymnasium and naumachia in connection with his Domus Aurea, or great palace. But there is no vestige of such constructions upon any part of the area occupied by these works upon the Esquiline Hill, the whole of which has been thoroughly explored; nor is there any spot suitable for the retention of a considerable body of water except this one, in the depression between the hills.

The complete excavation made down to the pavement of the substructures reveals modes of building in very different styles, and plainly shews that the whole mass cannot be attributed to one date or a few years. It also enables us to understand the nature of the stagna, the relation of the arena to them, and the provisions for introducing and exhibiting wild beasts.

First, then, it is seen, by the removal of earth filling the interior of the Colosseum to the depth of twenty-one feet, that the basement, containing complicated arrangements for the various uses of the theatre, is to a great extent composed of large blocks of tufa, which are evidently not of imperial date. There are plenty of instances of the adaptation of that material for foundations, when old sites were built over again, but not any of an original work reared by an emperor upon a new basement of tufa. The solution of this difficulty is most probably to be found, as has been proposed, in the conclusion that a previous structure of a similar kind existed on this site before the time of Vespasian or even of Nero. Pliny describes the theatre of M. Æmilius Scaurus, the step-son of Sylla, as the greatest work ever made by human hands, capable of containing *eighty thousand* people. The same number is recorded for the Flavian amphitheatre, and this is the only theatre in the world that would hold that number. Scaurus was curule ædile B.C. 58, and during his term of office entertained the citizens on a scale never before known; and Pliny blames him for spending such vast sums on exhibitions of a temporary nature. But a building of dimensions adequate to such a multitude, and three storeys high, as this is stated to have been, must have required a solid base to rest upon, which did not need to be removed, when the superstructure, having served its purpose, was swept away. The large quantity of tufa in the substructures was supplied, probably, from the remains of the wall of the second kingly period, which had once formed the defence of the south end of the Palatine close at hand. A circumstance which connects the site of the Colosseum with the name of Scaurus, is that the slope downwards from the Cœlian to the level on which the amphitheatre stands, was called Clivus Scauri. There is no difficulty in applying the term theatre to the amphitheatre; for, in an an inscription upon one of the marble seats found in the building, the Colosseum is called Theatrum.

The earliest parts of the structure being thus of tufa, the brickwork of Nero succeeded to them when the design of making his naumachia and arena was carried out. Around the central space occupied by them, the first galleries for spectators were commenced; and of that finest kind of brickwork which distinguishes the time of Nero; but the exterior was not finished in any part.

That the stone galleries and corridors were not of the original construction is shewn by there being no bond between them and the older brickwork; there is a straight and wide vertical joint where the two materials come together, which is conclusive as to the outer mass having been subsequently built on to the inner portion. The three styles sufficiently indicate three periods of construction: of tufa, brick, and travertine.

There is plain **proof of** other and later additions to the upper part of the amphitheatre. The highest gallery of all, for the women, was originally of wood; but this having been destroyed by fire caused by lightning in the time of Maximus, it was replaced in stone, and completed in twenty-three years under Gordianus III., A.D. 240.

This upper storey is built in a manner very inferior to the rest, being put together partly of old materials, with **pieces of** cornices, and of columns, or fragments of old **tombs** inserted in patchwork fashion. **And** to support the great additional weight at that enormous height, piers of travertine were introduced at short intervals, as if the architects were afraid to trust the soft tufa to bear so vast **a pressure;** these piers go right through the walls from top to bottom.

The arrangements connected with the naumachia are made intelligible since the clearing out of the area; we see the water-channels, which were filled and emptied at pleasure, and were **also** boarded over at will, so as to convert the whole internal space into an arena, or floor covered with sand, for athletic contests and wild-beast shows. There is a great central passage extending beneath the whole length of the building; and on each side of it are two canals parallel to it, and to each other, with an interval of about six feet between them. They were ten feet deep, **with a** passage ten feet high underneath **them;** so that their **soles did not go down** to the pavement of the **area, but were** reared upon substructures. They are, however, **of** unequal width, the canal nearest the centre being narrower than the other; while the **outer and** larger canal had its inner side **straight, and its outer side** curved, following the oval line **of the** building, so **as** to be widest in the middle, and tapering **off at** both ends. The narrower channel has been supported upon great cross-beams of timber resting upon the massive walls; the places in which these beams were inserted are seen at short intervals in the walls. The larger of the two was supported on brick arches. When the water was let in, it filled the channels; and as it probably overflowed also the space between them, it formed an unbroken liquid surface resembling a *stagnum* or lake, one on each side of the centre, about 300 feet long, by 50 wide in the middle. The vessels moving in parallel lines along the channels, when they came abreast, would be lashed together, and the attempt of one of the crews to board the other's ship constituted the naval fight.

Provision for stowing the moveable boards of the arena, when these water-spectacles were given, is seen in the stone corbels upon the wall in front of the podium, the lowest terrace of the theatre, about six feet below the present surface of the soil. These corbels run all round the building; and in some instances, as at the south end, are inserted into the old tufa wall, which is cut away to receive them.

The great mass of material underneath the corridors is of tufa; and in the interior are two walls of the same stone, in concentric curves, composing the outermost circle of the area. They are of the usual large blocks; but the inner one of the two has been faced with bricks, and it carries on its own inner side the largest of the canals. Between these two walls of tufa were placed the Pegmata—frames of wood, or lifts, on which the wild beasts when put into cages were raised to the level of the arena. In the sides of these walls are seen the grooves cut vertically in the stone for the lifts to work up and down; also deeper grooves about a yard long for the counter-weights, *pondera reducta*. Outside of these walls again, and under the path in front of the podium, are a number of chambers serving as dens for the wild animals; and in front of each is an opening large enough to allow the creatures to pass through into the cages attached to the lifts. But for beasts of the largest size, such as elephants or camelopards, there are four dens of greater dimensions, two on either side of the central passage. In front of the dens is a small channel for water supplied from the aqueducts, out of which the animals drank; and behind each one is a small cell about four feet square, opening from above, but not reaching lower than ten feet from the ground; this allowed a man to go down and feed the beasts in safety. Such attendants were called Catabolici, the den itself being a Catabolum.

In the passage connected with the dens are seen sockets let into the pavement for a pivot to work in; these were for the revolving posts or capstans round which were wound the cords which hoisted the pegmata. These contrivances, as parts of the stage machinery in a theatre, enable us to understand the descriptions given by historians writing in the time of the Empire, of the sudden appearance, simultaneously, on the boarded stage of numbers of wild beasts, which seemed to the spectators to spring out of the ground. Herodian and Ammianus Marcellinus both mention the exhibition of a hundred lions at once in this manner. Besides these provisions round the outer circle, there are lines of small square closets for lifts on both sides of the central passage, through which men and dogs could ascend from below by trap-doors on to the arena.

On the floor of this central passage is a remarkable fragment of an ancient wooden framework remaining, which has the appearance of the lowest portion of a cradle for a vessel to stand on, and also for it to slide on when requiring to be moved. It is laid in two lines with transverse beams; and on each side of the passage is a series of stone slabs which are perforated; these seem to have served for fixing the cradle for the vessels, so that they might stand upright. When the naumachiæ were exhibited there must have been some machinery for lifting up the ships, and placing them on the canals; and they must also have been removed when the water was let off, and the wooden floor replaced for the shows on the arena. Probably they never quitted the building, but were left in the vault as described, and hoisted up when required.

The term Pegma was not confined to the moveable apparatus connected with the wild animals, but was applied to any kind of theatrical contrivance of a shifting character introduced on the stage. Vast temporary structures several storeys high were exhibited, representing towers, and natural objects, hills with wood, and volcanoes. Martial mentions pegmata "rising" from the middle passage of the amphitheatre, and Seneca uses the same term for machines silently and imperceptibly hoisted aloft as amusements for the populace at the shows of his time. There is no doubt that this sort of scenery must have been prepared below in the spacious chambers of the substructure, and was sent up from the central way which divides the area into two halves. The framework laid down on the bottom is as well adapted for the sliding of such ponderous masses, as for the reception and movement of ships.

The waters of the stagna were let off by a great subterranean drain, which is seen issuing from beneath the arena, on the lowest level, at the south-east end of the amphitheatre, and is arched over. There are traces of the sluice-gate by which the water was penned up, and the rate of flow regulated; there are also remains of an ancient iron grating to prevent objects being swept away by the current. The drain, after skirting the foot of the Claudium on the Cœlian, turned sharply round to the west, and ran at a great depth close up to the Arch of Constantine, and then, making a second right-angle, followed the valley between the

Palatine and Cœlian to discharge itself into the Tiber. The new drain follows the same line.

Immediately over the mouth of this drain is another long passage, with a square-headed opening; this was the covered-way, by which the animals brought down in cages from the vivaria were introduced into the building, and they could thence be conveyed either right or left of the entrance, along the base of the outer tufa wall to their dens.

Above the passage again, and clear of the substructure, is an archway, the continuation of which formed one of the chief entrances: it was through this and a similar opening at the opposite end of the arena, facing the Palatine, that the State processions made their entry. The only one of the four great entrances that remains perfect is that on the north side, in the direction of the Esquiline, and it is through this one, as is believed, that the Imperial personages and court passed to their seats on the podium, which was the place of honour for those of highest rank in the State, including the Senators and Vestal Virgins.

To protect spectators sitting on the lowest range next the arena, a strong netting or trellis-work of metal, and gilded, was fixed in a strong frame of wood, surmounted by a revolving bar, which was overlaid with ivory, so that if a hunted beast sprang up from below and tried to cling to it with his claws, he should find no hold, and thus would fall back again on to the arena. This contrivance is represented by a rude delineation on marble, discovered in the excavations of the Colosseum, shewing the screen spoken of resting on the pavement in front of the podium. Below the pavement are seen the tops of a series of arches, with bars across the headings, which are intended for the dens of the wild beasts in the area, and in front of them some sort of performance is going on. Such rough kinds of carving or shallow incisions, called *graffiti*, usually made on the plaster-coating of walls, have frequently occurred in the ruins of Rome, and many of them have been transferred to museums.

The spectators were protected from the heat of the sun by an awning, *Velarium*, which was suspended by cords from the tops of masts. For supporting these masts, exposed to a strain necessarily very great, the contrivances were of an ingenious kind, and are still distinctly visible where the upper storey remains perfect. On the exterior wall, ten feet below the summit, there is a row of corbels projecting for the feet of the masts to rest upon, and holes are left in the cornice above through which the body of the masts passed; and on the inner side of the uppermost wall are other corbels, to which were lashed the stays for keeping them upright. From each mast-head a rope was stretched, sloping down inwards towards the arena, and upon these ropes the sections of the velarium were spread, running upon rings. At the bottom of the galleries next the podium are similar contrivances, evidently for supporting standing poles.

The awning was worked by a staff of seamen, who were detached for this purpose from the fleet stationed off Misenum, in the Bay of Naples, and hence the quarters provided for them within the walls were called *Castra Misenatium*. As this covering, requiring to be furled and unfurled according to the state of the weather and the position of the sun, was of immense weight, several hundreds of men were needed for the duty. The practice of shading theatres had been long before introduced; canvas was the material generally used, but afterwards the surface of the vela was decorated, and Pliny mentions an awning in Nero's time which was painted to resemble the blue sky, and was studded with stars.

The taste for shows similar to those exhibited in Rome

spread largely through the Empire, and buildings on the plan of amphitheatres must have been frequent in the chief cities. But it is probable that many of them continued to be constructed of wood, as had been the case at Rome till the time of Augustus. The structures of a permanent kind erected subsequently, whether in Italy or elsewhere, seem all to have followed the model of the Flavian amphitheatre, so perfect in its plan and all its arrangements. There are amphitheatres at Capua, Puteoli, Pompeii, at Verona, at Nîmes, Arles and Bordeaux, and on the eastern shore of the Adriatic at Pola in Istria. Such of these as have been excavated mostly exhibit the same provisions for the naval fights, with the conduits of aqueducts to supply the canals beneath the arena. At Pompeii, however, there were no aquatic shows, and no substructions under the stage; the dens for the wild beasts are therefore on the same level as the arena, and behind the podium instead of underneath it. The whole arrangements there indicate an early date, probably anterior to that of the Colosseum.

In one feature, however, the Roman amphitheatre differed from all the rest, namely, in having double corridors all round the galleries; the absence of this outer passage made a different adaptation of the stairs to the *vomitoria* necessary between this and the other amphitheatres, where the spectators went out straight through each archway.

The comparative dimensions of the three principal Italian amphitheatres are thus given in Neapolitan feet:—

	Colosseum.	Capua.	Verona.
Length of Exterior	639	645	522
Breadth of Exterior	527	530	417
Length of Interior	298	289	252
Breadth of Interior	186	174	149
Original height	174	169	91
Actual height of ruins	171	75	62
Number of Orders or Storeys	4	4	3
Number of Arches	80	80	72
Width of Arches	15	15	12½

Out of the eighty arches composing the outer circuit of the arcade of the Colosseum, forty-seven have perished. The most perfect portion of the exterior wall is upon the north-eastern side, opposite the Thermæ of Titus, on the Esquiline, where all four stages of the building are seen, representing with their columns the Doric, Ionic, Corinthian, and Tuscan orders of architecture respectively. The ruin was begun by earthquakes, which occurred at least five times between the fifth and eighteenth centuries; and the work of destruction was carried on by the Romans themselves during many centuries, for the sake of the valuable materials. Some of the largest palaces were reared by the Pontifical families out of the magnificent blocks of travertine facing the whole exterior, and the marble casing of the seats was burnt into lime for building purposes. Like other solid structures, it was also occupied during the times of anarchy in the Middle Ages as a military stronghold of different powerful clans; and it was not till 1728 that the misuse and continued spoliation of the amphitheatre was finally put an end to by the consecration of the whole of its remains.

CHAPTER XV.

PALACES OF THE CÆSARS.

DURING the time of the Republic the Pontifex Maximus, as holding the highest dignity in the State, and representing the sacred element of the kingly office, had the Regia assigned him as his residence. That building, under the northern corner of the Palatine, was the palace of the later Kings; it seems to have stood on the edge of the Forum Romanum, at the point of greatest distance from the Capitol. Julius Cæsar himself, as chief pontiff, occupied it till his death; but Lepidus, who succeeded him, resided chiefly in the provinces of which he held the government, and though in disgrace with Augustus and banished from Rome, still retained his office. When he died, B.C. 13, Augustus, as chief of the State, assumed the Pontificate, but declined to leave his own house on the Palatine, which had been the property of Hortensius the orator. Of this Suetonius says, "Octavius lived at first near the Forum Romanum, by the side of the steps of the ring-makers: he afterwards moved to the Palatine Hill, where he resided in a small house belonging to Hortensius, not remarkable either for its size or its ornamentation, the arcades being small, the pillars of peperino, and the rooms without either marble or mosaic pavement; he continued to use the same bed-chamber for both winter and summer during forty years." It was the wish or the policy of Augustus to live as a private citizen, either from real modesty and a love of retirement, or because this only stimulated the citizens to do him more honour, and to insist on providing him with a grand palace suitable to the position of the head of the Roman Empire.

Dion Cassius says, "The people planted laurels before his house on the Palatine, and hung a crown or wreath of oak-branches on the roof of it, as to the perpetual conqueror of the enemies of the State, and servant of the citizens; but they called his house a palace, and decreed that Cæsar should always live on the Palatine. He accepted some splendour, because it was right that the Emperor should inhabit such a house as would deserve the name of a palace."

In the course of excavations carried on over the northwest portion of the Palatine, a house has been discovered which answers very well to the residence of Augustus, as mentioned by these authors. There are two floors; the upper one is composed of a number of small chambers, which are built of concrete, faced with reticulated work, agreeing very well with the time of Hortensius. On the lower level, at the north end, state apartments have been added, and a great deal of ornamentation introduced. In front of the three chambers laid open is an area paved with mosaic-work of fine description, and with remains of an altar. The walls of the rooms are highly decorated with frescoes painted on a finely-prepared surface, representing Greek mythical subjects, domestic scenes, birds, candelabra, columns, flowers and fruits. They are admirably executed, and agree very well with the Augustan age of art: the whole fits in with the history that Augustus accepted some splendour. It seems also clear that his residence was near the spot where the cottage of Romulus had been; for Dion Cassius says that he dwelt in the Prætorium, which he chose out of all the hill, because Romulus lived there. And as the cottage of the founder of Rome is assigned by Varro to the Germalus, and by Dionysius to the corner as you turn from the Palatine Hill to the Circus, we must place the House of Augustus near the western border of the Palatine, certainly to the north west of the great foss which bounded Roma Quadrata on the south-east.

Tiberius had a palace on the Palatine close to that of Augustus, of which there are considerable remains, and in two divisions at different levels. The lower portion of it stands upon the Germalus, or platform, half-way down the hill, against the cliff of the upper part of the hill, on the side over the Circus Maximus. The other portion on the higher level is separated from the House of Augustus by the pavement of a street only; and here there are hypocausts under the floors of two chambers with the hot-air flue from a vaulted chamber below. Of the lower part the outer wall has fallen down, but the partition walls and the back walls against the cliff remain; among these is a fine mosaic pavement..

The construction of this House of Tiberius closely resembles that of the north wall of the Prætorian Camp, as seen from the inside, where there are sleeping-places for the guards built up against the wall: that camp was built by the same emperor. Tiberius added a library to this dwelling, as Augustus had connected one with the temple of Apollo, which was called the Palatine Library.

The next emperor, Caligula, also built on the Palatine, but at the opposite or northern end of the hill, where it touches the Forum. Suetonius says that this emperor used the temple of Castor and Pollux as a vestibule to his palace: part of it, therefore, must have stood on that low level just within the boundary-wall at the foot of the hill. There are considerable remains of his structures, both of the palace, and also of the bridge, which he threw across the valley in order to connect the Palatine and Capitoline Hills at a high level, and all these are of brick. Higher up on the face of the hill is a great mass of buildings, consisting of chambers, with a long and lofty vault, which supports the **pressure of** the earth overhead. It is through these that the Clivus Victoriæ with its pavement of basaltic lava passes, to gain the summit of the hill. High overhead against these chambers is a series of corbels, which carried a balustrade or screen of pierced white marble, a fragment of which, beautifully executed, remains. Whether these structures were **part** of the palace at the **lowest** level, subsequently added, is uncertain. Chambers of the time of Trajan and Hadrian are added on the east side of the *clivus*, or sloping paved road; **but it** seems that the summit of the Palatine was not large enough for the architects of the emperors, **and they** built great offices and guard-chambers against the cliffs all round, to gain space. This perpetual process of enlargement went on for two centuries, and is most conspicuously traceable on the face of the hill which fronts the Circus Maximus, **and on the** side opposite to the Cœlian. After Nero's Domus Aurea, which was converted into uses for the public benefit, there was no state palace built till Domitian's time. Vespasian resided sometimes on the Palatine, more frequently in the House of Sallust, which, with its gardens and stadium, had **become the property of the Crown.**

His son Domitian commenced the series of vast buildings which nearly cover the central portion of the hill in its greatest length from north-east to south-west. The ruins give an impression of the greatest magnificence. The name given to this palace seems to have been Ædes Publicæ, of which Pliny speaks in Trajan's time, and Ædes Imperatorum, as mentioned by Lampridius; **but when the** latter author wrote, **very** large **additions** had been made **to** it, and the whole southern half **of** the area was covered by **them.** The brick-stamps found in the walls of the earlier structures shew that Domitian began the work, and it was probably carried on by succeeding emperors, Nerva having inscribed the name Ædes Publicæ upon it. These buildings were continued by Commodus, of whose palace there are considerable remains, with the *stadium* (?) or *gymnasium* (?) excavated in 1877-80. This is the building which in the Regionary catalogue is called Sedes Imperii Romani in Regio X.[a]

On examining this great palace, it is plain that the architects found the level space on the summit of the Palatine insufficient for the execution of their grand plan. The surface on which they built was intersected by the ancient original foss, which was excavated to the width of a hundred feet, and to the depth of thirty feet, right across the hill, commencing upon the north-east side close to the Arch of Titus, and finishing on the south-west over against the Circus Maximus. This formed the defence of Roma Quadrata on the south side. When the line of buildings came to the dip of the foss, the architects disposed of the difficulty by laying down walls across the hollow, thus raising the surface to one level. The portion of the palace which is over the foss has for its foundations a series of these transverse walls about twenty feet apart, with a vault from one to the other.

Several compartments of this palace remain, by which its vast size and great beauty can be estimated. The two apartments which lie most to the south, or nearest the Circus, have been named the Academia, where recitations of literary

---

[a] Dr. Fabio Gori in his *Archivio*, vol. ii. p. 381, says that this building was the Pentapylon Jovis Arbitratoris of the Regionary Catalogue of Regio X., but this is very doubtful. Until the French nuns can be dismissed, and this part of the Palatine, where such important remains exist under the Villa Mills, is carefully excavated, nothing certain can be known about it.

compositions took place, and the Bibliotheca, which has portions of a low portico in white marble columns with capitals of the finest carving. This is backed by a lofty wall, behind which is the great banqueting-hall, answering to the Triclinium of a private house, and called Jovis Cœnatio. It terminates at the upper or southern end in a tribune or apse, in which there are remains of rich marble lining the walls, and an elaborate mosaic pavement, of which red, green, and yellow, form the staple colours, arranged in patterns. This is an example of the style of ornamented floor called Opus Alexandrinum, named so from Alexander Severus, who is said by Lampridius to have first invented this particular combination of stones, and to have introduced it into the " palace." On the western side of the hall is an oval bath of considerable beauty, with semicircular marble seats in the form of niches all round the basin, which was supplied from a fountain, still standing, like an island, in the centre. Adjoining the banqueting-hall on the north side is the grand court of the palace, the Peristylium, of the kind called Sicilia, a hundred and fifty feet long. It had a double row of marble columns on each side of the central space, forming two porticoes; the rest of the area seems to have been open to the sky, and was planted with shrubs and flowers.

The third great chamber in the series adjoins this court, and, from the analogy of the private Roman house, has been named by Signor Rosa the Tablinum, but is said by Professor Fabio Gori to be the Victoria Germaniana of Domitian. This seems to have served as the throne-room, in which the officers of State and foreign ambassadors were admitted to the imperial presence. On the east of the last-mentioned chamber is a smaller one, which is said to be the Lararium, or chapel of the palace : and on the western side stands the Basilica Jovis, the law-court of the emperors, the tribune of which is rectanglar, and is railed off from the body of the court by the original *cancelli*, or screen of white marble: within this the Cæsar is supposed to have sat and administered justice. A number of small chambers are ranged at the back of these halls, along the western side, probably *cubicula*.

There are subterranean passages leading to this from the palaces near the western face of the hill, so that there was a connection with those of Augustus and Tiberius, and Caligula.

Below ground, about the centre of the hill, and standing in the middle of the foss, are some chambers usually called the baths of Livia, but only on conjecture. The walls, however, answer to the style of the time of Augustus, and in their construction are provisions for heating purposes. They are roofed over at about fifteen feet from the bottom, and on the vault of the principal chamber are fresco paintings of great elegance upon a gilt ground. These consist of small groups of figures engaged in sacrifices, surrounded by deep borders in elaborate patterns: the whole being a good example of an *aureum lacunar*, in the time of Augustus.

In order to carry out the design of filling up the foss by throwing walls across it, and vaulting them over, these chambers have been cut through by the transverse walls of rough concrete, as supports to the great palace of Domitian reared above, which is thus made to stand at the natural level of the hill-top.

The central portion of the Palatine, being conventual property, has not been recently excavated; but to the east and south of the palace of Domitian there lie buried under modern buildings some very considerable remains of vaulted halls in good preservation, the interiors of which present proofs of rich decoration. Two of these chambers are octagonal, with dome-shaped roofs, which admitted light in the centre; their proportions are considered remarkably good. These buildings were excavated by the French about the time that the Villa Mills, now a convent, were built; they have been referred to the age of Augustus, but they seem rather to belong to the next century.

At the extreme southern end of the hill, there is a series of extensive remains belonging to the times of later emperors, which cover the cliffs facing both the Aventine and the Cœlian. On the south-western side, overlooking the Circus in the valley below, is a double balcony or exedra, consisting of two apses, placed back to back; the outer one of which commanded the view of the Circensian shows, and the inner one the private stadium, or *gymnasium*, of the palace. The roofing of this structure is a fine specimen of the style called *testudinaceum*, from the pattern of the medallions inserted in it, which resemble the form of the tortoise's back. The stadium, or gymnasium, answers in shape to others in existence, being semicircular at one end, and rectangular at the other. It is also of the usual length, 606 feet, but very narrow; and it could only have been intended for foot-races, not for chariots, but the passage for the foot-races has not been found. A colonnade of marble bounded it on either side, executed out of the finest materials, and in the purest taste; the north end is finished with pilasters. Midway down the course, on the east side, is another exedra connected with the stadium, or gymnasium, by a separate colonnade; it is of very great height and span, and was occupied by the *ludi-magistri* and the *lanistæ*, who owned and trained the competitors. At its base, on either side, are chambers richly painted in fresco, which were for the use of those engaged in the gymnastic contests. The Emperor Commodus, according to Herodian, built a gymnasium, and it must have been this one on the Palatine.

Adjoining these remains, still farther to the south-east, and occupying all that angle of the hill, is a vast mass of buildings, forming another great palace, which is attributed to the reigns of Commodus and Septimius Severus. This is in a state of greater ruin than the work of Domitian, and it is impossible to trace out its component parts. Nothing is separately distinct beyond some hypocausts and hot-air flues. On the side facing the Cœlian, a terrace or platform of considerable area projects into the valley, reared upon substructures in several storeys. Its construction affords a good example of the manner in which the imperial architects enlarged the surface of the Palatine beyond the natural limits to find room for additions to the palaces. The spot for this particular enlargement seems chosen with great judgment; nothing can exceed the beauty of the situation, which commands the view of the Alban and Sabine Hills, the distant Apennines, and the Campagna with the aqueducts. There was attached to the palace at this corner an out-flanking structure, rising from the level at the foot of the hill to a great height, called the Septizonium. This was the work of Septimius Severus, who seems to have been the last Emperor that built upon the Palatine. As its name denotes, it was reared in seven stages, in as many different styles of architecture, after the pattern of the Colosseum. Probably it served the double purpose of a tomb for the imperial family, and of a gate-house to the palace; and it was placed in this conspicuous position in order to proclaim to the countrymen of Severus, as they entered Rome by the Via Appia, that a citizen from the African province was lord of the Roman world. One of the fragments of the Marble Plan represents the curve of the Circus Maximus at its eastern extremity, with the Septizonium behind it. After serving as a fortress during the Middle Ages, a portion of this monument was still standing in 1575, when it was pulled down to supply materials for additions to the Vatican Church.

On the face of the hill parallel to the Circus are additional remains connected with imperial work. Westward from the double exedra just mentioned is another of large dimensions, but without a roof; and farther on in the same direction, the whole slope of the hill is covered with fragments of buildings of the Ædes Imperatorum. Among these stands a range of columns belonging to a portico of white marble, and of great beauty; and behind it are Excubiæ, or chambers of the soldiers of the imperial guard. The walls of these compartments are coated with the usual fine preparation of powdered marble mixed with sand, on which frescoes were executed; but here **the men have amused** themselves with carving names and jests upon the surface, the names **being chiefly in** Greek letters. Among **these was found a caricature of the** Crucifixion, representing a human figure, with the head of an ass, fastened to a cross, and a man standing by in the act of worship, **with the in**scription in Greek, "Alexamenos adoring God." The portico is attributed to the time of Septimius Severus.

Besides the great ranges of buildings on the Palatine, which were public property, and contained the official residence of the head of the State, there were other houses on a palatial scale, owned in some instances by great families, from branches of which sprang some of the later emperors. There were also near the city imperial villas, or country houses, of great splendour, the remains of which in some cases may be identified.

The House of Mæcenas, with its gardens in the Esquiline quarter, or fifth Regio, was made in the old burial-ground of the common people, the Esquiliæ, which therefore was outside of the city, lying between the agger of Servius and the outer agger, the unfinished rampart of Tarquin II.

This property came to Augustus, and passed on to the other Cæsars in succession. Adjoining it was the House of the Lamiæ, with still larger gardens, which came into the possession of Tiberius, and with those of Mæcenas formed part of the domain of the crown in the time of Caligula. The embassy sent to that emperor by the Jews was received by him here, as is related by Philo, a member of the deputation. He says, "Caligula sent for the keepers of these two villas, which were near the city and each other (whither he had retired three or four days previously), and ordered them to open the doors of the several apartments in the pleasure-houses, as he intended to stroll through the whole of them, and then bade us come to him." This part of the Esquiline Hill has yielded more specimens of valuable objects of art than any other district of Rome, and in laying down the deep drains for the new quarter of the town springing up here, seven fine statues were brought to light, with a rich pavement of marble and alabaster, forming the floor of the chamber in which they were found in the house of the Lamiæ. The bases of a colonnade or portico remained on this pavement, probably one side of an atrium.

In the course of excavations for the new city the site of the House of Mæcenas has been discovered, which was hitherto considered doubtful. Its remains are found a little to the south of S. Maria Maggiore, at the southern end of the agger of Servius Tullius, where it joins the cliff of the Esquiline. The house stood upon the sloping banks of the agger cut away to receive it, part of it being within and part without the ancient municipal boundary, so that one face of it touched the street-way laid down in the inner foss, and the other face the street in the outer foss. The only part at all perfect that has been found is a room with an apse at one end, resembling a small theatre, which seems to have been lighted from above. It has sham windows in the walls of the apse, which are beautifully painted on the plaster with views of a garden, as if seen through them, probably representing the garden of Mæcenas outside.

There are paintings of the same character at the paternal mansion or villa of the Empress Livia, situated at Prima Porta, near Rome. Round the apse are ranged steps, but they are not calculated for sitters, being too narrow, and not all of the same height. It has therefore been concluded that this building was a kind of green-house for special plants grown in terra-cotta vases or wooden boxes—a practice which is known to have existed among the Romans. Nero had connected these gardens with his Golden House, and from the tower of Mæcenas witnessed the great fire which swept away the structures he had reared between the Palatine and the far-side of the Esquiline.

The Gordiani had a splendid villa on the Via Prænestina, about three miles from Rome, which is marked by the mediæval tower called Tor dei Schiavi, or Tower of the Slaves. Annexed to it was a mausoleum for the family burial-place, which was never used, all the princes of that name having died at a distance from Rome. Their biographer describes this villa as very magnificent, which is borne out by the remains, and by the accounts of the rich marbles found there when the excavations were made. There was a portico supported by two hundred columns of the four most curious and costly varieties of marble; three of the chambers were an hundred feet long, and there were baths of great beauty and extent. The ruins present a round temple with a domed roof, a circular chamber, or Laconicum, belonging to the Thermæ, and a reservoir of considerable size. The site of the villa seems to have been chosen on account of the nearness of the abundant reservoirs supplied by the great Claudian aqueduct.

The Sessorium, originally a detached fortress at the extreme south-eastern angle of the fortification of Tarquinius Superbus, with its own foss on the side towards the city, was afterwards a palace and imperial residence. It was some time in the occupation of the family of Verus, or Varius, to whom is referred the construction of the Circus Varianus, just outside the city wall at this spot, and also with probability the Amphitheatrum Castrense, which is half-engaged in the wall of Aurelian. Both of these places were for the amusement of the soldiery. The style of the palace buildings still existing belongs to the second century. In the fourth century it was occupied by Helena, mother of Constantine the Great, who, after making a pilgrimage to Jerusalem, founded the Basilica of the Holy Cross of Jerusalem, using in the process the earth which she had brought from that city for the purpose. This church, still standing, was made out of one of the great halls of the palace, called the Prætorium, a large oblong building of the second century, with side-aisles still traceable; but it occupied only the central portion of the hall, within which narrow aisles were made to carry the roof: it terminates in an apse. There are also standing in the garden the massive walls of another great hall, or Basilica, likewise ending in an apse, which is supported by thick buttresses of the fourth century, added after it had been shaken by an earthquake.

The Lateran Palace was another of the great family houses which came into the possession of the emperors, and like the last-mentioned, standing outside the city, was in early times part of the outer defences. The Laterani were descendants of L. Sextius Sentinus Lateranus, the first Plebeian consul, B.C. 366, and they were still of importance in the time of Nero, against whom Plautius Lateranus, when consul elect, joined in a conspiracy with Piso. In consequence of this rebellion the property owned by the family was confiscated, and their "splendid palace," as Juvenal calls it, passed into the hands of the Emperor. The name occurs again on the list of consuls in the reigns of Antoninus Pius and Septimius Severus; but whether any of these Laterani recovered their forfeited inheritance is uncertain. A writer of the fourth century seems to imply that the Empress Fausta, wife of Constantine, resided in the Lateran while on her visits to the city. But this would signify that the palace was at the Emperor's disposal, and it gives some support to the current tradition that Constantine bestowed the Lateran upon the See of Rome.

A portion of this building that remains in its ruined state is incorporated in the wall of Aurelian, which keeps a straight line westward from the Sessorium to this point, and then suddenly makes a right-angle to the south, in order to include the projecting mass of the palace. At the western end of this projection the line recedes again considerably, and this part of the building is better preserved than the rest, the doors and windows of the first century being distinctly visible, though walled-up. Within this angle are several vaulted chambers, and remains of a building three or four storeys high, of different periods, from the first century to the fourth.

The ruins of a fine hall of the time of Nero remain in the precincts of the monastery, the arches of which are lofty, and peculiar in construction; and again in the garden, between the hall and the southern front of the palace upon the city wall, partition walls have been excavated, shewing that the whole of this considerable space was built over.

The original basilica, or great hall of this palace, was on the northern side, on the site now occupied by the church of S. John Lateran; in the alterations of the church indications of the ancient splendour of the basilica have been brought to light. Under the monastery also, in the fifteenth century, were found the remains of a rich building, consisting of arches, chambers, mosaic pavements, coloured walls, columns, marble panels, and statues.

The Popes lived in the Lateran as their principal residence for a thousand years, but after their return from Avignon, in 1377, they abandoned it for the Vatican. Their palace occupied the ground to the north of the Lateran church, on the side farthest removed from the wall of Aurelian. This building, having been burnt down, was replaced at the end of the sixteenth century by the present structure, now a museum.

ALPHABETICAL INDEX.

ÆRARIUM, Treasury, in basement of Tabularium, of square vaulted chambers, connected with Temple of Saturn, 123; steep steps from, leading to upper storey of Tabularium, 124.

Alba Longa, reputed parent of Roman colony, tradition of, confirmed by similarity and peculiarity of ancient wells, 17.

Alban lake, formerly a crater, 2.

Almo river, in valley between Palatine and Aventine, 29; liable to sudden floods, 33; called also Aqua Crabra, 37.

Amphitheatrum, of Statilius Taurus, the first in stone, 145; amphitheatres common in chief cities of Empire, 160; of Pompeii, had no substructions or naumachia, *ib.*; largest in Italy, compared with Colosseum, *ib.*; Amphitheatrum Castrense, at the Sessorium, half-included in the wall of Aurelian, 174.

Anastasia, S., church of, on western slope of Palatine, over buried tower of Kings, and shops of Circus Maximus, 27.

Anio Vetus, second aqueduct, taken from river Anio above Tivoli, 101; 43 miles long, *ib.*; water of inferior quality, *ib.*; follows Aqua Marcia below Tivoli, *ib.*; enters at Porta Maggiore, 102; one branch along wall of Aurelian to Prætorian Camp, another branch at foot of Nero's arcade, *ib.*

Anio Novus, ninth aqueduct, 62 miles long, liable to impurity, 110; arcade of 109 feet high, *ib.*; three dams in each place forming lochs, built for, in bed of Anio, 111; runs in open cutting on left bank of river, *ib.*; joins Claudian at Ponte Lupo, *ib.*; within city, on Neronian arcade, the two aqueducts in one channel, 112; at castellum over arch of Dolabella, 50 feet high, *ib.*; supplied Claudium and Colosseum and Palatine, *ib.*; carried to Aventine from Cœlian by Trajan, and from Palatine to Capitoline at high level by Caligula, 113; ran into all 14 Regions of city, *ib.*

Apollodorus of Damascus, architect of Trajan's Forum, 135.

Appius Claudius, constructs Via Appia, B.C. 312, 87.

Aqua Appia, oldest aqueduct, 11 miles long, 99; underground except at Porta Capena, *ib.*; seen by Frontinus 50 feet deep, 100; sources in stone-quarries, *ib.*; unfiltered and liable to be choked, *ib.*; supplies Piscina Publica, first public bath, under cliff of Pseudo-Aventine, 114; mouth, in cave under Aventine, 101.

Aqua Marcia, third aqueduct, 61 miles long, source of, below Subiaco, 103; on right bank of Anio to Varia, *ib.*; below Tivoli on high bridges, 104; after Piscinæ on 7 miles of arcade, *ib.*; specus of, one of three visible at Porta Tiburtina, *ib.*; branch of, to Cœlian, ending in reservoir above Porta Capena, *ib.*; excellence of its water, *ib.*; re-introduced by an English company under Pius IX., 1870, to high district of city, 114.

Aqua Tepula, fourth aqueduct, source of, near Via Latina, 105; intercepted by A. Julia, afterwards separated, but carried on same arcade, *ib.*; smallest channel of all, and had no branch, 106.

Aqua Julia, fifth aqueduct, 15 miles long, source of, under Mons Algidus, 106; on same arcade with A. Marcia and Tepula, *ib.*; western branch of, to Cœlian, *ib.*

Aqua Virgo, sixth aqueduct, 14 miles long, supplied Thermæ of Agrippa, 106; source of, in reservoirs near Collatia, 107; course of, traced by respirators, *ib.*; enters Rome under Pincian hill, *ib.*; branch from, in large pipe through Via Condotti to Thermæ of Alexander Severus, *ib.*; still supplies lower city, 108.

Aqua Alsietina, seventh aqueduct, 22 miles long, supplied Naumachiı of Augustus, but unfit for drinking, 108; source of, in Lacus Alsietinus, *ib.*; renewed by Trajan and Paul V., as Acqua Paola still supplies Leonine city, 109.

Aqua Claudia, eighth aqueduct, 46 miles long, 109; source, below Subiaco, 110; ran on right bank of Anio, and crossed it along with Aqua Marcia, 111; arcade crosses that of Marcian, *ib.*; inscription on Specus over Porta Maggiore records work of Claudius, 112.

Aqua Felice, work of Sixtus V., partly on arcade of Marcian and Claudian, 113; branches at Porta Maggiore to Lateran and Ghetto, *ib.*; main channel to Porta S. Lorenzo and higher town, 114.

Aquarii, staff of workmen employed in aqueducts, 95.

Aqueducts, study of, necessary, 93; an important part of defences of city on eastern side, *ib.*; have been traced to walls, and shewn on chart, *ib.*; knowledge of older aqueducts gained from Frontinus, *ib.* 94; none constructed till B.C. 312, *ib.*; list of nine in first century, *ib.*; **seven later** ones in third century, *ib.*; **fourteen** remaining in sixth century, *ib.*; channel of, or specus in stone cemented, later on of concrete faced with brick, 95; forms of, pointed, square, round, *ib.*; average size of, 5 feet by 2½, *ib.*; filtering-pool of, or Piscina, at source, and repeated with Castellum Aquæ, *ib.*; force of current broken by sharp angles, 96; ventilated by shafts, or respirators, *ib.*; are carried in tiers, and cross at right angles, *ib.*; accumulation of, at Porta Maggiore, *ib.*; skilfully brought round heads of valleys to Campagna, 97; arcades of, begin below Tusculum, *ib.*; pass through subterranean Piscinæ above arcades, *ib.*; height above sea of, at Porta Maggiore, 98; final reservoir of each, or Castellum, whence distributed through city, *ib.*; net-work of channels to interchange supplies, *ib.*; heads of distribution, 99: water rented by owners of houses, free to poor, *ib.*; calculated volume of, and daily quantity, *ib.*; only two of ancient, now in use, 113; chief use of, to supply Thermæ, 115.

Arch of Drusus, close to Porta Appia, carries aqueduct of Caracalla across road, 87, 119.

Arch of Janus Quadrifrons, in Velabrum, still standing, 18; approached from Forum by branch of Via Nova, 82.

Arch of Septimius Severus, in Forum, on site of that of Tiberius, 125; inscriptions on, with sculptures of Parthian and Persian wars, 126; name of Geta on, **erased** by Caracalla, *ib.*; in Velabrum erected by guild of silversmiths, 133.

Arch of Titus, in valley north-east of Palatine, where Via Sacra and Via Nova met together, 83.

Arcosolium, recess in wall of tomb, with sarcophagus below; grave of martyrs in catacombs, 145.

Arx, citadel of Rome, cut off from rest of Palatine by foss, 11; the place of safety for settlers around it, *ib.*; fortified on same principles as other cities in Italy, 12; usually a hill with sides scarped into cliffs, *ib.*; on highest ground, with town around it also fortified,

ALPHABETICAL INDEX.

ib.; called by Roman writers Roma Quadrata, *ib.*; compared with Tusculum and Varia, 14; each of Seven Hills had its own Arx, 41.

Atrium Minervæ, entrance to Forum of Nerva, on side of Forum Romanum, with effigy of goddess still standing, 132.

Aurelian, wall of, necessary to protect Rome in the third century, 67; begun by him, 271; finished by Probus, 280 A.D., *ib.*; first complete line of masonry round city, 68; 50 feet high, with towers connected by arcaded corridors, *ib.*; half-a-mile of corridor perfect on south side, 69; wholly of brick, but stately in appearance, *ib.*; strides over buildings in its course without destroying them, *ib.*: towers added to gateways by Honorius made fortresses of them, 70; forced by Goths at Porta Salaria, 409 A.D., *ib.*; restoration of, by Theodoric, and revenues granted for the purpose, 71; towers at three gates rebuilt by Theodoric, 71, 72; repairs of, by Belisarius, 537 A.D., enable Rome to stand siege by Goths, *ib.*; total destruction of, intended by Goths, hindered by Belisarius, who repairs wall in 25 days, 73; traces of hasty repairs near south-east corner of city, 74; gates of, barred by portcullis added to door on hinges, *ib.*; penetrated by Lombards in eighth century, *ib.*; restored by Pope Hadrian I. and Leo IV., 75; survey of, by Swiss ecclesiastic, when perfect, in ninth century, 76, 77; enumeration of towers, battlements, &c., *ib.*; list of gates in, in Procopius and Itinerary, compared with modern, *ib.*, 78.

Belisarius, general of Justinian, occupies palace on Pincian, 60; forces Goths to evacuate Rome, 72; stands prolonged siege, *ib.*; repairs wall, and stands second siege, 73; hasty work of, traceable in Aurelian's wall, 74.

Bibliotheca, of Trajan, attached to temple in his Forum, 134; of Augustus, called Palatina, and of Tiberius, attached to his palace on Palatine, 164.

Bibulus, tomb of, remaining, stood just outside Porta Ratumena, at issue of Via Flaminia from second wall of Kings, 84.

Campus Martius, level plain on bank of Tiber, north of Capitol, often flooded, 24; not part of town anciently, 59; without Pomœrium, but occupied with public buildings and grounds, 60.

Capitolium, signified keep of city, whether on Palatine or Saturnian Mount, 20; properly applied to small temple in every arx, 21.

Castra, Prætoria, of Tiberius' time, fine example of brickwork, 7; square projection from line of defence on old earthwork, 63; dismantled after mutiny of guards under Constantine, *ib.*; soldiers' barracks, 19 of, supplied by aqueducts, 99; Misenatium, quarters of seamen employed on awning of Colosseum, 159.

Catabolum, den for wild beasts under Podium of Colosseum; Catabolici, attendants on dens, 156.

Catacombs, burial-places sometimes made in galleries of worked-out quarries of pozzolana sand, 3.

C. Cestius, pyramid as monument of, near Ostian gate, engaged in Aurelian's wall, 69.

Cicero, describes journey to Modena by three routes, 85; second Philippic of, spoken in Temple of Concord, 123.

Cippus, name of boundary-stones marking out Pomœrium, 65; of mile-stones, or Milliaria, along great roads, 92; of record connected with aqueduct, 192; of monumental stones in tombs, as in that of Augustus, 142, 149.

Circus, Maximus, in valley between Palatine and Aventine, 32, 35; **spectacles in**, of wild beasts and naumachiæ, 251.—C. Varianus, outside city wall at Sessorium, for amusement of soldiery, 174.

Clamps, of iron or bronze, for fastening large stones, 3; in wall of Servius, found near railway-station, 50; and in wall of Robur Tullianum, 139.

Clivus, Capitolinus, road up slope of hill from Forum, paved with basalt, 30, 82; pavement of, still existing, winding up from Arch of Septimius Severus, 124.—C. Sacer, ascending portion of Via Sacra from Forum, 83.—C. Scauri, slope on western side of Cœlian, descending to Colosseum, 112, 153.—C. Victoriæ, **on branch of** Nova Via up to Palatine, 82; **passes** through palace, under **vault**, with original pavement, 165.

Cloaca, great sewer attributed to Tarquin I. by Dio, 55; drains off three springs in valley **between** Capitol and Palatine, 122; original arch of visible under Basilica Julia, 128; connected with drain from Mamertine prison, 139.

Colosseum, not all reared by Flavian family, 151; plan of amphitheatre conceived by Augustus, followed by Nero, *ib.*; stagnum at, part of Nero's golden house, 152; substructures of, shew different styles and dates, *ib.*; basement of tufa blocks, earlier than Empire, attributable to Scaurus, 153; is called on inscription, Theatrum, *ib.*; brick galleries of, with naumachia and arena assigned to Nero, *ib.*; third period of, in stone, shewn by vertical joint between it and brickwork, *ib.*; additions to upper storey of, ill-built, 154; canals in, for naumachia filled, and covered over at pleasure, ten feet deep, *ib.*; boards of arena removed and stowed away on corbels, 155; dens in, supplied with water from aqueducts, 156; central passage in, provided with frame-work as cradle for ships, *ib.*; great drain from, at south-east end, for waters of stagnum, 157; beasts shewn in, introduced **by subterranean** way into basement, 158; only one of amphitheatres, with double corridors round galleries, 160; of eighty arches in outer circle, forty-seven destroyed, 161; four stages of, with columns of different orders, *ib.*; much injured by earthquake, *ib.*; stones of, used for building palaces, *ib.*; a fortress in middle ages, *ib.*

Columbarium, burial-place named from niches to contain many bodies in small space, 143; instance of, with nine tiers of niches, for two urns, 144; some assigned to servants of Cæsars, *ib.*; names in, same as mentioned by S. Paul, *ib.*

Comitium, meeting-place in Forum of Comitia Curiata, marble screens of, existing, 126; sculptures on, described, 127.

Concrete, of rough stone and lime-mortar, oldest example of in wall on south-west side of Palatine, 5; earliest dated instance of, in Emporium, B.C. 175, *ib.*; forms chief **mass of walls faced** with cut stones or brick, 6.

Crassus, M. Licinius, triumvir, husband of Cæcilia Metella, killed 53 B.C., 148.

Crepido, raised footpath for passengers along roadways, 88, 92.

Dei Consentes XII., portico in marble, to contain images of, under Tabularium, 124.

Dioscuri, group of, reining horses, in bronze, on Quirinal, 120.

Dolabella, arch of, on Cœlian, ear-

ALPHABETICAL INDEX.

liest dated building of Christian era, 9; carries castellum and piscina of aqueduct, 112.

Domitian, institutes Agon Capitolinus, literary contest at celebration of Lustrum, 149.

Elephants, four dens for, of larger size, in central passage of Colosseum, 156.

Emplecton, name for earliest masonry, with stones laid lengthwise and crosswise, 13.

Emporium, port of city on Tiber below Aventine, 5; enclosed by Claudius within Pomœrium, 164.

Ennius, fragment of, mentions Roma Quadrata, 12; statue of, and tomb in vault of Scipios, 147.

Esquiline Hill, named from groves of Æsculus, 40; few remains of early defences on, *ib.*; great part of, occupied by Nero's golden house, 41; arx of, at north-western point, *ib.*

Exarch, title of lieutenant of Eastern Emperor in Italy, 71; Smaragdus, erects column in Forum to Phocas, 126.

Exedra, semicircular balcony, on four sides of baths of Titus, 117; in baths of Caracalla, 119; in baths of Diocletian, 120; double, on Palatine, with roof of tortoise-back pattern, 169.

Forum Romanum, made in foss at foot of Capitoline, 24; dimensions of, 122; began outside Porta Saturni, *ib.*; buildings remaining in, described, 123—130; eastern side still unexcavated, *ib.*

Forum Boarium, cattle-market, outside gate of Janus, 24; round temple in, close to Tiber, called Vesta's, is of Hercules, 133.

Forum Olitorium, vegetable-market, west of Capitol, adjoins theatre of Marcellus, 25.

Forum of J. Cæsar, north-east of Forum Romanum, immense cost of site, 131; very slight remains of, *ib.*; statue of founder discovered on site and preserved, *ib.*

Forum of Augustus, east of Forum of Julius Cæsar, 131; tufa wall of remaining, part of second wall of Kings, *ib.*; Temple of Mars Ultor in, with four columns visible, 132; arches in honour of Germanicus and Drusus, *ib.*

Forum of Vespasian, or Forum Pacis, from Temple of Peace in it, 135; largest in Rome, from Forum of Nerva to Temple of Antoninus in Forum Romanum, 136.

Forum of Nerva, or Transitorium, south of Forum of Augustus, 26, 132.

Forum of Trajan, north-east of Capitoline, partly cut out of rock on Quirinal, 133; apse of, at east end, remains, with three tiers of shops on face of hill, *ib.*; Temple of Trajan in, on north side, with library, 134; Basilica Ulpia in, had largest columns in Rome, *ib.*; great magnificence of whole Forum, shewn on coins, *ib.*; column of Trajan still standing, of white marble, 127 ft. high, *ib.*; connected with Forum of Augustus by triumphal arch, 135; sculptures from this arch now on Arch of Constantine, *ib.*

Foss, in primitive defences, 100 ft. wide, 30 deep, 11; traced round Capitoline, 25; Fossæ Quiritium, in Festus, work of Romans and Sabines, round city on two hills, 29.

Fratres Arvales, college of, with sacred grove, buildings and inscriptions, on Via Campana, 90.

Frontinus, Curator Aquarum under Trajan, 93; writer of history of Aqueducts, 94, 99, 111.

Gabii, defences of, give good idea of primitive walled town, 86.

Gallienus, Arch of, at north-east end of Esquiline, near S. Maria

Maggiore, 49; weak reign of, encouraged barbarians, 67.

Germalus, terrace on south-western slope of Palatine, formed by earth thrown down in scarping cliff, 15.

Geta, name of, erased from Arch of Septimius Severus and elsewhere, after his murder by Caracalla, 126.

Gordiani, Emperors, youngest of completes Colosseum, A.D. 240, 154; splendid villa of, on Via Prænestina, 173.

Græcostasis, adjoining Temple of Concord on edge of Forum, meeting-place of ambassadors, 123.

Graffiti, scratchings, or shallow carvings on stones or plaster, as in Colosseum, shewing screen before podium, 159; remarkable one, in guard-chamber on Palatine, caricaturing Crucifixion, 170.

Green-house, supposed, in house of Mæcenas, 173.

Hadrian I., Pope, reigns 23 years, A.D. 772—795; employs revenues in restoring walls, 75.

Height above sea, of Seven Hills, 98.

Hortensius, house of, on Palatine, residence of Augustus for forty years, 162; decorated by order of Senate, 163; three chambers added by Senate still remain, with fine frescoes, *ib.*; situated near hut of Romulus, and therefore chosen by Augustus, *ib.*

Julius Cæsar, plans of, for improving Rome, 62; Temple of, in Forum, 128; Basilica of, in Forum, burnt, but restored and enlarged by Augustus, *ib.*; shows of, with wild beasts and naumachia, in Circus Maximus, 151; lived in Regia as Pontifex Maximus till his death, 165.

Jupiter Victor, Temple of, in peperino, on Palatine, 2.—J. Stator, Temple of, near Porta Mugonia, on Palatine, 18.—J. Feretrius,

Temple of, in tufa, at top of steps of Cacus on Palatine, 20.

Lacus, signifies reservoir, or fountain, 99; loch, or pool, made by damming Anio, 111; basins, as Lacus Curtius, and Lacus Juturnæ in Forum, 122, 128, 129.

Lamiæ, house of, with gardens, came to Tiberius, 171; occupied with villa of Mæcenas by Caligula, *ib.*; Jewish deputation received in, by Caligula, 172.

Laocoon, group of, at Baths of Titus, found on north side of Esquiline, 118.

Lateran, fortress and palace, detached from Cœlian, 36; separated by foss from Cœlian, now filled up, 38; shewn to be outwork beyond city, by tombs of first century, *ib.*, 140; named from L. Lateranus, first plebeian consul, 174; confiscated to Emperors on rebellion of Plautius Lateranus, *ib.*; given by Constantine to Popes, 175; remains of, incorporated in wall of Aurelian, *ib.*; great hall of, on site of church of S. John Lateran, *ib.*; residence of Popes for 1,000 years, is now a Museum, 176.

Lector, officer in great households, recited literary works, 146, 166.

Leo IV., Pope, restores defences, 75; connects transtiberine quarter with Leonine city, *ib.*

Lepidus, Triumvir, Pontifex Maximus, banished by Augustus, retained his office, succeeded by Augustus, B.C. 13, 162.

Loculus, space built in wall of tomb for one body, 145; use of, in tomb of Statilius Taurus, shews cremation disused in second century, *ib.*

Lombards, attack city, injure, but do not capture it, 74.

Lupercal, spring in cave of, near Circus Maximus, supplied Arx with water, 16.

ALPHABETICAL INDEX. 183

Mæcenas, house of, made in burial-ground of Esquiliæ, 171; devolved to Augustus and later Cæsars, *ib.*; site of, at south end of great agger, and partly on it, 172; one room of, remains, with apse and fine wall-paintings, *ib.*; garden of, connected with Nero's golden house, 173.

Mamertine Prison, name of, from Mamers, i.e. Mars, or Ancus Martius (?), 137; remains of vestibule, called Prison of S. Peter, in two small chambers, one above other, *ib.*; six larger chambers to north-east, partly of original tufa, 138; floor of, raised 6 feet, as liable to floods from Tiber, *ib.*; two portions connected by passage with drain below, joining Cloaca Maxima, 139; part of Robur Tullianum in larger cells, known by great tufa blocks, clamped, *ib.*

Marble, never used commonly for building-material, 9; a facing to grand buildings in slabs, sometimes blocks, *ib.*; cornices and columns wholly of, *ib.*; earliest mention of, B.C. 150, *ib.*; Temple of Hercules and Mausoleum of Hadrian overlaid with, *ib.*; marks of marble slabs on brick walls of Thermæ of Caracalla, 10; finest from Africa, *ib.*; wharf on Tiber for landing of, called Marmorata, *ib.*; of Devonshire highly esteemed, *ib.*

Marble Plan of Rome, engraved on slabs, hung on brick wall under porch of Temple of Rome, 136; fragments of, all found on same site, on three different scales, preserved in Capitoline Museum, *ib.*

Marcellus, nephew of Augustus, buried in Mausoleum, 142.

Marcus Aurelius, sculptured in Comitium, remitting taxes, and burning records of debt, 127.

Mars Ultor, Temple of, in Forum of Augustus, 131; vowed by Augustus for victory at Philippi, 132.

Mausoleum, of Augustus, in Campus Martius, mound of earth, on marble base and planted, 141; adorned with obelisks still in Rome, *ib.*; vestibule of, contained plates engraved with Gesta Augusti, i.e. **Ancyran** Marbles, *ib.*; made of central vault and thirteen smaller cells, *ib.*; Cippi of many Cæsars in, 142; Emperor Nerva last buried in, *ib.*—M. of Hadrian in Trastevere, circular, with square base, *ib.*; of concrete, faced with peperino, once cased with marble, *ib.*; central chamber in form of cross, *ib.*; afterwards a fortress of Popes, and joined to Vatican by covered way, 143.—M. of Alexander Severus, two miles outside Rome, circle of masonry covered with mound, *ib.*

Media, Via, **central** passage below arena in Colosseum, contained moveable scenery, 167.

Milliarium, milestone, invented by C. Gracchus, 92. — Milliarium Aureum, a gilt column, placed in Forum by Augustus as central milestone of Empire, 81; central mass of, round brick pedestal, close to Arch of S. Severus, remaining, 82, 125.

Mons Aventinus, fortified by nature and art, 32; part of it called Lauretum, from bay-trees, 33; assigned to conquered Latins by Ancus Martius, *ib.*; first included in Pomœrium by Claudius, *ib.*; Wall of Kings on, 50 ft. high, 12 ft. thick, 34, 35; forts on, to defend Porta Raudusculana of Kings, 89.

Mons Cælius, or Querquetulanus, from oak-trees, named after Cæles Vibenna, 35; inhabitants of Alba removed to, *ib.*; Lateran not naturally part of, 36; strong ancient fortress on, 37; Claudium, at first a fortress, was the Arx, 42; connected with Esqui-

line by bank and wall across valley, and with Pseudo-Aventine, 51.

Mons Capitolinus, hill **of Saturn,** joined to Palatine **within** one wall before Numa, 23; smallest of seven hills, 24; **not walled** on north side, 25, 29.

Mons Janiculensis, not part **of city,** but southern portion **occupied very early as outpost,** 42; a **strong fortress in ancient and modern times,** 43; foss of, **visible from** summit to Tiber on **east side,** 44; added to city by **Augustus as** Regio XIV., 64.

Mons Palatinus, always believed to be site of original city, 11; this confirmed by rudest masonry on portions of it, *ib.*; central position of, among seven hills, *ib.*; diamond, or lozenge shape of, *ib.*; 170 ft. above sea, contains 65 acres, *ib.*; only north-western portion, **or** one-third **of,** at first occupied, *ib.*; divided by a great foss into two, *ib.*; had three gates, 17; presents examples of all styles, 22; assigned by Senate as residence of Cæsars, 163.

Mons Pincius, northernmost spur from table-land, fortified by foss and wall, 44; called *Collis Hortulorum*, and is still a garden, *ib.*

Mons Vaticanus, fortress on, with scarped cliffs, 44.

Monte Cavallo, in front of Quirinal palace, adorned with group of Dioscuri in bronze, 120.

Monuments, usually placed along public roads and near gates of city, 69.

Mortar, **of rock-sand** with fresh lime, **sets hard as stone,** 3; none in primitive walls, 4; not used generally till two or three centuries B.C., 5.

Muro Torto, bulged wall, fine specimen of reticulated-work, against north-east cliff of Pincian, 5, 60.

Necropolis of Rome, district so called, between Via Latina and Via Appia, 146.

Nymphæum of Alexander Severus, on Esquiline, **name** applied to entrance **to women's** baths, 121.

Ollæ, urns of earthenware to contain human ashes, 143; immense numbers of, in small space, 144.

Opus Quadratum, earliest specimen in wall of Romulus on Palatine, 4; style of, lasted about 100 years, *ib.*; usually called Etruscan, *ib.*; second stage of, in wall of Latins on Aventine, Pulchrum Littus, tower under S. Anastasia, and wall of Servius Tullius, *ib.*; great rudeness of, in wall on north-west side of Palatine, 13; important as confirming truth of legendary history, *ib.*; occurs in small temple **on** Palatine, 20.

Opus incertum, or antiquum, first use of lime-mortar, 5; occurs at Emporium, *ib.*; passes into reticulate-work, when concrete is introduced, 6.

Opus reticulatum, good example of, in the Muro Torto on Pincian, 5; faced with diamond-shaped blocks of tufa, 6; looks like brick, but is of stones flat outside, wedged at back, set in fresh concrete, *ib.*

Opus lateritium, succeeds stone in time of Augustus, 6; earliest of thin tiles, very hard, *ib.*; best in first century, *ib.*; finest specimen in Nero's arcade of Claudian aqueduct, *ib.*; declines after early part of second century, 7; age of, can be tested by number of bricks in a foot, *ib.*; in first century, 9 or 10 to a foot, in fourth, not more than 4, *ib.*; can be dated also from consular stamps on bricks, 8.

Opus mixtum, of bricks and rough stones in alternate layers, 8; occurs in walls of Rome and Circus of Maxentius, A.D. 310, at Pompeii, and Hadrian's villa at Tivoli, *ib.*; prevalent in later Empire, but no criterion of date, *ib.*; commonly used in Gaul and Britain, *ib.*

pus signinum, cement for lining channels of aqueducts, 9; impermeable by water, made of pounded tiles and fresh lime, *ib.*

pus musivum, mosaic-work, in house of Augustus on Palatine, visible, 163.

pus Alexandrinum, mosaic-work in coloured patterns, designed by Alexander Severus, 167.

stia, port of Tiber, early colony of Rome, 89.

ɪlace of Tiberius on Palatine, close to house of Augustus, 164; construction of, corresponds to Prætorian Camp built by him, *ib.*—P. of Caligula, at north end of Palatine, next to Forum, *ib.*; **part** of, at low level, with Tem**ple** of Dioscuri as vestibule, *ib.*; **part** at high level joined to Capitol by bridge partly standing, *ib.*; lofty vault adjoining, under which Clivus Victoriæ runs, 165.—P. **of** Domitian, covers central por**tion** of Palatine; magnificence of, *ib.*; carried on by later Emperors, called by Nerva Ædes Publicæ, 166; site for, provided by filling great foss, *ib.*; ruins of, contain Academia, Bibliotheca, 166; great banqueting-hall of, with apse and mosaic pavement, 167; oval bath in, with marble seats and fountain, *ib.*; grand court of, with two marble porticoes, *ib.*; throne-room of, chapel, and hall of justice, with marble railing, *ib.*; chambers under, or baths of Livia, with fine paintings on vault, 168.— P. of later Emperors, remains of, on south-west and south-east cliffs, 169; gymnasium of, with mar-

ble colonnade, and exedra, work of Commodus, *ib.*; terrace on substructures, example of enlargement of surface, 170; guard-chambers of, with inscriptions by soldiers on walls, 171.

Pallantian gardens, attached to Sessorian palace, where Aqua Marcia divided, 104; arcade of Claudian aqueducts ends at, 109.

Pater Patriæ, title of Augustus, inscribed on monument to him in his Forum, 131.

Pegmata, lifts for cages of beasts in Colosseum, remains of grooves for working, left in tufa walls below arena, 155, 156; applied to other theatrical contrivances on stage, described by Martial and Seneca, 157.

Peperino, stone of Mons Albanus, named from nodules in it, 2; wall **of** Servius Tullius, Mamertine Prison, Temple of Jupiter Victor, built of, *ib.*

Peristylium Sicilicum, **grand court** in palace of Cæsars, open to **sky**, with double colonnade, 167.

Piscina Publica, first public bath, under cliff of Pseudo-Aventine, 115; fed by Aqua Appia, and had no warming apparatus, *ib.*

Podium, lowest terrace in amphitheatre for spectators of highest rank, 155, 158; protected from beasts in arena by strong trellis-work of metal, *ib.*

Politorium, taken by Ancus Martius; Latins from, transferred to Aventine, 33.

Polygonal masonry, of lava, not cemented, 5; rare in Rome, only on Viminal, and perhaps in Emporium, *ib.*

Pomœrium, space *post murum*, between outer and inner rampart, 43; was limit of the Urbs, 65; lost signification of military boundary in late times, *ib.*; length of, under Vespasian, nearly agrees with wall of Au-

relian, 66; last mention of, A.D. 467, *ib.*
Pondera reducta, counterweights for hoisting machinery, sliding in grooves under arena of Colosseum, 155.
Pons Fabricius, bridge over Tiber to Trastevere across the island, 27, 30.
Pons Palatinus, next below P. Fabricius, now P. Rotto, 30.
Pons Sublicius, ancient wooden bridge, from Aventine to Trastevere, remains of, visible in bed of Tiber, 34, 43, 90, 101.
Pons Ælius, under Hadrianum, built by Trajan, now bridge of S. Angelo, 91, 142.
Pons Janiculensis, next below P. Ælius, now P. Sisto, 76.
Pons Milvius, over Tiber on Via Flaminia, Goths had a camp there, 85.
Ponte Nomentano, bridge over Anio, two miles from Rome, 85.
Ponte di Nono, fine ancient bridge of sperone and tufa, with original pavement, on Via Gabina, 86.
Ponte di S. Mauro, over dam of loch in Anio, 144 ft. above the water, 111.
Porta Romana, gate of Palatine nearest Forum, 17; road from, up Clivus Victoriæ, *ib.*; from steps of Capitol, 135 yards, 23.
Porta Mugonia, gate of Palatine, on north-east, 18; called "old gate" in Livy, Porta Palatii by Ovid, *ib.*
Porta Janualis, gate below Palatine, named from statue of Janus, 18; not on hill, but barrier in outer defences, *ib.*; probably connected with drawbridge over stream, *ib.*
Porta Saturnia, gate into Capitol from Forum, 30, 122; tufa jambs of, remaining, 82.
Porta Flumentana, gate on western side of Capitoline, near Tiber, liable to be flooded, 30.

Porta Carmentalis, gate near southwest point of Capitol, named from altar of goddess Carmenta, also called Scelerata, 31.
Porta Collina, gate of Servius on north end of Quirinal, 47; weakest point of defences, 48; commencement of Viæ Salaria and Nomentana, 85.
Porta Viminalis, middle gate in agger of Servius, near Thermæ of Diocletian, 49.
Porta Esquilina, southernmost of three gates in agger of Servius, 47, 49; name also given to outer gate in agger of Tarquin by Frontinus, *ib.*, 59, 63.
Porta Querquetulana, gate in line of Servius, in foss between Cœlian and Esquiline, 52.
Porta Raudusculana, gate of Servius, in gorge between S. Balbina and S. Sabba, 89.
Porta Capena, under Cœlian cliff, with tower, at entrance of Via Appia into city, 52; pavement of Via Appia discovered at, 3 yards wide, 53; carried Aqua Appia over its arch, *ib.*, 100.
Porta Ratumena, gate in agger connecting Capitoline with Quirinal, 84.
Porta Trigemina, gateway of Kings, commencement of Pulchrum Littus, 27; starting-point of Via Ostiensis, 89; near it, at Salinæ, mouth of Aqua Appia, 99, 100.
Porta Triumphalis, built across foss of second city of Kings, is now porch of church of S. Angelo, 25; was starting-place for grand processions entering city, and ascending Capitol, 28.
Porta Flaminia, northernmost point of city, now P. del Popolo, 60; Goths before it, in siege of A.D. 537, 72; stood on slope of hill, to east of modern gate, 77.
Porta Pinciana, name still retained, now closed, restored by Theodoric, 72.

Porta Salaria, name still retained, at weakest point of defences, 48; forced by Goths, *ib.*, 70.

Porta Nomentana, little to south-east of modern P. Pia, 77.

Porta Chiusa, closed gate to road on south side of Prætorian Camp, 49, 77; connected with branch of Via Tiburtina, 86.

Porta Tiburtina, now P. S. Lorenzo, in wall of Aurelian, corresponding to P. Viminalis in line of Servius, 59; inscription on arch of, records restoration of A. Marcia, Tepula, Julia, by Augustus, 62; old arch and gate of, walled up in new works of Honorius, 70; arch of, carries three ancient and one modern aqueduct, 96.

Porta Prænestina, also Labicana, now P. Maggiore, 49, 59; forms with Claudian aqueduct important part in fortifications, 63; road to Gabii passes through, 86; Aqua Claudia and Anio Novus carried over, 96; Anio Vetus enters at, almost level with ground, 102; gateway of, with inscription, is monument of Claudius's completion of aqueducts, 112, 148.

Porta Asinaria, gate near Lateran, little westward of modern P. S. Giovanni, 78.

Porta Lateranensis, between P. Asinaria and Metronia, walled up, but traceable, 77.

Porta Metronia, between P. Lateranensis and Latina, replaced by new gate close to it, 78.

Porta Latina, name preserved, long closed, 78; near it old pavement of V. Latina exists, 87.

Porta Appia, now S. Sebastiano, restored by Theodoric, 71; principal entrance from south, 87; outside of, first milestone from P. Capena found, 88; three columbaria close to, 143.

Porta Ardeatina, between P. Appia and Ostiensis, standing, but closed, 77; of finest brickwork of Nero's time, 88.

Porta Ostiensis, now S. Paolo, 34; restored by Theodoric, 72; fine example of sixth century, with round towers, *ib.*

Porta Portuensis, in Trastevere, rebuilt by Honorius, replaced by P. Portese, within line of Aurelian's wall, 96.

Porta Janiculensis, or of Pancratius, in Trastevere, now P. S. Pancrazio, 78.

Porta Aurelia, in Trastevere, site of doubtful, probably an inner gate, near Pons Ælius, 76, 91.

Porta Septimiana, in Trastevere, work of Septimius Severus, gate from Regio XIV. to north, 76.

Portcullis, used in gates of Rome, grooves for, in six of them, 74.

Portus Augusti, new port of Tiber near Ostia, projected by Augustus, 90; soon silted up and superseded by new harbour of Trajan, with channel still navigable, *ib.*

Primitive wall, necessary round Palatine, 14; probably always partly visible, as mentioned in Cassiodorus, *ib.*; afterwards covered by ruins from hill-side, now again exposed to view, *ib.*; exactly corresponds to Etrurian remains, *ib.*

Pseudo-Aventine, south-east portion of Aventine, divided by natural valley made into foss, 32; approach to, protected by ancient forts, *ib.*, 35; had arx on it, 41.

Pudens, family house of, against cliff of Viminal, 40; on site of citadel of Viminal, 42; name of, with Claudia, mentioned by S. Paul, occurs in Columbarium, 144.

Pulchrum Littus, part of second wall, of tufa, along Tiber for half-a-mile, 27; Cloaca inserted into it, and therefore more recent, *ib.*; a protection against floods, and a military rampart, **28**; pierced to receive mouth of river Almo, 29.

Pulvis Puteolanus, rock-sand, or pozzolana, quarries of, miles long in Campagna, 3; galleries of, sometimes converted to catacombs, *ib.*

Pumice-stone, very light, used for vaulting, 3; thrown up from Mount Vesuvius, forms into beds, and is quarried, *ib.*; occurs in vaults of Pantheon and Colosseum, *ib.*

Quirinal Hill, not called Mons, but Collis, promontory from high table-land, 38; Sabine name for, Agonalis, or hillocky, 39; has scarped cliff at royal palace, and old tufa wall, *ib.*; horn-work at north-east end of, foss at foot, *ib.*; king's palace site of arx, **42**.

Regia, residence of kings, afterwards of Pontifex Maximus, 129, 130; occupied by J. Cæsar till his death, *ib.*; given up by Augustus to Vestal Virgins, *ib.*; site of, corresponds with church of S. Maria Liberatrice, *ib.*; stood at edge of Forum, under cliff of Palatine, 162.

Regiones, wards of **city, four in** time of Servius, increased to **fourteen** under Augustus, 64; R. XIV., or transtiberine quarter, occupied by Goths, and **defences** mostly destroyed, 65; R. VIII., called Forum Romanum Magnum, containing all the Fora except Vespasian's, 131.

Robur Tullianum, part of cell of, **work of Servius** Tullius **in Ma**mertine **Prison,** remains with holes left by **iron clamps, 139.**

Romulus, cottage of, on **Palatine,** preserved to late ages, 21.

Rostra, raised platform for speakers; Vetera, at western end of Forum, **125**; R. Nova, at eastern end, **128**.

Sabines, in possession of Mons Saturnius before Rome founded, 15; fusion of, with Romans, 16, 23, 24; held Quirinal also, 39.

Salinæ, salt-wharves on Tiber, where A. Appia discharged itself, 99, 101.

Sallust, the historian, house of, with gardens and circus made in foss at north-east end of Quirinal, 39; stood on **horn-work** or fort to defend the hill, 48; reservoir of aqueduct under, 49; became Crown property, and was residence of Vespasian, 165.

Saracens, in ninth century, unable to attack city walls, spoil Vatican and St. Peter's, 75.

Scaurus, M. Æ., B.C. 58, built wooden theatre for 80,000 people, 153.

Schola Xantha, at foot of Tabularium, row of chambers for ser**vants** of curule ædiles, reared by A. F. Xanthus, 124.

Second wall, of city on two hills, can be traced out, 25; remains of it, of tufa, under modern street, 26; portion of, 50 ft. high and 12 ft. thick, still standing, *ib.*; buried tower under S. Anastasia, 27; carried from Tiber to western side of Capitoline, 28.

Sei Deo, **seive** Deivæ, inscription on altar on Palatine, 21; formula dictated by reverence, 22.

Selce, basaltic lava, issued from crater, now the lake of Albano, **2**; several streams of, across Campagna, *ib.*; used for pavements, 3.

Septa, a vast building, polling-place of Comitia Centuriata, in Campus Martius, 60; arcade of, under houses in Corso, near Pantheon, 107.

Septizonium, latest addition to Palace of Cæsars, **170**; work of Sept. Severus, at south-east corner of Palatine, *ib.*; seven storeys **of, in** different styles, *ib.*; a fortress in Middle Ages, *ib.*

ALPHABETICAL INDEX. 189

Servius Tullius, did not build continuous wall round Seven Hills, 46; connected hills by short agger, with gate and fort in each, *ib.*; great agger of, with wall and foss, described by Dionysius, 47; modern measurement verifies dimensions of foss, *ib.*; agger ends against cliff of Esquiline, where ground is steeper, 50; wall of, near railway station, 12 ft. thick, of large blocks, clamped with iron, *ib.*; similar wall at bottom of foss, under buried church of S. Clemente, 51, 52; same wall backing short agger between Cœlian and Pseudo-Aventine, 52; whole course of great agger and wall, with sites of gates, traced out, 54; houses built into bank by cutting it away, in first century, 80.

Sessorium, fortress and palace of, at south-east angle of wall, 36, 38; in garden of, aqueducts enter city, 57; A. Marcia, Tepula, Julia, traced from, to P. S. Lorenzo, *ib.*; strength of fortification of, 62; military amphitheatre connected with, 63, 174; became residence of Empress Helena, *ib.*; great hall of, made into Church of S. Croce, *ib.*

Sette Sale, seven chambers with two piscinæ, regulating flow of water to baths of Titus, 117.

S. Maria in Cosmedin, church of, in Forum Boarium, made out of two temples, 133.

Sperone, stone from Gabii, 2; arches of Cloaca Maxima, and the Tabularium, built of, *ib.*

Spolia Opima, offered by Romulus, after killing king of Cæninenses, 20.

Stadium, of 606 ft., for foot-races, attached to palace on Palatine, 169.

Steps, flights of, three on Palatine, 19: one to site of Arch of Constantine, one to Forum, one to Circus Maximus of gigantic size, cut in natural rock, called Steps of Cacus, *ib.*; cut from deep foss-ways to top of bank, 80.

Suovetaurilia, sacrifice attending lustrum, sculptured on screen of Comitium in Forum, 127.

Sylla, adds to fortifications, 59; extends wall from Pulchrum Littus along Tiber, 60; his fortress and palace on Pincian, *ib.*; his work ends at Medici Villa, 61; exercises right to extend Pomœrium, 66.

Tables, XII., laws of, fix width of streets at gateways, 87; forbid interment within city, 140.

Tabularium, great building at foot of Capitol towards Forum, record-office of both ancient and modern Rome, 23; connected with Treasury under it, and Senate-house, 122.

Tarpeian rock, one of two eminences of Capitoline, within stone's cast from Palatine, 15; separated from northern eminence by natural depression, 23; is of hard stone, tufa, and peperino, 24.

Tarquinius Priscus, builder of Cloaca Maxima and Circus Maximus, 55.

Tarquinius Superbus, agger of, with great foss, mentioned by Pliny and Dionysius, 56; tradition that it was unfinished, *ib.*; and not completed except by wall of Aurelian, 57; argument from Frontinus, and position of aqueducts on outer rampart, *ib.*; length of, from Sessorium to Prætorian Camp, 2,600 yards, 58; design of, to join on to defences at north end of Quirinal and Pincian cliff, *ib.*; magnitude of work caused rebellion, *ib.*; suspended, and never renewed, *ib.*; three gates in, the doubles of gates in agger of Servius, 59.

Temple of Antoninus and Faustina,

height of base of, proves Forum Romanum to have stood at level of old foss-way, 83.

Temple of Concord, in front of Tabularium, podium of remains, 123; used as vestibule to Senate-house and Tabularium, *ib.*; from steps of, decrees of Senate published, *ib.*

Temple of Dioscuri, in Forum, with three columns standing, 83; original tufa foundations of, visible, existing columns of fabric rebuilt by Augustus, 129; used as vestibule to palace of Caligula, 164.

Temple of Saturn, in front of Tabularium, three columns of, standing, with inscription, 123; connected with Treasury-vaults by doorway and stone steps, *ib.*; rebuilt by S. Severus, 124.

Temple of Vespasian, on edge of Forum, near Tabularium, with eight columns standing, 124; built by Domitian, restored by S. Severus, 125.

Temple of Vesta, the shrine of Roman and Sabine peoples combined, 24, 25, 129; circular basement of, in Forum, visible, committed by Numa to care of Virgins, *ib.*; reached by flood of Tiber in ancient and modern times, 16; shewn on coins as small circular building, 130.

Theodoric, Ostrogoth, King of Italy, restores Roman buildings, 70; visits Rome, and assigns revenues for repairs, 71; re-constructs three gate-fortresses, 72.

Thermæ, introduced to rich private houses only under Republic, 115; earliest public, of M. Agrippa, connected with Pantheon, 116.—T. of Titus, on Esquiline, made out of Nero's palace, *ib.*; opened in his reign, but finished by Trajan, 117; plan of, still discernible, *ib.*—T. of Commodus and S. Severus, in southernmost part of city, 118; supplied by Aqua Aurelia and Severiana, *ib.*—T. of Caracalla, or of Antonines, magnificent remains of, *ib.*; provided with arena and stadium, 119; fed by Aqua Antoniniana, branch of Marcian, *ib.*—T. of Diocletian, on Viminal, largest and best preserved, *ib.*; had places for 3,000 bathers, *ib.*; great hall of, made into noble church, 120; supplied by Aqua Jovis from Marcian, and covered 30 acres, *ib.*—T. of Constantine, on southern part of Quirinal, destroyed, *ib.*; adorned by bronze group of horses, now near Quirinal palace, *ib.*; list of, in fourth century, mentions eleven thermæ, 121.

Tombs, great magnificence of, 140; forbidden within city proper, *ib.*; Esquiliæ, burying-ground for poor, Campus Martius for rich, *ib.*; cruciform specimen of, at Cento Celle, 144; form of, called Arcosolium, a recess arched over, 145.—T. of Statilius Taurus in Esquiliæ, test of painting-art under Augustus, 145; frescoes in, illustrating Æneid, of great merit, 146.—T. of Scipios, earliest example of Roman burial-place, *ib.*; in two storeys, upper one used for family meetings, *ib.*; poet Ennius buried in same vault, 147; sarcophagus in, of P. C. Scipio Barbatus, with earliest Latin inscription, 303 B.C., *ib.*— T. of Eurysaces the Baker, at Porta Maggiore, formerly enclosed by tower of Honorius, *ib.*; stones of, represent instruments of baker's trade, *ib.*; not touched by Claudius in rearing monument of aqueducts, 148.— T. of Cæcilia Metella, on Via Appia, a circle, of travertine and concrete, *ib.*; became citadel to fortress of Gaetani, 149.—T. of Q. S. Maximus, enclosed in tower of Porta Salaria, *ib.*; with

ALPHABETICAL INDEX. 191

figure of youthful poet and his prize verses, *ib.*

'or dei Conti, mediæval tower east of Forum of Augustus, 26.

'or delle Milizie, mediæval tower on cliff above Forum of Trajan, 133.

'or Fiscale, three miles from Rome, tower with five tiers of aqueducts through it, 96, 102.

otila, Ostrogoth, throws down one third of defences, 73; retreats before Belisarius, returns and besieges him, *ib.*

Transitorius, name given to house of Nero, as stretching from Palatine over Esquiline, 116; to Forum of Nerva, as connecting Forum of Augustus with Forum of Vespasian, 132.

Travertine, stone from Tibur, good quality, large blocks of, 2; tomb of Cæcilia Metella, and outer wall of Colosseum, built of, *ib.*

Tufa, red soft sandstone, 1; first walls of Palatine built of, *ib.*; found on other hills of Rome, and in Campagna, *ib.*; cleaves into square blocks, *ib.*; *Opus quadratum* of, without cement, 4; in oblong blocks on Palatine, 4 ft. by 2, 13.

Vallis Murcia, named from its myrtles, between Palatine and Aventine, site of Circus Maximus, 32; traversed by stream of the Almo, or Aqua Crabra, 37.

Velabrum, low-lying district, near Arch of Janus and Tiber, 133.

Velarium, awning over spectators in Colosseum, 159; stretched from masts, standing on corbels, and running through cornice at summit, *ib.*; worked by large staff of seamen from fleet at Misenum, *ib.*; usually of canvas, but also decorated to resemble sky and stars, *ib.*

Velia, western spur of Esquiline cut off by foss, and added to Palatine, 27; foss still existing, Via del Colosseo made in it, *ib.*

Vertical joints, between blocks in primitive wall on Palatine, leaving fissure open through two courses of stone, 13; occur in Colosseum between galleries and brickwork, shewing the outer mass to have been built subsequently on to the inner, 153.

Viæ Stratæ, reckoned among wonders of Roman construction, 55, 79; built of basaltic lava in polygonal blocks, *ib.*; in Rome were originally foss-ways in valleys between the hills, *ib.*; and along each side of connecting banks, 80; at first only track-ways on the soil, *ib.*; later such roadways became streets in modern sense, by building houses against banks, *ib.*; streets usually 20 feet below natural level, *ib.*; being deep and narrow, not suited for carriage-traffic, 81; in second century, new streets made by filling the fosses to convenient height, *ib.*; Pliny states number of cross-streets at 265, 82; street from Porta Saturni to right hand, traced through Forum, 82; branches off to Palatine by Clivus Victoriæ, and to Circus Maximus, *ib.*; left-hand branch, under Arch of Severus, continued as Via Sacra, 83; past Basilica of Constantine and Arch of Titus to Summa Sacra Via, *ib.*; method of construction given by Vitruvius, 84; immense durability of, *ib.*; width within city, except at gates, four yards, 82; the means of uniting provinces with Rome, 91; made as direct as possible, and works of, ineffaceable, 92; stations all along, with post-horses, *ib.*; length of, from Britain to Jerusalem, *ib.*

Via Flaminia, issued by Porta Flaminia, constructed, B.C. 220, 84;

went along shore of Adriatic, and as V. Æmilia, to Milan, and east and west through Gallia Cisalpina, *ib.*, 84, 85.—V. Cassia and Clodia branched from, on left hand, *ib.*

Via Salaria, issued by Porta Collina, went past Antemnæ to Ancona, 85.

Via Nomentana, out of Porta Collina, to Nomentum of Sabines, joined V. Salaria, 85.

Via Tiburtina, out of city by Porta Esquilina, out of wall by Porta Tiburtina to Tivoli, 86; branch of it by Porta Chiusa, in sunk road or V. Cupa, *ib.*; continued as V. Valeria to Adriatic, as V. Sublacensis to Subiaco, *ib.*

Via Prænestina, out of city by Porta Esquilina, out of wall by Porta Prænestina, 86; same as V. Gabina, *ib.*; branches from, V. Labicana, and Collatina, *ib.*

Via Latina, branches from V. Appia within walls, out by Porta Latina, 87; many tombs along it, *ib.*; through Tusculum to Campania, joining V. Appia, *ib.*

Via Appia, out by Porta Appia, earliest road, B.C. 312, 87; starts from Porta Capena, and is three yards wide, 88; crossed Pontine marsh to sea-coast, through Campania, Samnium, Apulia, to Tarentum and Brundusium, *ib.*; lined for miles with monuments, *ib.*

Via Ardeatina, out by Porta Ardeatina, of finest brickwork, 88; paving of, still visible, 89; ran to Ardea in Latium, *ib.*

Via Laurentina, out of city by Porta Raudusculana, of walls by Porta Ardeatina, ran to Laurentum on coast, 89.

Via Ostiensis, out of city by Porta Trigemina on Tiber, 89; original pavement of, visible at pyramid of Cestius, *ib.*; crossed Decimo by ancient bridge of eleven arches, remaining, *ib.*

Via Portuensis, from Janiculan side, by Porta Portuensis, now destroyed, 89; approached from city by Pons Sublicius, 90; ran to Portus Augusti at mouth of Tiber, *ib.*; branch of, Via Campana, *ib.*

Via Aurelia Vetus, out by Porta Janiculensis, starting from Porta Aurelia, inner gate near Mausoleum of Hadrian, 91; ran to Alsium along Mare Inferum to Pisa, Genoa, and Forum Julii in Transalpine Gaul, *ib.*—V. Vitellia, branch of, to sea-coast, *ib.*—V. A. Nova, under Janiculan hill, throwing off branch, V. Cornelia, to north, joined V. Anio Vetus, 3½ miles from wall, *ib.*

Viminal Hill, spur from table-land, cliff, supported by wall of split tufa without mortar, 40; house of Pudens built against cliff of, *ib.*

Visigoths, enter city, A.D. 410, by Salarian gate, 48.

Vitiges, King of Ostrogoths, expelled from city by Belisarius, returns and besieges him, 72; plants six camps on eastern, one on western side of Tiber, 73.

Vivaria, receptacles of wild beasts, brought thence to be exhibited in Colosseum, 158.

Vomitoria, passages for ingress and egress from corridors to seats in Colosseum, 160.

CHAPTER I.
MODES OF CONSTRUCTION.

PLATE I.

I. Opus Quadratum.—Squared Work, A.U.C. 3, B.C. 750.

This example is from the Wall of Romulus, at the northwest corner of Roma Quadrata. In this kind of construction each stone is four feet long, two feet wide, and two thick, in other words, it is an oblong block of tufa stone consisting of two squares of two feet each, and the weight of the whole is one ton, or a load for a one-horse cart. There is reason to believe that these measurements are not *strictly* accurate; the length is about 3 feet 1 inch, which is an Etruscan measure not corresponding *exactly* to Roman feet; the edges of the stones are often worn, so that it is difficult to be quite certain of the measurement. (See p. 4.)

II. Opus Incertum.—Irregular Work.

The Latin names are those of Vitruvius, and they really apply to the *visible construction only*, that is, of the *surface* of the wall.

After the time of the Kings and the introduction of lime-mortar into use, the mass of the wall was always of rubble-walling, or concrete, and it was only faced with the ornamental construction. This irregular construction, or rather ornamentation of the surface of the concrete wall, came into use in the time of the later Republic, and prepared the way for the more regular *opus reticulatum* of the time of Augustus. The example here given is from the Emporium on the bank of the Tiber, near the *Marmorata*. (See p. 5.)

Modes of Construction.—Plate I.

I. Opus Quadratum.—Squared Work, A.U.C. 3, B.C. 750.

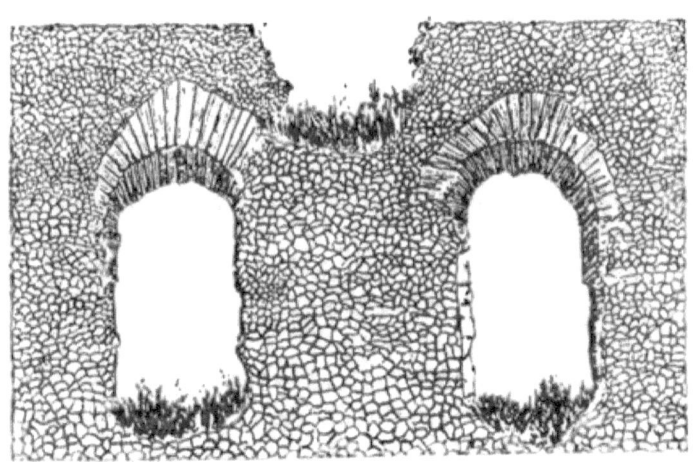

II. Opus Incertum.—Irregular Work, A.U.C. 558, B.C. 195.

PLATE II.

III. Opus Reticulatum.—Reticulated, or Net-work.

This came into use in the time of Augustus; the example is from his Mausoleum, as a dated example, but it continued in use for a century, only in the earlier examples the joints between the diamond-shaped blocks are wider, in the later they are very fine. We find it in the *Muro torto* of the time of Sylla, and it goes on to the time of Hadrian, A.D. 120, but in the time of Trajan and Hadrian the reticulated-work is enclosed in a framework of brick, as in the great villa at Tivoli, and in chambers of his time on the Palatine, at the north-east corner. (See p. 6.)

IV. Opus Lateritium.—Brickwork.

This example is of the best period, that is, of the time of Nero, and is from the arcade of his aqueduct on the Cœlian Hill; in the arches of this *ten* bricks to the foot can be counted, mortar included.

The lower part of the wall in this instance is mediæval work of a comparatively late period.

The buildings of the time of the Early Empire can be distinguished by the thickness of the bricks, and of the mortar between them.

First century, nine or ten to the foot.
Second century, seven or eight.
Third century, five or six.
Fourth century, four only, as in modern brick walls.

These measurements apply specially to the arches, where the bricks support a weight; in the walls, where they are laid flat, more mortar is used, consequently there are not so many bricks to the foot. (See p. 7.)

Modes of Construction.—Plate II. 197

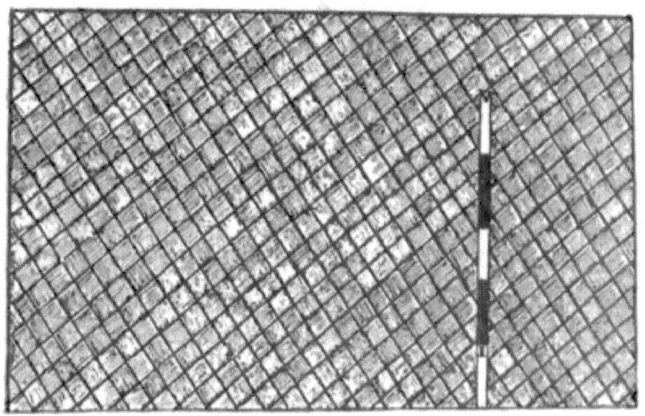

III. Opus Reticulatum.—Reticulated, or Net-work,
A.U.C. 725, B.C. 28 to A.D. 118.

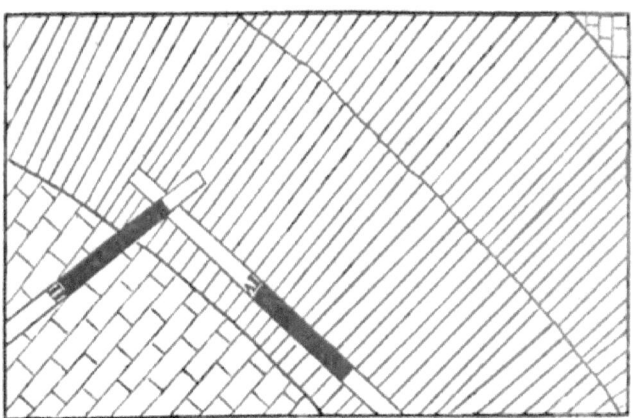

IV. Opus Lateritium.—Brickwork, A.U.C. 810, B.C. 57.

PLATE III.

Roma Quadrata.

I. The surface, which is *oblong* (not square), is left white; the cliffs on three sides, north, east, and west, and the great foss on the south, are shaded.

a a a a. Walls of the Kings, on the surface; the one near the north-west corner is usually called the "Wall of Romulus."

b. Supposed site of the Porta Mugionis, or Sacri Portus.

c c c. Pavements of old roads.

d. A piece of wall of the Kings, on the lower level of the Germalus.

e. Remains of a very early temple, supposed to be of Jupiter Feretrius, on the top of the steps of Cacus.

f. Porta Romana, at the foot of the Clivus Victoriæ.

f*. Summit of the Clivus Victoriæ.

g. Probable site of the Templum Victoriæ.

h. Site of ancient altar near that of the house of Romulus.

i. Arch of Titus on the Via Sacra.

k. Modern entrance to the "Palaces of the Cæsars," formerly to the Villa Farnesi.

l l l l. Lower Cliff.

m m m m. Upper Cliff.

n n. Germalus, with road on lower level.

o o. Outer side of great Foss.

p p. Inner side of great Foss.

q q. Sloping paved road up to City.

II. Details on the sides of Roma Quadrata.

A—B. Ancient reservoir of rain-water behind the Wall of Romulus.

C—D. Section at the south-east corner, with ancient stone-quarry behind the southern wall.

E—F. Steps of Cacus.

Roma Quadrata.—Plate III.

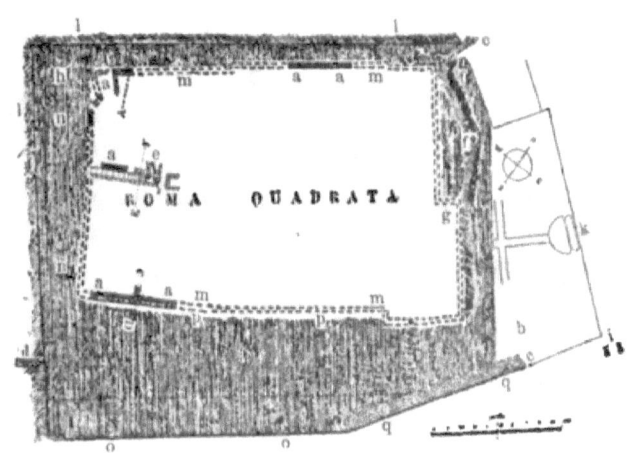

I. Plan of the Surface and the Sides.

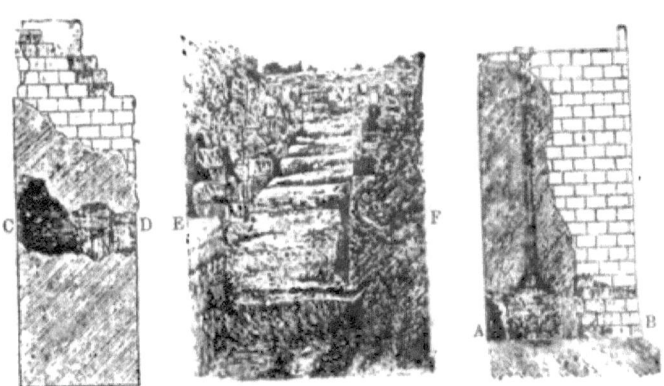

II. Details of the Sides of the Primitive City.

PLATE IV.

ROMA QUADRATA.

Details of the great Foss, on the southern side, which crossed the hill from near the Arch of Titus to the Germalus, near the Circus Maximus. (See p. 12.)

III. BATH-CHAMBERS OF LIVIA, with a painting of the time of Augustus on the vault of the inner chamber.

A—B. LONGITUDINAL SECTION. This is near the middle of the great Foss.

C—D. TRANSVERSE SECTION.

E—F. PLAN, with the modern steps down to it in the curve. (1, 1). The walls of these chambers, of the time of Augustus, with a painting of his time on the vault over (2). These walls, of the time of Augustus, are cut through on the east and north sides by rough concrete walls of the time of Domitian, to make a larger level surface for his great palace (3, 3, 3, 3).

IV. Section of the great Foss at the west end, near the Germalus, with a house built of squared stones of the time of Sylla standing on the bottom of the foss, and a colonnade of small columns (or a portico) standing on the surface of the ground, at the back of the tribune of the great hall of the palace of Domitian.

Roma Quadrata.—Plate IV.

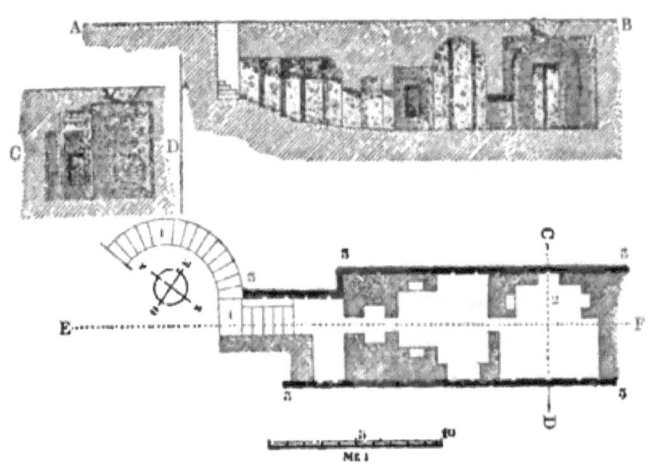

III. BATH-CHAMBERS OF LIVIA, MADE IN THE GREAT FOSS.

IV. SECTION OF THE GREAT FOSS AT THE WEST END.

PLATE V.

PLAN OF THE CITY ON THE TWO HILLS.

A. Roma Quadrata on the Palatine.

B. The Capitoline Hill.

C. The Quirinal Hill.

D. The Viminal Hill.

E. The Esquiline Hill.

F. The Celian Hill.

G. The Aventine Hill.

h h h h. Fossæ Quiritium.   (See Festus.)

a^1 a^1. Wall of Romulus (twelve feet thick where perfect).

a^2 a^2. Great Foss on the south side of Roma Quadrata, to isolate it from the rest of the Palatine Hill.

a^3. Southern part of the Palatine, afterwards THE CITY, as distinct from the citadel; the latter *only* was called Roma Quadrata.

a^4. The Velia, originally a promontory from the Esquiline Hill, cut off by the Quirites by means of one of their great fosses.

The City on the Two Hills.—Plate V.

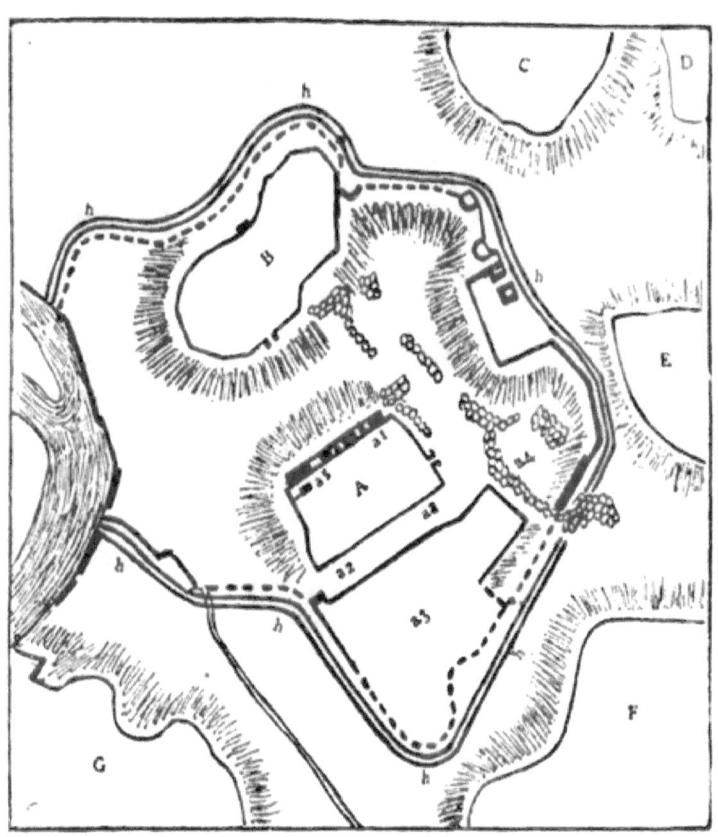

PLAN OF THE CITY ON THE TWO HILLS.

PLATE VI.

I. Forum of Augustus.

REMAINS of one of the towers of the second wall of Rome, towards the east, built of tufa in the usual style of the walls of the Kings; one side has been cut away to make room for a house in the sixteenth century, and the lower part is buried, as in other instances. It now stands behind the houses near the corner of two streets, and is best seen in the yard of the Caffè del Palladio. The wall of the time of Nerva, of travertine, between his forum and that of Augustus, is built into this old tower, and is one-third the height and of the thickness, as shewn in this view.

II. Part of the Second Wall of Rome, with Gateway.

PART of the Forum Transitorium of Nerva, and wall on the southern side with a gateway. The column here shewn supports the figure of Pallas, or Minerva, which appears to have had a wayside altar under it against the old wall. The lower part of the column is buried to one-third of its length owing to the filling-up of the foss-way, as shewn in dotted lines. This gate of the old wall of the Kings has been closed from the time of Nerva.

The City on the Two Hills.—Plate VI.

I. Tower in the Forum of Augustus.

II. Forum Transitorium of Nerva.

PLATE VII.

III. CLOACA MAXIMA. SECTION.

THIS is visible in the Forum Romanum, under the platform of the Basilica Julia. Another part is visible near the Arch of Janus, and the church of S. Giorgio in Velabro. The mouth of it is also visible in the Pulchrum Littus on the bank of the Tiber, near the round temple of Hercules, commonly miscalled of Vesta, about a hundred yards above the mouth of the river Almo.

IV. PULCHRUM LITTUS, a wall of the Kings on the bank of the Tiber, for the double purpose of a fortification against an enemy arriving in boats; and to keep out the great floods of the river, when the water was obliged to pass *over* this wall to begin with (and when each stone was a ton weight it was not easy for the floods to move it) the walls of buildings within could only be flooded from above, not undermined, and thus the floods could do much less damage. The arch through the wall is the mouth of the small river Almo, which is called by other names in different parts of its course; where it passed through the Circus Maximus it was called Euripus.

N.B. The six-foot rule, with each foot painted black and white alternately, shewn in the left-hand corner, indicates that the view is taken from one of Mr. Parker's photographs; he intended this to be always used as a scale, but the photographers either from carelessness, or from prejudice, frequently did not use it.

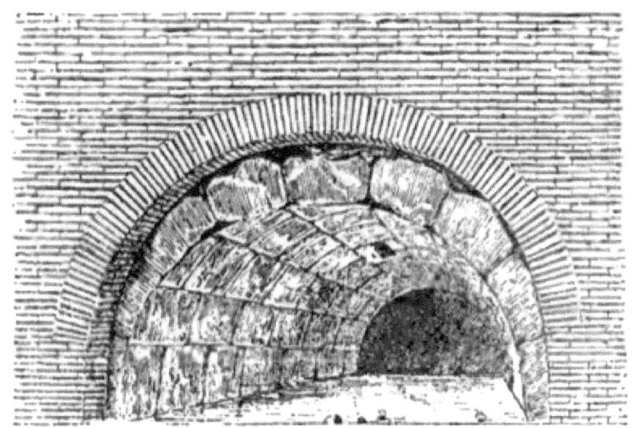

III. Cloaca Maxima, part visible in the Forum Romanum.

IV. Pulchrum Littus, and exit of River Almo into the Tiber.

PLATE VIII.

I. WALL OF THE LATINS, ON THE AVENTINE.

THIS wall is built of the usual large blocks of tufa, but differing slightly from the wall of Romulus on the Palatine, the edges of the stones being chamfered. In this two arches have been inserted, probably for a catapult and a balista; one remains perfect, and is seen in the view, of the other only one jamb remains. This wall is on one of the forts to defend the original Porta Ostiensis, and is near the church of S. Prisca; there are remains of another fort on the other side of the road under S. Sabba; the two stood on the outer corners of a gorge, at the narrow end of which was the gate, where now four roads meet.

II. MURO - TORTO.

THIS celebrated part of the wall of Rome is at the north-east corner, built against the cliff at the end of the Pincian Hill, to prevent the earth or tufa from slipping down; being on the edge of the great outer foss, and the soil rather loose, it began to give way when the builders had got about half-way up the cliff, and hangs over more than three feet (a), so as always to look dangerous; but as the builders who watched it saw that it did not go any farther, they had the courage to build the upper part of the wall upon this distorted part (b). (See p. 61.)

This is shewn by the layers of stone, which slope in the part that overhangs, but are horizontal in the upper part.

I. WALL OF THE LATINS, ON THE AVENTINE.

II. MURO-TORTO.

PLATE IX.

Porta Capena.

I. Exterior of the Western Tower of the Gate, with the pavement of the Via Appia, and the raised path by the side of the road, as shewn in the excavations of 1868. This lower part of the ancient tower has a mediæval tower built upon it, and is now used as the gardener's cottage. The aqueduct passed over the gate and through this tower. The earth on the side appearing as four steps, was only thrown up in that manner for the convenience of the workmen.

A. The Aqueduct.   B. Pavement of the Via Appia.
C. Bank of earth on the northern side, shewing the depth.

II. Interior of the same Tower, with the wall of the time of Appius Claudius remaining on two sides of it, and the aqueduct passing through this chamber after having passed over the gate. From this point it has been traced both ways; on the eastern side from the great reservoir (formerly miscalled a *vivarium*) under the Claudium, and on the western side under the north wall of the Pseudo-Aventine to the great reservoir under S. Sabba, and from thence to the final reservoir in the Porta Trigemina on the bank of the Tiber.

a. The Aqueduct.   b. Bed of *opus signinum* or *coccio pesto*, the peculiar hard cement made with broken pottery, and used only for the Aqueducts.   c. Wall in the style of the walls of the Kings.   d. Modern wall.   e. Modern plaster.

The City on the Seven Hills.—Plate IX.

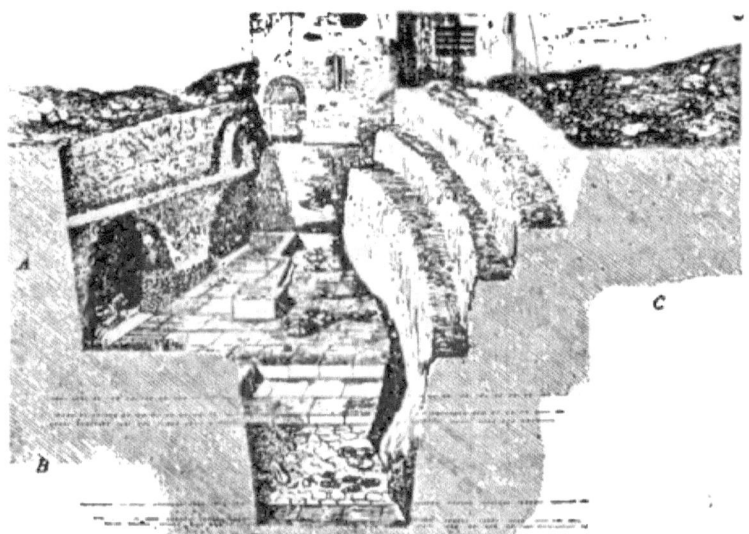

I. PORTA CAPENA. EXTERIOR OF THE LOWER PART OF THE WESTERN TOWER OF THE GATE, WITH THE EXCAVATIONS OF 1868.

II. PORTA CAPENA. INTERIOR OF THE WESTERN TOWER OF THE GATE, WITH THE AQUEDUCT PASSING THROUGH IT.

PLATE X.

III.—A. PART OF THE AQUEDUCT near the Porta Capena, still remaining in the lower part of the tower, as shewn in Plate IX. It passed over that gate and across the valley at the north end of the Pseudo-Aventine.

B. Section of the eastern tower of this gate, which remains, with part of the aqueduct passing through it, shewn by the hollow space left for it. (See the previous plate.)

C. Part of the arcade of the aqueduct, and of the pavement of the *crepido*, or raised footpath by the side of the Via Appia. It has been traced from this point to its mouth at the Porta Trigemina. (See p. 53.)

IV. PART OF THE RAMPART AND WALL OF SERVIUS TULLIUS IN 1870, near the railway station, with large black figures painted on each stone by order of the Baron Visconti for Pope Pius IX., to prevent the stones being moved. This preserved it in its place for two or three years, but this part has now been all swept away to enlarge the railway. Many other parts of this great rampart have been brought to light since that time; the existence of it, with the enormous foss at the foot of it, was not known, and had not been known for many centuries. On another part very near this, there was a row of houses of the time of Augustus built on the top of the rampart or bank, with gardens going down the slope to the edge of the foss. The latter was found to be 100 feet wide and 30 feet deep, agreeing exactly with the history of Dionysius from the old family legends. (See p. 50.)

III. Part of an Aqueduct.

IV. Rampart of Servius Tullius, near the Railway Station.

PLATE XI.

V. PART OF THE AGGER, or Rampart, and Wall of Servius Tullius, near the church of S. Antonio Abate, with the Porta di S. Lorenzo, or Tiburtina, in the distance.

This was excavated by the Municipality about 1875, for making the foundations of this part of the new city on the *chess-board plan*, ignoring entirely, and wantonly destroying, the remains of the ancient city.

VI. HORN-WORK at the north end of this great Rampart, or the north-east corner of the City on the Seven Hills. Upon the south-west corner of this great horn-work the house of Sallust was built; this is marked by a small square space on the plan. The Via di Porta Pia passes on the southern side, and is shewn on the plan. The foss of Sallust is seen on the northern side; this was used by the Emperor Aurelian for horse-exercise when he resided in the house of Sallust, which had come to the Crown in default of heirs, according to the Roman law. An aqueduct of the time of Augustus is shewn on the lower bank, leading to a *castellum aquæ* (cistern or reservoir) under the house of Sallust. (See p. 47.)

V. Agger or Rampart, and Wall of Servius Tullius.

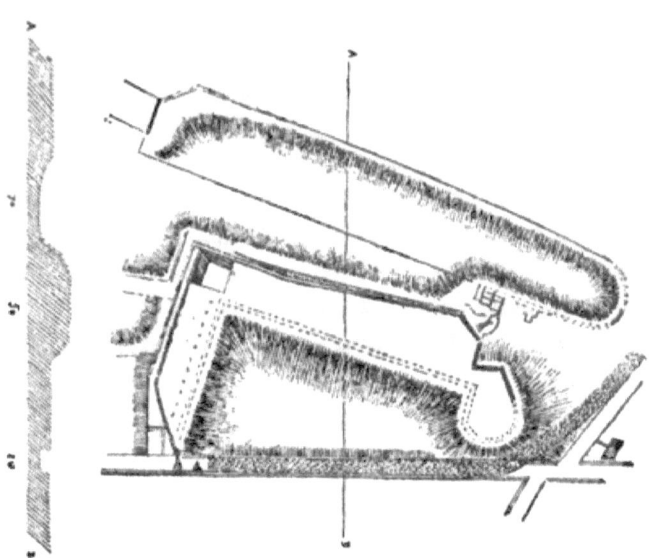

VI. Plan of the Horn-work at the north end of this Rampart.

PLATE XII.

I. Part of the Outer Wall of Rome and Rampart of Tarquinius II.

This was left unfinished in consequence of the successful rebellion under Brutus, which ended in the Republic.

This part is between the Prætorian Camp and the Porta Tiburtina, with part of the wall of Aurelian built against it, and sometimes upon it, but no corridor within it, as in other parts where there is no rampart. (See p. 56.)

II. Section of the Wall and Rampart.

This is the only part of the rampart of Tarquinius the Second that remains sufficiently perfect to be understood by ordinary readers; it can be traced by experienced eyes in many parts, especially between the Sessorium (now S. Croce) and the Prætorian Camp. Between the Prætorian Camp and the Pincian Hill there is a gap of more than a mile in length in which there is no rampart, this is now chiefly in the gardens of the Villa Ludovisi; in that part the wall of Aurelian is on the level ground, and has the corridor for the sentinel's path within the wall quite perfect, and the towers on the exterior nearly so; but this wall without the rampart did not prove a sufficient defence, and this is the weak point at which Rome has always been taken.

    a. Level of the Rampart within the Walls.
    b. Section of the Rampart.   c c. Wall of Aurelian.
    d. Wall of Tarquinius II.   e. Modern road outside of the wall.   f. Vineyard made in the old outer foss.
    g g. Section of the Wall of Tarquinius II.

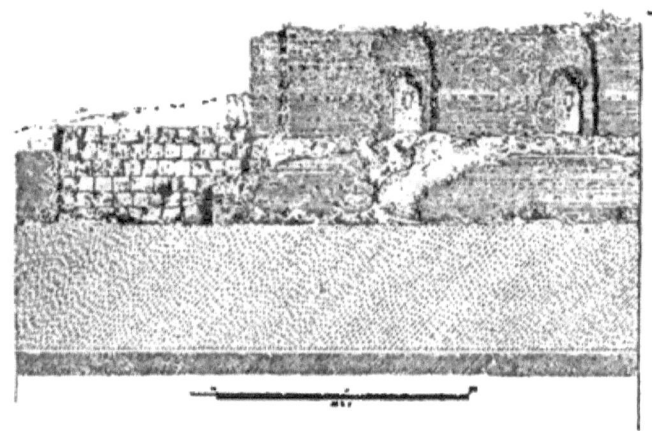

I. Part of the Outer Wall of Rome of Tarquinius II., between the Prætorian Camp and the Porta Tiburtina.

II. Section of the same part of the Wall and Rampart.

PLATE XIII.

I. Porta Maggiore.

THIS is the principal gate of Rome on the eastern side, on the high table-land from which the seven hills are in reality great promontories in the valley of the Tiber. The deep and rapid stream of the Tiber was a sufficient defence on the western side, especially where the bank was supported by the massive wall called the *Pulchrum Littus*. At this great gate several roads met, and it was called by various names, according to whether persons were going from Rome or entering into it. This was the entrance through the outer wall not into THE CITY, but into the *pomœrium* only, in part of which the great burial-ground of the time of the Kings and of the Republic was made. The gate was called Esquilina, as the entrance into the Exquiliæ;—Prænestina, by those coming from Preneste (see p. 69);—Labicana, by those coming from Labicum; and—Sessoriana, because it entered into one corner of the great garden of the Sessorian Palace.

II. Porta Asinaria.

THIS gate is on the southern side, near the east end, and between the old Lateran Palace of Aulus Plautius Lateranus, of the time of Nero, and the Sessorian Palace of the Kings, originally a detached fort, in which S. Helena, the mother of Constantine, resided for many years, and where she built the church of S. Croce in Gerusalemme, so called because she had brought earth from Jerusalem to be laid in the foundations, and under the altar had placed a piece of what she believed to be the true cross on which Christ was crucified. The gate led direct to the villa of the Asinii, between the Lateran and the Sessorium.

I. Porta Maggiore.

II. Porta Asinaria.

PLATE XIV.

III. Porta Appia, now called di S. Sebastiano.

This gate, in the outer wall of Aurelian, is just a mile from the Porta Capena, in the inner wall of Servius Tullius; it was restored by King Theodoric, and the two gateway-towers are of his time—the square parts of these towers below, with the gateway, are built of square blocks of marble taken from the Temple of Mars, that stood outside of the original gate near this spot. This temple was in ruins in the time of Theodoric (see p. 71), and he had ordered that in such cases the materials should be used for the repairs of the walls that he continued to use. The upper and round part is of the same character as the towers at Ravenna; the inner side is in a ruinous state, but the passage over the gate from one tower to the other is still practicable for a good climber. The battlements have probably been renewed in the fifteenth century.

IV. Wall of Aurelian.—Exterior.

This shews the most perfect part that remains, with the only tower of his time that is perfect; it is on the exterior of the Ludovisi gardens, and on the inner side the corridor for the sentinel's path is more perfect than in almost any other part. The part here shewn is on the level ground between the Prætorian Camp and the Pincian Hill.

III. Porta Appia, or di S. Sebastiano.

IV. Wall of Aurelian.—Exterior.

PLATE XV.

V. THE CORRIDOR FOR THE SENTINELS' PATH.

THIS part is near the Porta Appia, in a large vineyard within the Porta Latina. The inner side of one of the towers is seen in the foreground. These towers are flat at the top, and had a catapult and a balista placed upon each in time of siege, and steps up from the corridor in every instance, so that the guards could go from one tower to the other in perfect safety, and be ready to receive an attack at any point that was threatened. (See p. 68.)

There are altogether some miles of this corridor remaining, but it was not made in all parts; where the old earthen rampart was left there was no place for it. (See Plate XII.)

VI. ANOTHER PART OF THE CORRIDOR OF AURELIAN.

THE great wall is remarkably perfect in the interval between the Prætorian Camp and the Pincian Hill, now chiefly in the gardens of the Villa Ludovisi. In this part there is no earthen rampart behind it, so that the wall was the only defence, and notwithstanding that being apparently sufficient, it was always there that the enemy succeeded in making a breach, and from which Rome was taken. In modern days, since the use of artillery, this is only what might have been expected, but in earlier times, before the use of gunpowder, the great wall of the Empire would seem to have been sufficient; indeed, in defending Rome against the enormous army of the Goths, Belisarius found it sufficient by constant vigilance, but when the battering-ram could be applied, it appears that a breach was soon made.

V. Wall of Aurelian, inner side, with the Corridor for the Sentinels' path.

VI. Wall of Aurelian, interior.

PLATE XVI.

I. Part of the Via Appia, near Ariccia.

The streets of Rome are so thoroughly undermined, and the old streets buried to such a depth, that it is useless to try and give illustrations of them. The roads, on the other hand, are an endless subject; there are remains of them all over the old Roman Empire. The most important was long considered to be the Via Appia; of this the exit from Rome was the Porta Capena, in the Wall of Servius Tullius, the remains of which have already been given (see Plates IX., X.). It passed through the Porta Appia in the outer wall, just a mile from the old wall. An important portion of this ancient road, where it passes across a swamp near Ariccia, is very distinct, and is built as a causeway.

II. Pons ad Nonum, or Ponte Nono, on the Via Gabina.

This ancient bridge has its name from being just nine miles from the original gate in the old wall of Rome, but it is only eight miles from the gate in the outer wall, on one of the old roads where it crosses a river liable to floods, and is therefore of great length. The level of the road has evidently been raised very much at a more recent period, and the bridge raised to correspond with it. There was no parapet wall to protect horses or carriages in the dark until quite recently, since the photograph was taken from which this engraving is made. The early remains of the Porta Capena have shewn that the style of the buildings of the time of Appius Claudius, who made this road (A.U.C. 441, B.C. 312), was very much the same as in the time of the Kings.

I. Part of the Via Appia, near Ariccia.

II. Ponte Nono, on the Via Gabina.

PLATE XVII.

I. Arcade of the Claudia and Anio Novus,
FIVE MILES EAST OF ROME,

in the district popularly called Roma Vecchia (or old Rome), at the east end of which are the principal *castella aquæ*, where the aqueducts emerge from the hills, and the arcade begins. These great reservoirs are chiefly subterranean. The height of the arcade from the ground is raised almost immediately: at first it is very low, but as the level of the ground becomes lower, and that of the aqueduct must be kept nearly level, the height from the road rapidly becomes higher, until it is frequently thirty or forty feet from the ground, and in places even more, where it passes over a stream. The specus, or stone conduit, of the Claudia carried immediately on the arches, is clearly visible in this view, and over it the specus of the Anio Novus of Nero, which is built of concrete, and faced with the beautiful brickwork of his time, and in part with reticulated work. (See pp. 99 and 109.)

II. Arches of Nero, near the Porta Maggiore.

This arcade and porticus is between the western wall of the great garden of the Sessorian Palace, now of S. Croce, and the Cœlian Hill. It was continued along the northern side of that hill for more than a mile, to the great central reservoir at the west end of the Cœlian, carried on arches twenty feet from the ground, and having the Arch of Dolabella used as part of the substructure at the north-west corner. It will be seen that the arches of the part across the great foss are double, one over the other, to keep the watercourse level. The water is that of the Claudia and Anio Novus, united in the two great twin-reservoirs called the Gemelli, made in what had been the foss of the time of the Kings.

The Aqueducts.—Plate XVII.

I. Arcade of the Claudia and Anio Novus, near Roma Vecchia.

II. Arches of Nero, near the Porta Maggiore.

PLATE XVIII.

III. Septizonium, or Sette Sale, on the Esquiline Hill.

These were the great reservoirs, supplied by several aqueducts, for the palace of Nero and for the Thermæ of Titus and of Trajan, built over that palace. Various conjectures have been made about this name of Septizonium: the most probable is that it was called after the seven half-arches, or zones, between the reservoirs on the outer face. There was another Septizonium on the low ground between the Cœlian and the Palatine, of which the lower storey exists, though still buried; all that was above ground was destroyed by Pope Leo X., as building-materials for the great church of S. Peter on the Vatican, along with some other ancient buildings of the Empire.

IV. Interior of a Castellum Aquæ, one of the great Cisterns or Reservoirs of the Aqueducts.

There are nine such chambers in the Sette Basse. It was at first said that there were seven only, and that it was named from them, and that the two outer ones were piscinas or filtering-places only. The latter is probably true; the one on the south side certainly was a filtering-place, for the vault over it remains with an opening in the centre, and the surface is ornamented with a mosaic pavement, shewing that there was an upper chamber; perhaps the whole of these numerous reservoirs were of two storeys. There was sometimes only an open arcade between two of these chambers or cisterns, more frequently there was a wall with apertures at different heights, so that the water, running in at one end and out at the other, was kept in perpetual motion, to purify it more thoroughly.

III. Septizonium, or Sette Basse, on the Esquiline Hill.

IV. Interior of a Castellum Aquæ, or Reservoir.

PLATE XIX.

I. The Pantheum, or Entrance-hall to the Thermæ of Agrippa;—the Front with the Portico.

This fine portico is an addition to the original plan of the time of Agrippa and Augustus by later emperors, as recorded in the inscription just above the colonnade in front. It has been several times *repaired*, but not altered. The original brick Front, of the time of Agrippa (but not of the time of the first foundation), remains perfect behind this portico, which is built up against it. The turrets are mediæval additions. (See p. 116.)

M. AGRIPPA . L. F. COS . TERTIVM . FECIT

IMP. CAES. L. SEPTIMIVS . SEVERVS . PIVS . PERTINAX . ARABICVS . ADIABENICVS . PARTHICVS . MAXIMVS . PONTIF. MAX. TRIB. POTEST. X. IMP. XI. COS. III. P. R. PROCOS. ET .

IMP.CAES. M. AVRELIVS. ANTONINVS . PIVS . FELIX. AVG.TRIB. POTEST. V. COS. PROCOS. PANTHEVM . VETVSTATE . CORRVPTVM . CVM . OMNI . CVLTV .
RESTITVERVNT

II. Back of the Pantheum.

This shews the original construction and fine cornice, and parts of the walls that connected the great entrance-hall with the other parts of these extensive Thermæ. These walls still remain; they have been made more visible since the photograph was taken (from which this engraving is copied) by pulling down the house of a baker which had been built over them. There are also considerable ruins of the walls of the bath-chambers, which shew the great extent of the whole structure. Considerable excavations have been made in this place in 1881.

The Thermæ.—Plate XIX. 231

I. THE PANTHEUM—FRONT WITH PORTICO.

II. PANTHEUM AT THE BACK, TIME OF AGRIPPA.

PLATE XX.

III. Thermæ of Caracalla.

PART of the *porticus* on the side of the Via Appia, begun by Caracalla, finished by Alexander Severus (Lampridius, 32). The lower part of this was excavated by Mr. Parker in 1878, to explain the meaning of the word *porticus:* it is used by Lampridius in describing this addition, which consists of a *double arcade* one over the other, with a bath-chamber under each arch.

IV. Part of the Hot-air Chamber on the Western Side of the Thermæ.

THESE Thermæ are of enormous extent, and better known than any other, because they are so much more perfect, and have so often been described at all periods. But there is good reason to believe that others were equally large, even as early as those of Agrippa, in the time of Augustus; although each succeeding Emperor, at intervals of about half-a-century, seems to have tried to outdo what his predecessors had done. Of those of Titus and Trajan the ruins are of the same enormous extent. Those of Commodus and Septimius Severus appear to have been of about the same extent, although they have been so thoroughly destroyed that the only remains of them are now underground. Of those begun by Diocletian and completed by Constantine, there are still large remains, though in a very ruinous state; the extent of them may be seen by the railway-station being made in a comparatively small part of them.

III. Thermæ of Caracalla, part of the Porticus added by Alexander Severus.

IV. Thermæ of Caracalla, part of the Sudatorium, or Hot-air Chamber.

PLATE XXI.

I. Forum Romanum, General View from the Palatine Hill, looking north.

THE three columns on the left hand are the celebrated columns of the Temple of Castor and Pollux—beyond these is the platform of the Basilica Julia, with the series of brick bases erected by Signor Rosa where *he imagined* the old columns of the arcades were situated.—At the further end of this are some brick arches of a later period, on the line of the original basilica, which went from west to east, and was almost destroyed in a great fire; it was then rebuilt by Augustus, who enlarged it so much that "what had been the length became the breadth;" the platform now goes from north to south. The corner of the Municipium (shewn to the right in this view) is the due north point of the Forum Romanum—to the left of this is a street down the middle of the Forum, part of the Via Nova. The great building at the end of the view is the Municipium, still used by the Municipality; under it is the Tabularium, the arches all walled up excepting one, which has been re-opened. Under this is the Ærarium, or public treasury in the time of the Kings and of the Republic, of which some of the small square windows are seen behind the modern road up to the Piazza del Campidoglio. The bell-tower of the Municipium is the highest point in Rome, from which there is a splendid view. On the right in this view is the arch of Septimius Severus, near the further end;—in front, part of the Temple and Rostrum of Julius Cæsar. (See p. 122.)

1. Forum Romanum, General View from the Palatine in 1878.

PLATE XXII.

II. A View of one of the Rostra in the Forum,

Of the time of Constantine, from a sculpture on his arch.

It represents the principal rostrum near the Temple of Saturn. The two seated figures, one at each end, holding a staff, are statues of gods—in the centre stand the orators, protected by a low screen of pierced marble (called *transenna*), addressing the citizens from a raised platform; the crowd at each end are the citizens—the building in the background is the Tabularium. (See p. 125.)

III. Sculpture from one of the Marble Walls.

THE principal figure is the Emperor Marcus Aurelius Antoninus (much mutilated); he is addressing the citizens, when they interrupt him by crying out *octo! octo!* demanding *eight gold pieces*, which he gave them (as related by Dion Cassius, lib. lxxi. c. 32). The figure of the Emperor is seen standing on the rostrum, with coins dropping from his right hand (which, with the head, are unfortunately destroyed); the two foremost figures of the citizens are each holding out a hand, one with five fingers extended, the other with three, and the money is seen falling into them.

This engraving is from a photograph, taken at the time of the excavation of these marble walls in 1872. (See p. 126.)

The Forum Romanum.—Plate XXII.

VIEW OF A ROSTRUM IN THE FORUM, FROM THE ARCH OF CONSTANTINE.

III. THE EMPEROR MARCUS AURELIUS ADDRESSING THE CITIZENS.

PLATE XXIII.

Forum of Trajan.

The *three* tiers of shops at the east end of this Forum, against the cliff of the Quirinal Hill.

1. On the level of the ground, with part of the old pavement of the Forum remaining in front of them; there are several of these shops more or less perfect.

2. On the first floor, or half-way up the cliff, where a sort of bazaar was formed. The Rows, or shops, on the first floor of the houses at Chester, were probably an imitation of these, as Chester was a Roman city. In the Forum of Trajan the passage was at the back of the shops, which extended to the edge of the cliff. The flight of stone steps from the level to this gallery still remains; though in a bad state of repair, it can still be used.

3. On the top of the cliff, and on the summit of the hill. These have been converted into stables for the cavalry barracks, made in what had been in the Middle Ages a nunnery, and this continued till the time of Pius IX. The steps or staircase from the gallery on the first floor to the upper part have been destroyed, but there are distinct marks of them in the walls. The whole of these are clearly shewn in the drawing from which this plate is engraved.

- A. Plan of the lower storey.
- B. Passage behind the Shops, on the first floor.
- C. Upper storey.   D. Part of the Quirinal Hill.

- a. Pavement of the Forum.
- b b b. Stairs from one storey to the other.
- x. Level of the ground at the summit of the cliff.
- y. Modern buildings.

Forum of Trajan.—Plate XXIII. 239

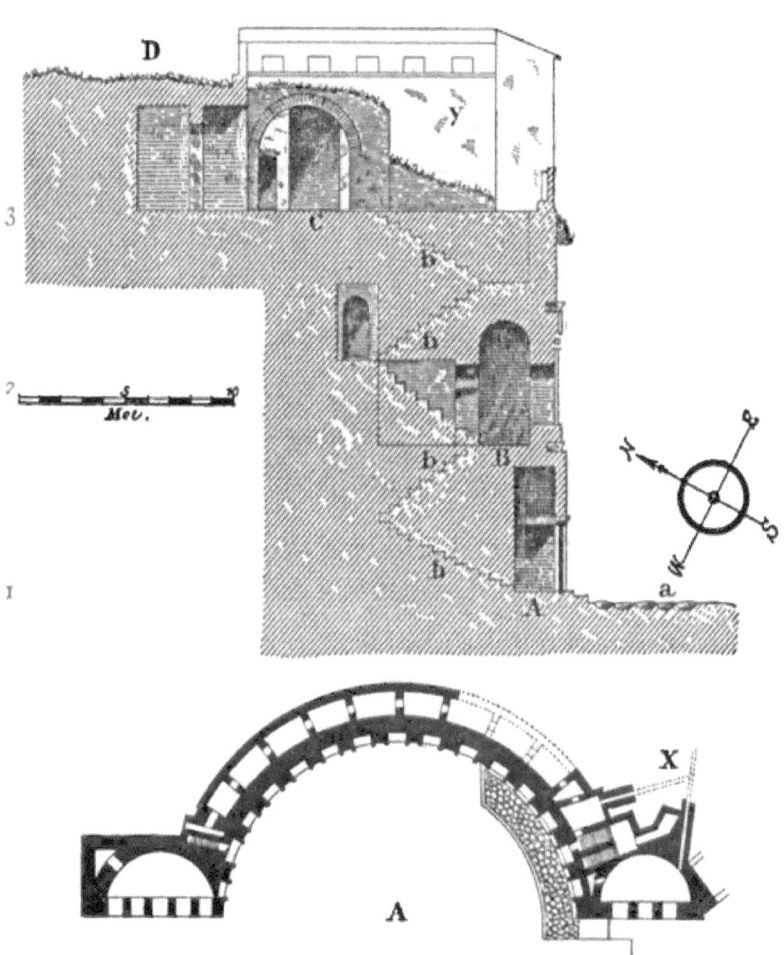

THE THREE TIERS OF SHOPS AT THE EAST END.

PLATE XXIV.

I. COLUMBARIA in a public burial-vault on the Via Appia, between the Porta Capena in the *inner* wall, and the Porta Appia in the *outer* wall. Near to the latter (now in the Vigna Codini), with the steps down to them, are two similar burial-vaults in the same vineyard, all of the first century, one of which is of the servants of Augustus, and has the names and offices of the deceased engraved on each. Similar columbaria are usually found in all large Roman tombs, more especially those which were public burial-places and those for the public officials, such as the officers of Cæsar's household, to which this belonged. (See p. 144.)

II. TOMB of the Lateran family of the first century, on the west bank of their garden, within the present walls of Rome. The Lateran was originally a separate fortress, probably on the Celiolum, or "little Celian," separated from the Cœlian Hill by a wide and deep foss, only filled up by order of Signor Rosa in the time of Pius IX., by bringing there the earth that he had dug out from the Palatine in searching for statues for Napoleon III. This tomb was originally circular, and faced with reticulated-work, but two wings were added to it about a century afterwards. Both are full of *columbaria*, or places for the cinerary urns.

The Mausolea and Tombs of Rome.—Plate XXIV.

I. Columbaria in a public Burial-vault on the Via Appia.

II. Tomb of the Lateran Family.

PLATE XXV.

III. Tomb of the Baker Eurysaces and his Wife Aristia, at the Porta Maggiore.

THIS celebrated and curious tomb represents all the implements employed in baking bread; those which are chiefly seen are the basins for kneading the dough, or (as some say), the ovens. At the outer end, now destroyed, were the effigies of the baker and his wife, which are preserved and built up in a wall on the opposite side of the road; they should be replaced at the outer end of the tomb. The whole was buried for many centuries, in one of the great round towers, to defend the gate of the time of Honorius, which was destroyed in 1838, and the old part of the gate brought to light, together with this tomb. It stands between the two ancient roads, the Via Labicana and the Via Nomentana, which have been originally foss-ways, and the tomb was made at that level of the ground. The roads have now been filled-up to the present level, and the lower part of the tomb is about ten feet below that level. The foss-ways were not intended for carriages, or carts on wheels. After long opposition throughout all the latter part of the time of the Republic, public convenience eventually prevailed, and these hollow ways were filled up to the level, but this was not done until the second century of the Empire. (See p. 147.)

The Mausolea and Tombs of Rome.— Plate XXV.

III. Tomb of the Baker Eurysaces and his wife Aristia.

PLATE XXVI.

I. General View of the Exterior, North-east side, in 1870.

This side is the only one that is perfect; the two lower storeys are of the time of the Flavian Emperors; the upper storey was originally of wood, and was burnt about a century afterwards, and then built of stone, as now seen in this part.

II. Part of the Interior, brought to light by the excavations made by the Italian Government at the request of Mr. Parker, but under the direction of Signor Rosa. This view shews the enormous depth of the chambers, and passages, and canals, supplied by the aqueduct used for the naval fights, beneath the arena, and for the use of the performers in the theatrical exhibitions, and the immense walls that were necessary to support the floor of boards, covered with sand, called the arena. Some of the walls are built of the large blocks of tufa of the time of the Kings, brought from the south end of the Palatine in the time of Sylla. These inner walls are faced with brickwork of the time of different Emperors; some of it is of the time of Nero, who included the Colosseum in his enormous palace (see p. 153). Under the galleries are seen the dens for the lions, and other animals of about that size. A small stream of water ran in front of these for the animals to drink; there were a hundred of them, and during the great exhibition at the time of the dedication, it is recorded that at the word of the Emperor a hundred lions leapt on to the stage, or arena, at once.

I. COLOSSEUM, VIEW OF THE MOST PERFECT PART OF THE EXTERIOR IN 1870.

II. COLOSSEUM, PART OF THE EXCAVATIONS IN 1878, SHEWING THE INNER WALLS TO SUPPORT THE FLOOR AND THE DENS.

PLATE XXVII.

III. Probable restoration of part of the substructure at the time of the dedication, when the lions and other animals used to leap on to the arena.

This shews—

1. A lion which has just come out of his den into an iron cage.

2. A cage with a lion in it, being pulled up by cords and pulleys to the level of the arena, on which he leapt, as recorded by contemporary authors.

3. A cameleopard leaping out of a cage on to the arena. This animal is mentioned as one of those that were then exhibited.

Above this is seen the arcade of the lower gallery for spectators, and the recesses under it left for the actors to take refuge in at the time of the fight of wild beasts, or in bull-fights. Also part of the screen of lattice-work in front of the gallery; but this is not *in situ*.

The Colosseum.—Plate XXVII.

III. COLOSSEUM, PROBABLE RESTORATION OF PART OF THE SUBSTRUCTURE.

PLATE XXVIII.

I. CHAMBERS of the House of Hortensius, afterwards of Augustus, excavated by Signor Rosa for Napoleon III., about 1870. This kind of reticulated-work is of the time of Sylla, or Julius Cæsar. Similar small chambers occur in many houses of that period at Pompeii. In this house, and in all the palaces of the Emperors of the first century, the chambers of the ground-storeys only had walls of stone or brick, and these were always small, as for bed-chambers. The state apartments, on the upper floor, were usually of wood until after the time of the great fire of Nero, which spread so rapidly from that cause. The same thing may be seen in many houses at Pompeii, where the apertures left for the great beams of the upper floor can still be seen.

II. CHAMBERS OF THE PALACE OF TIBERIUS.

THIS palace almost joined on to that of Augustus, which had been originally the house of Hortensius, the orator, of the time of Cicero. It was separated from it only by a narrow street, the pavement of which remains visible, but the palace was of considerable extent. In addition to the part on the upper surface of the Palatine, another part is on the lower level of the Germalus; there are remains of a hot-air chamber on that level communicating with the hypocaust under the floor of another room on the higher level, which also remains visible. The construction of the walls of this agrees exactly with those of the guard-chambers at the back of the northern wall of the Prætorian Camp, which is of the time of Tiberius. Suetonius mentions that only three palaces were allowed to be built on the original part of the Palatine, those of Augustus, Tiberius, and Caligula, of all of which there are considerable remains.

I. Chambers in the House of Hortensius, afterwards of Augustus.

II. Part of the Palace of Tiberius on the Palatine Hill.

PLATE IV*.

ROMA QUADRATA.

I. A CAVE-RESERVOIR of rain-water, near the north-west corner, with two wells descending into it from the summit of the hill, the lower part of each of which is a hollow cone.

II. Another cave-reservoir at Alba Longa, also with a similar well descending into it. This cave is on the bank of the lake of Albano, and close to the small monastery called Palazzuolo. An open aqueduct conveys water to it, of which there are considerable remains by the side of the road.

III. Remains of Walls of the Kings at the east end of the Capitoline Hill. These remains were brought to light by the excavations of 1878 (?); they had previously been concealed in the cellars of the monastery of Ara Cœli. Part of them had evidently been the original fortifications of that end of the hill; they stood partly against the cliff, and in part upon a great bed of clay, as shewn in this view, taken from a photograph.

Roma Quadrata.—Plate IV*.

I. Reservoir of Romulus on the Palatine Hill.

II. Cave-reservoir and Well at Alba Longa.

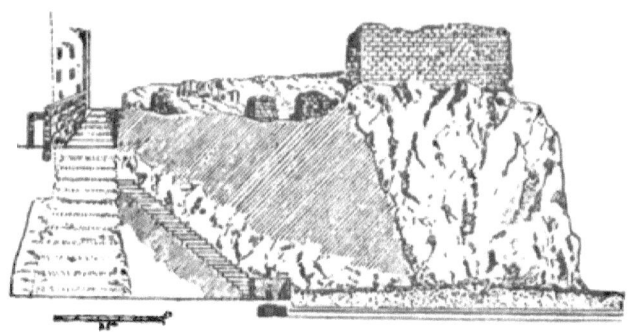

III. Remains on the East End of the Capitoline Hill.

WORKS ON
Mediæval Architecture and Archæology,

PUBLISHED BY

MESSRS. PARKER AND CO.
OXFORD,
AND 6 SOUTHAMPTON-ST., STRAND, LONDON.

A B C OF GOTHIC ARCHITECTURE.
By JOHN HENRY PARKER, C.B., Hon. M.A. Oxon, F.S.A. Lond., &c. *Second Edition.* 264 pp., square 16mo., with 200 Woodcuts, cloth, 3s.

"It is scarcely necessary to say that this is a good and useful little book. The author of the well-known 'Glossary of Architecture' was not likely to fail in his A B C, and has produced a short and admirable view of the growth and progress of Gothic architecture in England, illustrated at every stage with accurate woodcuts of well-chosen examples. Its size is suited to the pocket, and it will be an invaluable *vade mecum* for every one who visits old churches or other old buildings, whether as student or excursionist."—*The Academy, Sept.* 24, 1881.

THE GLOSSARY OF ARCHITECTURE ABRIDGED.
A CONCISE GLOSSARY OF TERMS USED IN GRECIAN, ROMAN, ITALIAN, **AND** GOTHIC ARCHITECTURE. By JOHN HENRY PARKER, C.B., M.A., F.S.A. A New Edition, revised. Fcap. 8vo., with nearly 500 Illustrations, in ornamental cloth, 7s. 6d.

ARCHITECTURAL MANUAL.
AN INTRODUCTION TO THE STUDY OF GOTHIC ARCHITECTURE.
By JOHN HENRY PARKER, C.B., M.A., F.S.A., with 200 Illustrations, and a Topographical and a Glossarial Index. *Sixth Edition, with Additions.* Fcap. 8vo., in ornamental cloth, 5s.

GOTHIC ARCHITECTURE.
AN ATTEMPT TO DISCRIMINATE THE STYLES OF ARCHITECTURE IN ENGLAND, FROM THE CONQUEST TO THE REFORMATION: with a Sketch of the Grecian and Roman Orders. By the late THOMAS RICKMAN, F.S.A. *Seventh Edition*, with considerable Additions, chiefly Historical, by JOHN HENRY PARKER, C.B., M.A., F.S.A., and numerous Illustrations. Medium 8vo., cloth, 16s.

[1181.4.50]

ARCHÆOLOGY.

THE DOMESTIC ARCHITECTURE OF THE MIDDLE AGES,
FROM THE CONQUEST TO HENRY VIII. By the late T. HUDSON TURNER and J. H. PARKER, C.B. *Second Edition.* 4 vols., 8vo., profusely Illustrated, cloth, £3 12s.

Separately.

—— Vol. I. FROM THE CONQUEST TO THE END OF THE THIRTEENTH CENTURY. With numerous Illustrations. By T. HUDSON TURNER. *Second Edition.* 8vo., cloth, 21s.

—— Vol. II. FROM EDWARD I. TO RICHARD II., (the Edwardian Period, or the Decorated Style). 8vo., cloth, 21s.

—— Vol. III. FROM RICHARD II. TO HENRY VIII., (or the Perpendicular Style). With numerous Illustrations. By J. H. PARKER, C.B. In 2 Parts. 8vo., 1l. 10s.

MILITARY ARCHITECTURE,
Translated from the French of E. VIOLLET-LE-DUC, by M. MACDERMOTT, Esq., Architect. With the Original French Engravings. Second Edition, with a Preface by JOHN HENRY PARKER, C.B., F.S.A., &c. Medium 8vo., cloth, 10s. 6d.

"The archæological interest of this book is very great. Like all M. Viollet-le-Duc's works, it is done thoroughly and illustrated with designs which in themselves are of no small value to the student. . . . Perhaps the most interesting part, however, of this work is Mr. J. H. Parker's Preface to the Second Edition."—*John Bull.*

MEDIÆVAL GLASS PAINTING.
AN INQUIRY INTO THE DIFFERENCE OF STYLE OBSERVABLE IN ANCIENT GLASS PAINTINGS, especially in England, with Hints on Glass Painting, by the late CHARLES WINSTON. With Corrections and Additions by the Author. *A New Edition.* 2 vols., Medium 8vo., with numerous coloured Engravings, cloth, £1 11s. 6d.

MEDIÆVAL ARMOUR.
ANCIENT ARMOUR AND WEAPONS IN EUROPE. By JOHN HEWITT, Member of the Archæological Institute of Great Britain. The work complete, from the Iron Period of the Northern Nations to the Seventeenth Century. 3 vols., 8vo., 1l. 11s. 6d.

EARLY BRITISH ARCHÆOLOGY.
OUR BRITISH ANCESTORS: WHO AND WHAT WERE THEY? An Inquiry serving to elucidate the Traditional History of the Early Britons by means of recent Excavations, Etymology, Remnants of Religious Worship, Inscriptions, &c. By the Rev. SAMUEL LYSONS, M.A., F.S.A., Rector of Rodmarton. Post 8vo., cloth, 5s.

ARCHÆOLOGY AND ARCHITECTURE.

THE ARCHÆOLOGY OF ROME.

THE ARCHÆOLOGY OF ROME. With Plates, Plans, and Diagrams. By JOHN HENRY PARKER, C.B.

Part 1. PRIMITIVE FORTIFICATIONS. *Second Edition*, 8vo., with 59 Plates, cloth, 21*s*.

Part 2. WALLS AND GATES. *Second Edition, nearly ready.*

Part 3. CONSTRUCTION OF WALLS. *Second Edition, in the Press.*

Part 4. The EGYPTIAN OBELISKS. *Second Edition*, 8vo., cl., 5*s*.

Part 5. THE FORUM ROMANUM ET MAGNUM. *Second Edition, Revised and Enlarged*, 41 Plates, 8vo., cloth, 10*s*. 6*d*.

Part 6. THE VIA SACRA, was originally published with Part 5, it will now be separated, and the New Edition is nearly ready, with THE TEMPLE OF ROMA, AND THE MARBLE PLAN OF ROME originally under the Porticus of that Temple, with Twenty-three Plates, giving outlines of all the fragments of this, now in the Capitoline Museum.

ALSO a complete account of the Excavations in Rome from A.D. 1485 to the present time.

Part 7. The COLOSSEUM. 8vo., cloth, 10*s*. 6*d*.

Part 8. The AQUEDUCTS OF ANCIENT ROME. 8vo., cloth, 15*s*.

Part 9. TOMBS IN AND NEAR ROME, and

Part 10. FUNEREAL AND EARLY CHRISTIAN SCULPTURE. 8vo., cloth, 15*s*.

Part 11. CHURCH AND ALTAR DECORATIONS IN ROME. 8vo., cloth, 10*s*. 6*d*.

Part 12. THE CATACOMBS OF ROME. 8vo., cloth, 15*s*.

Part 13. EARLY AND MEDIÆVAL CASTLES, with an Account of the Excavations in Rome, &c. *Nearly ready.*

Part 14. THE MEDIÆVAL CHURCHES. *Nearly ready.*

A PLAN OF ROME, ANCIENT AND MODERN, in colours, shewing the differences of level; the Seven Hills; the lines of the Aqueducts, and their Reservoirs; the natural streams of water; the Line and Station of the Railway; and the new Streets, especially the VIA NAZIONALE. *Second Edition, nearly ready.*

ARCHITECTURAL TOPOGRAPHY.

MEDIÆVAL SCULPTURE.

A SERIES OF MANUALS OF GOTHIC ORNAMENT. No. 1. STONE CARVING. 2. MOULDINGS; 3. SURFACE ORNAMENT. 16mo., price 1s. each.

ENGLISH CHURCHES IN COUNTIES.

OR, AN ARCHITECTURAL ACCOUNT

OF EVERY CHURCH IN THE

DIOCESE OF OXFORD:	DIOCESE OF ELY:
OXFORDSHIRE, BERKSHIRE, BUCKINGHAMSHIRE. 8vo., cloth, 5s.	BEDFORDSHIRE, CAMBRIDGESHIRE, HUNTINGDONSHIRE, SUFFOLK. 8vo., cl., 10s. 6d.

Its Dedication.—Supposed date of Erection or Alteration.—Objects of Interest in or near.—Notices of Fonts.—Glass, Furniture, —and other details.—Also Lists of Dated Examples, Works relating to the County, &c.

CANTERBURY CATHEDRAL.

THE ARCHITECTURAL HISTORY OF CANTERBURY CATHEDRAL. By Professor WILLIS, M.A., F.R.S., &c. With Woodcuts and Plans. 8vo., cloth, 10s. 6d.

WESTMINSTER ABBEY.

GLEANINGS FROM WESTMINSTER ABBEY. By GEORGE GILBERT SCOTT, R.A., F.S.A. With Appendices supplying Further Particulars, and completing the History of the Abbey Buildings, by Several Writers. *Second Edition, enlarged, containing many new Illustrations by O. Jewitt and others.* Medium 8vo., cloth, gilt top, **10s. 6d.**

WELLS.

ILLUSTRATIONS OF THE ARCHITECTURAL ANTIQUITIES OF THE CITY OF WELLS: 32 Photographs, Folio size, in portfolio, price 3*l*. 3*s*.; or separately, 2*s*. 6*d*. each.
  Also 16 Photographs, in 8vo., reduced from the above, in a case, price 15*s*.; or separately, 1*s*. each.

GLASTONBURY ABBEY: 9 Photographs, Folio size, in portfolio, price 1*l*.; or separately, 2*s*. 6*d*. each.

DORSETSHIRE: 23 Photographs, Folio size, in portfolio, price 4*l*. 4*s*.; or separately, 2*s*. 6*d*. each.

ENGLISH TOPOGRAPHY.

OXFORD.—A HAND-BOOK FOR VISITORS TO OXFORD. Illustrated by One Hundred and Forty-five Woodcuts by Jewitt, and Twenty-six Steel Plates by Le Keux, and a new coloured Plan. *A New Edition.* 8vo., ornamental cloth, 12s.

——— THE VISITOR'S GUIDE TO OXFORD. With many Illustrations, Crown 8vo., in ornamental wrapper, 1s.; cloth, 1s. 6d.

——— GUIDE to ARCHITECTURAL ANTIQUITIES in the Neighbourhood of Oxford. *New Edition, in preparation.*

DOVER.—THE CHURCH AND FORTRESS OF DOVER CASTLE. By the Rev. JOHN PUCKLE, M.A., Vicar of St. Mary's, Dover. Medium 8vo., cloth, 5s.

SANDFORD.—AN ACCOUNT of the PARISH OF SANDFORD, in the Deanery of Woodstock, Oxon. By EDWARD MARSHALL, M.A. Crown 8vo., cloth, 3s.

By the same Author.

CHURCH ENSTONE.—AN ACCOUNT of the TOWNSHIP OF CHURCH ENSTONE, Oxon. Crown 8vo., cl., 3s.

IFFLEY.—A HISTORY OF THE TOWNSHIP OF IFFLEY, OXFORDSHIRE. A New Edition. Crown 8vo., cloth, 4s.

WORKING DRAWINGS OF CHURCHES, WITH VIEWS, ELEVATIONS, SECTIONS, AND DETAILS.

Published by the Oxford Architectural Society.

WARMINGTON CHURCH, NORTHAMPTONSHIRE. Royal folio, cloth, 10s. 6d.
 A fine thirteenth-century Church. About 115 feet by 47.

SAINT LEONARD'S, KIRKSTEAD, LINCOLNSHIRE. Small folio, 5s.
 A small Church in the Early English style. 42 feet by 19.

MINSTER LOVELL CHURCH, OXFORDSHIRE. Folio, 5s.
 A very elegant specimen of the Perpendicular style. To hold 350 persons.

LITTLEMORE CHURCH, OXFORDSHIRE. *Second Edition*, with the designs of the painted Glass Windows. Folio, 5s.
 A small modern Church, in the Early English style. Size, 60 feet by 55 and 40 feet high. Cost 800*l.* Holds 210 persons.

SHOTTESBROKE CHURCH, BERKS. Folio, 3s. 6d.
 A good and pure specimen of the Decorated style.

WILCOTE CHURCH, OXFORDSHIRE. Folio, 3s. 6d.
 A small Church in the Decorated style. Size, 50 feet by 20. Estimated cost, 364*l.* Holds 160 persons.

ST. BARTHOLOMEW'S CHAPEL, OXFORD. Folio, 3s. 6d.
 A small Chapel in the Early Perpendicular style. Size, 24 feet by 16. Estimated cost, 228*l.* Holds 90 persons.

STRIXTON CHURCH, NORTHAMPTONSHIRE. Folio, 5s.
 A small Church in the Early English style. Calculated for 200 persons; Cost about 800*l.*

OXFORD BURIAL-GROUND CHAPELS. Folio, 10s. 6d.
 1. Norman. 2. Early English. 3. Decorated.
 Separately, each 5s.

Sixpence per Sheet.

OPEN SEATS.
3. Steeple Aston.
4. Stanton Harcourt; Ensham.

PATTERNS OF BENCH ENDS.
6. Steeple Aston. Sheet 1.
7. Ditto. Sheet 2.

OAK STALLS.
8. Beauchamp Chapel.

FONTS.
10. Heckington, (*Decorated*).
11. Newenden, (*Norman*).

REREDOS.
12. St. Michael's, Oxford.

PULPITS.
15. Wolvercot, (*Perpendicular*).
16. Beaulieu, (*Decorated*).
17. St. Giles', Oxford, (*Decorated*); with Coombe, (*Perpendicular*).

STONE DESK.
20. Crowle Church, (*Norman*).

THE CALENDAR OF THE PRAYER-BOOK IL-
LUSTRATED. (Comprising the first portion of the "Calendar of the Anglican Church," with an Appendix on Emblems,
illustrated, enlarged, and corrected.) With upwards of Two
Hundred Engravings, from Mediæval Works of Art. Fcap.
8vo., *Sixth Thousand*, ornamental cloth, 6s.

INVENTORY of FURNITURE and ORNAMENTS
REMAINING IN ALL THE PARISH CHURCHES OF
HERTFORDSHIRE in the last year of the Reign of King
Edward the Sixth: Transcribed from the Original Records,
by J. E. CUSSANS, F.R.Hist.Soc. Cr. 8vo., limp cloth, 4s.

PARISH CHURCH GOODS IN BERKSHIRE,
A.D. 1552. Inventories of Furniture and Ornaments remain-
ing in certain of the Parish Churches of Berks in the last year
of the reign of King Edward the Sixth: Transcribed from the
Original Records, with Introduction and Explanatory Notes
by WALTER MONEY, F.S.A., Member of Council for Berks,
Brit. Arch. Assoc., and Hon. Sec. of the Newbury District
Field Club. Crown 8vo., limp cloth, 3s. 6d.

DOMESDAY BOOK, or the Great Survey of England
of William the Conqueror, A.D. MLXXXVI. Facsimile of the
part relating to Oxfordshire. Folio, cloth, price 8s.

THE TRACT "DE INVENTIONE SANCTÆ
CRUCIS NOSTRÆ IN MONTE ACUTO ET DE
DUCTIONE EJUSDEM APUD WALTHAM," now first
printed from the Manuscript in the British Museum, with Introduction and Notes by WILLIAM STUBBS, M.A., Regius
Professor of Modern History. Royal 8vo., price 5s.; Demy
8vo., 3s. 6d.

SKETCH OF THE LIFE OF WALTER DE MERTON,
Lord High Chancellor of England, and Bishop of Rochester;
Founder of Merton College. By EDMUND HOBHOUSE, for-
merly Bishop of Nelson, New Zealand; and Fellow of Merton
College. 8vo., 2s.

ARCHÆOLOGICAL WORKS.

THE PRIMEVAL ANTIQUITIES OF ENGLAND AND DENMARK COMPARED. By J. J. A. WORSAAE. Translated and applied to the illustration of similar remains in England, by W. J. THOMS, F.S.A., &c. With numerous Illustrations. 8vo., cloth, 5s.

DESCRIPTIVE NOTICES OF SOME OF THE ANCIENT PAROCHIAL AND COLLEGIATE CHURCHES OF SCOTLAND, with Woodcuts. 8vo., 5s.

HISTORICAL MEMORIALS OF BEAUCHIEF ABBEY, near Derby. By S. O. ADDY, M.A. 4to., 15s.

OUR ENGLISH HOME: Its Early History and Progress. With Notes on the Introduction of Domestic Inventions. Third Edition. Crown 8vo., 3s. 6d.

ART APPLIED TO INDUSTRY: A Series of Lectures by WILLIAM BURGES, F.R.I.B.A. Medium 8vo., cloth, price 4s.

PROCEEDINGS OF THE ARCHÆOLOGICAL INSTITUTE AT WINCHESTER. 8vo., 10s. 6d.

MEMOIRS ILLUSTRATIVE OF THE HISTORY AND ANTIQUITIES OF THE COUNTY AND CITY OF YORK. With 134 Illustrations. 8vo., cloth, 10s. 6d.

MEMOIRS ILLUSTRATIVE OF THE HISTORY AND ANTIQUITIES OF THE COUNTY AND CITY OF OXFORD. 8vo., cloth, with Illustrations, 10s. 6d.

PROCEEDINGS OF THE ARCHÆOLOGICAL INSTITUTE AT NORWICH. 8vo., cloth, 10s. 6d.

www.ingramcontent.com/pod-product-compliance
Lightning Source LLC
Chambersburg PA
CBHW031951230426
43672CB00010B/2126